Paradoxes
of Group Life

Kenwyn K. Smith

David N. Berg

In Full Collaboration

Paradoxes
of Group Life

Understanding Conflict,
Paralysis, and Movement
in Group Dynamics

Jossey-Bass Publishers

San Francisco • Oxford • 1990

PARADOXES OF GROUP LIFE
Understanding Conflict, Paralysis, and Movement in Group Dynamics
by Kenwyn K. Smith and David N. Berg

Copyright © 1987 by: Jossey-Bass Inc., Publishers
                     350 Sansome Street
                     San Francisco, California 94104
                              &
                     Jossey-Bass Limited
                     Headington Hill Hall
                     Oxford OX3 0BW

Library of Congress Cataloging-in-Publication Data

Smith, Kenwyn K.
   Paradoxes of group life.

   (Jossey-Bass management series) (Jossey-Bass
social and behavioral science series)
   Bibliography: p. 267
   Includes index.
   1. Social groups. 2. Paradox. I. Berg, David N.,
1949–   . II. Title. III. Series. IV. Series:
Jossey-Bass social and behavioral science series.
HM131.S569   1987   302.3   86-33706
ISBN 1-55542-046-X (alk. paper)

Manufactured in the United States of America

The paper in this book meets the guidelines for
permanence and durability of the Committee on
Production Guidelines for Book Longevity of the
Council on Library Resources.

JACKET DESIGN BY WILLI BAUM

FIRST EDITION
      First printing: April 1987
      Second printing: January 1988
      Third printing: November 1990

Code 8717

A joint publication in
The Jossey-Bass Management Series
and
The Jossey-Bass
Social and Behavioral Science Series

To our mothers and fathers
with thanks for your loving parenting

Contents

Preface

Paradoxes of Group Life is the result of our collaboration on the importance of paradox for understanding group dynamics. We arrived at this topic of mutual interest from very different directions. Berg's introduction to paradox was firmly grounded in his experience with groups and their struggles with ambivalence, contradiction, paralysis, and movement. He found paradox in the expressions and actions of people in groups and in his own experience in collective situations. For Smith, the importance of paradox was most powerfully presented in a tradition of philosophy and social thought that explored concepts such as framing, negation, and self-reference. He was most struck by the influence of paradox on our understanding of the world in which we live.

As we searched the literature on group dynamics for theory and research that could speak to our developing interest, we found less than we expected. Two decades of work on group development had produced *descriptions* of the course of group life, descriptions that fit much of our own experience, but the *conceptualization* of these observations seemed limited by the framework used to understand, in particular, issues involving conflict, opposition, and contradiction. We also found ourselves disappointed with explanations of paralysis and movement in groups. The literature was clearer on *where* groups were going than on *how* they managed to get there. In our work we were constantly faced with groups that experienced themselves as being stuck, and while there was a great deal written about how to make groups more effective, productive, and successful, there was little theoretical work on the collective conditions attending paralysis and movement.

So we set out to examine the role of paradox in group life and to write about the results of that examination. What emerged was a paradoxical conceptualization of group life that deepened our understanding of the nature of conflict and opposition in groups and of the processes of paralysis and movement. This book is a description and elaboration of this way of thinking about paradox in group dynamics.

It is also the expression of a collaborative relationship, the nature of which is both difficult to describe and important to convey. In the spring of 1982, we gave ourselves the gift of four weeks together to explore the possibility of making good on our wish to collaborate on a project that would give expression to our ten-year-old friendship. There are no simple ways to describe the intertwining of two minds as they struggle with ideas and emotions related both to their project and their relationship. Our profession and the mechanics of graphic presentation conspire to cast our relationship in familiar "rank order" terms, perhaps as a way of expressing unconscious disbelief at the notion of full and equal collaboration. Yet this is our experience of writing this book. Neither of us could have written it alone. And as we attempted to respond to the questions that inevitably arose from inside as well as outside about "who did what," it became increasingly impossible for us to *know* the answer to the question of our separate contributions.

Having lived the joys and frustrations of so close a collaboration has enriched our work tremendously. One short chapter from the story of our collaboration illustrates the often unconscious ways we found to express and subordinate our respective individualities in the service of our joint undertaking. In the early stages of the project, we would write together. One of us would take pen and paper and the other would dictate ideas. Our styles were very different, and each of us struggled to persuade the other to change his style to match our own. At the height of these "stylistic" struggles, we would often take a break. During one of these breaks, we created our own version of basement handball, complete with rules to cover the ball ricocheting off the clothes dryer. The games were intensely competitive and provided an absorbing break from our intellectual work. Near the end of one week's work we noticed a link between our writing and our handball: Whoever won at handball on a given occasion inevitably acquiesced on the writing.

What had begun as a process of articulation, an act of recording and organizing the insights gleaned from years of work with groups, quickly became a process of discovery as we collaboratively reflected on both our experiences and our favorite theories about life in groups. The more we wrote, the more we found ourselves engaged in a conversation not only with each other but with the words and ideas we had begun to formulate. Successive outlines, drafts, and chapters actually helped us discover aspects of our understanding that were implicit in each of us separately and in our relationship. The publication of *Paradoxes of Group Life* represents our desire to move this conversation to a wider audience.

Who Should Read This Book?

We have written this book for both students of human behavior in groups and practitioners who manage the complex dynamics of groups in everyday life. By students we mean those in formal educational programs, such as graduate classes in organizational behavior, management, psychology, sociology, education, and social work, as well as those who study the behavior of groups simply in order to understand the entities in which they participate. Practitioners for whom we believe this material is relevant include those who manage work groups, those who deal with groups in their communities (for example, journalists, community organizers, and school board members), and those for whom the group is the fundamental social unit in their professional practice (for example, classroom teachers, lawyers dealing with the courts and juries, social workers involved in social and human reparation, and organizational consultants involved in planning and change processes).

Overview of the Contents

The book is organized into three major parts. Part One is primarily devoted to theoretical and conceptual background. Chapter One introduces the concept of paradox and suggests that our understanding of what happens in groups can be enhanced by the addition of a paradoxical perspective. In Chapter Two we explore the presence of paradoxical dynamics in social thought in this century, beginning with a selective review of psychotherapeutic practice at the individual, group, and family levels and ending with an examination of theory and research on small groups. In Chapter Three we look across the broad legacy of paradoxical thought in an attempt to distill its essential, underlying philosophical elements, focusing particularly on issues of negation, self-reference, and double bind. Chapter Four presents a paradoxical conception of group dynamics, tracing the sources of paradox and the processes through which paradox manifests itself in group life.

Part Two is the heart of the book. Here we explore twelve group paradoxes organized into three clusters. Chapter Five examines the paradoxes associated with belonging (identity, involvement, individuality, and boundaries). Chapter Six looks at the paradoxes of engaging (disclosure, trust, intimacy, and regression). Chapter Seven is concerned with the issues surrounding speaking in small groups (authority, dependency, creativity, and courage). Chapter Eight looks at the ways "frames" for understanding are imported into groups and exported from any group to other groups in which the individuals are involved. Chapter Nine examines the influence of group context on the twelve group paradoxes and, in particular, how the conflictual nature of intergroup relations, with its own paradoxical elements, shapes members' experience of the groups to which they belong.

Part Three addresses the implications of a paradoxical conceptualization for theories of group movement and for the ways members, leaders, and consultants think about group behavior. Chapter Ten looks at what paradoxical theory has to say about the way groups move from one condition to another and how they release themselves from that which paralyzes them. It is not a chapter about where groups move, but rather about how they move. The final chapter, Chapter Eleven, presents a case in which we include the thoughts and decisions of a consultant working with numerous interconnected groups in an organization to illustrate how paradoxical theory informed his understanding and action.

These eleven chapters represent an attempt to step back and reflect on the struggles we all encounter in our experiences in groups, as members, leaders, and interventionists. It is our contention that through this reflection we will come to understand more clearly those forces that draw us into the repeated oscillations of enchantment and despair that characterize our relationship to group endeavor. Our intention is to make more visible those hidden and troublesome group dynamics that become comprehensible when examined from a paradoxical perspective. We believe that many of our solutions to practical problems have been limited by our ways of thinking about groups. Familiar prescriptions for handling conflict and contradiction in groups often merely displace the problems they attempt to solve. This book offers a way to think about groups that we hope will open up new possibilities for the way we act in them.

Acknowledgments

There are many people we would like to thank for their role in this project. First, we want to thank Sara and Robin, whose support, encouragement, enthusiasm, and patience have helped make our family lives and our collegial work mutually reinforcing. Second, Rachel Golden Berg's eighteen months have been a source of inspiration and discipline for her father. Both her laughter and her pain have added perspective at important moments throughout the final drafting of the manuscript. Third, we would like to thank our colleagues, clients, and students whose lives, thoughts, and actions have been our teachers. Fourth, a special thanks to Karen Donegan who worked tirelessly on the manuscript in its final stages and to the editorial staff at Jossey-Bass for supporting us in this undertaking from its early days. Last, we want to thank those members of our field, past and present, who have courageously affirmed the importance of individual and collective self-examination as a source of insight in the process of social science research and especially Clayton P. Alderfer for being our link to that tradition.

David N. Berg   Kenwyn K. Smith
Bethany, Connecticut   *Philadelphia, Pennsylvania*

February 1987

The Authors

David N. Berg is associate professor of organizational behavior at the Yale School of Organization and Management. He received both his B.A. degree (1971) in psychology and his M.A. degree (1972) in administrative sciences from Yale University and his Ph.D. degree (1978) in psychology from the University of Michigan. He has been at the Yale School of Organization and Management since 1977; between 1979 and 1981, he was director of professional studies there. He has worked with school systems, public agencies, private corporations, and a variety of professional practices and has a special interest in the nonprofit world.

Berg's professional interests include group and intergroup relations, clinical research methods, organizational diagnosis, and the use of experiential methods in teaching and learning. His previous books include *Failures in Organization Development and Change* (1977, with P. H. Mirvis) and *Exploring Clinical Methods for Social Research* (1985, with K. K. Smith).

Kenwyn K. Smith is associate professor of organizational behavior and management at the Wharton School, University of Pennsylvania. He received a B.A. degree (1965) and an M.A. degree (1970), both in psychology, from the University of Queensland, Australia, and an M.A. degree (1973) and a Ph.D. degree (1974) in organizational behavior from Yale University. Smith, who began his professional life as a high school teacher of mathematics, worked for several years as a clinical psychologist before entering the field of organizational behavior. He has been a member of the faculty at the University of Melbourne and the University of Maryland.

Smith's main research interests have been in group dynamics, intergroup relations, conflict management, and organizational diagnosis and change, with a special focus on how people, groups, and organizations make sense of their worlds and how their actions shape their experiences of reality. His empirical work has been done in organizations such as the telecommunications industry, educational systems, psychiatric hospitals, design and engineering facilities, manufacturing organizations, and community settings. Smith's books include *Groups in Conflict: Prisons in Disguise* (1982), *Exploring Clinical Methods for Social Research* (1985, with D. N. Berg), and *Group Relations and Organizational Diagnosis* (forthcoming, with C. P. Alderfer, L. D. Brown, and R. E. Kaplan).

Paradoxes
of Group Life

Part One

Locating Paradox

In the first part of this book we introduce the concept of paradox, review its role in twentieth-century thought about human behavior, and explicate a theory of group relations based on paradoxical thinking.

We start with the observation that people's experiences in groups are filled with tensions and conflicts that are hard to manage. Yet the majority of theories about group dynamics ignore the theme of conflict entirely or deal with it in a rather superficial manner. This leads us to the question of what framework would enable the topic of conflict in groups to be productively understood. We turn to paradox as a guiding conceptualization.

In defining and exploring paradox in general, it is evident that how we, as humans, think about our experiences in collective life is as important to us as the actual experiences themselves. If we think according to one set of principles, our experience of life can be radically different from the experience of someone who uses an alternate set of principles. This raises many questions that demand a theoretical and conceptual exploration. We undertake this by first looking at the writers who have applied paradoxical thinking to human actions. This takes us to the general work of individual and group psychotherapists and to the field of family therapy in particular. After reviewing the contributions a paradoxical perspective has made to their work, we move to the issue of what can be added to our understanding of groups by acknowledging the paradoxical side of collective life.

As we do this we are drawn into several philosophical issues relevant to how we conceive of our experiences in groups. In Part One, we provide the conceptual and theoretical ground for understanding group processes when using a paradoxical approach.

1

Defining Paradox

> We stand in a turmoil of contradictions without
> having the faintest idea how to handle them: Law/
> Freedom; Rich/Poor; Right/Left; Love/Hate—the
> list seems endless. Paradox lives and moves in this
> realm; it is the art of balancing opposites in such a
> way that they do not cancel each other but shoot
> sparks of light across their points of polarity. It
> looks at our desperate either/ors and tells us they
> are really both/ands—that life is larger than any of
> our concepts and can, if we let it, embrace our con-
> tradictions.   —*Mary C. Morrison*

In the last few years, there has been a resurgence of interest in groups, especially groups in organizations. Stimulated in
part by observations of other cultures, academics and practitioners alike have begun to look upon groups as the essential
units in organizations. We have created quality circles, quality
of work life committees, and semiautonomous and self-manag-
ing work groups with the belief that groups will help solve some
of the nagging problems of organizational life: low morale, poor
motivation, unmet needs, and low productivity.

Quotation from "In Praise of Paradox," by Mary C. Morrison
taken from *The Episcopalian*, January 1983 and used by permission of
the author.

We look to groups and their potential to create synergy to realize a number of our aspirations for collective life, ranging from a greater sense of psychological community in an era of high social mobility to a productive edge in a world of international economic competition. As we once again turn to groups to solve some of our problems and to realize some of our aspirations, we often forget the problematic aspects of group life that caused our interest to ebb the last time around. We tend to overlook the experiences in groups that led people and organizations to look elsewhere for their solutions, often back to the individual or the state.

We forget common complaints such as "committees don't work," "groups take too much time," and "I could do it better myself," and we appear to ignore our mixed emotions about participating in and leading groups. Those whose interest in groups has peaked again seem to focus on the creativity, energy, productivity, and satisfaction possible in groups and pay less attention to the frustration, hostility, compromise, slowness, and periods of "stuckness" that also punctuate life in groups. There is a tendency to forget or ignore the problems *created* by groups while attending to the problems we hope will be *alleviated* by them. In a way, we find ourselves caught in a paradox, for remembering what we know about groups is both enabling and disabling. Attention to the difficult and problematic aspects of life in groups makes it possible to manage them more effectively, but the memories generated by this attention may dissuade us altogether from connecting with groups.

In this book, we want to step back and reflect on the struggles we all encounter in our experiences in groups, as members, leaders, and interventionists. It is our hope that through this reflection we will understand more clearly those forces that draw us into the repeated oscillations between enchantment and despair over groups. Our intention is to make visible those hidden and troublesome group dynamics that become comprehensible when examined from a paradoxical perspective. Our goal is to enable those who work with and in groups to find release from the dynamics that often paralyze group members, the group as a whole, and relations among groups. In this way, the book is about paradox and group movement. It is a book that offers a way to think about groups that can open up new possibilities for action in groups.

Experiences in Groups

To lay the groundwork for the theoretical emphasis of this book, we begin by illustrating the types of group situations that concern us. Consider the following three examples:

The president and four vice-presidents (all men) of a medium-sized manufacturing company created an "operating committee" of the various directorial-level management personnel: sales, training, research, manufacturing, quality control, and finance (also all men). They wanted this group to "run the day-to-day operations of the company" so that the senior group could concentrate on long-range planning, since the company had the capital but not the strategy for dramatic growth in the next five years.

The monthly meetings of top management (president, vice-president, and directors) were now augmented by biweekly operating committee meetings. In trying to define the scope of the operating committee's responsibilities in the firm, the members found themselves repeatedly confronting the same internal disagreement. Some members felt that the committee needed to find out whether the president really intended to give them any authority, believing that it was likely that their committee would be given minimal decision-making authority and that its meetings would be a waste of time. Another "faction" advocated taking as much responsibility as they could. "If they want us to run the company, let's do it until they slap our wrists."

The operating committee meetings proved

frustrating to both subgroups, and no course of action, no matter how much it was intended to "split the difference" between the two positions, generated enough commitment and energy for anything constructive to be accomplished. Both factions began to feel that the committee was a sham.

*   *   *

The four men and four women had been together for seven weeks in one of six ongoing study groups in a graduate management course. Each study group was to meet on a regular basis, outside class time, to work on assigned cases and to learn about groups by reflecting on and analyzing their own behavior. These "extra" meetings were hard to schedule, with always at least one member absent or late, and were stiff and perfunctory. Finally, one of the women said that she was thinking about not coming to group meetings anymore because she was not getting anything out of them.

In the discussion that followed, three of the four men expressed frustration because nothing of importance was happening in their group. The women exchanged glances, and finally one of them said that she thought that much was happening but that the members did not trust each other enough to talk about it. She mentioned subgroups, leadership, and the question of how much socializing the group wanted to do as examples of what was "happening." One of the men began to express his view that the women were fishing for something to "get heavy" about; another woman in the group said that she was tired of always bringing up these issues and not getting a response (the men did not respond at all on most occasions, and the women responded privately, outside the group). She said it made her seem "needy" or "different," and she was tired of "being made to feel that way." There was silence. One man left, claiming that he had another study group meeting to go to. The women together tried to decide whether to go to the professor to ask his help, since it looked like the group was falling apart. They could not reach a decision, but they agreed that it made them angry that none of the men "cared enough" to even think about the question.

* * *

Everyone on the faculty was looking forward to the arrival of the new dean, who was seen as a potential peacemaker by a faculty whose conflicts had escalated to unbearable levels. No matter which side of a particular dispute faculty members found themselves on, they were weary of all the conflict, factionalism, and intrigue. Many members of the faculty had already contacted the new dean offering their views of the situation and their suggestions for constructive action.

When he arrived, the dean invested a great deal of time in watching and listening before he acted. It was clear to him that many of the problems that the faculty complained about were rooted in practices and policies that attended only to the individuals on the faculty and not to considerations of the faculty as a group. After careful thought, the dean began to announce (and live by) certain administrative practices designed to reduce suspicion, mistrust, and backroom conspiracies, exactly the problems brought to his attention upon his arrival. He appointed a committee to draw up faculty guidelines for the work that the faculty as a group conducted. He published minutes of meetings, eliminated backdoor approaches to decision making, and slowly began to put an end to secret, special deals on hiring, salary, course assignments, and research support.

Soon faculty members were meeting to complain privately about the dean. Their needs were

not being met. They began to feel that the dean
had "usurped" too much power. Within three years
of his arrival, the "new" dean was the target of a
variety of behaviors designed to undermine his authority. As faculty meetings deteriorated and professors became more and more frustrated with the
group's inability to function, they began to meet in
small, informal subgroups (some called them "ca-
bals"). Finally, the dean himself was forced to
meet with individual faculty members to get important decisions made and committed to; as these
private meetings multiplied, the complaining intensified. Unhappy again, faculty members began to
write to the university's president questioning the
advisability of renewing the dean's term and suggesting that he be replaced by someone better able
to handle the destructive politics and internal divisions that now characterized the faculty.

When we examine naturally existing groups in organizations such as these, several observations strike us: (1) a great
deal of energy seems to be invested in getting groups "unstuck,"
even though it is not always obvious what produced the paralysis in the first place; (2) the very people who desire change
often act in ways that reinforce the things they want altered;
(3) relationships in decline continue to deteriorate while each
party waits stubbornly for the other to make the first move; and
(4) groups keep themselves enmeshed in paralyzing "we-they"
dynamics despite their expressed interest in wanting to avoid
such problems. One very noticeable feature of groups that are
stuck is the presence of conflict that leaves individuals, the relationships among members, or the group as a whole split into opposing sides. As each faction struggles to assert its dominance,
the other seems to find sufficient strength to restore the balance
of power among the parts, re-establishing the paralyzing conflict
but with a sense of heightened intensity. We also notice that
when social scientists are pulled in to help, the parties in conflict usually ask for assistance in *resolving* the situation. Yet our

experience is that attempts to resolve conflicts produce only temporary relief. The conflict seems either to reappear at another time or to shift to another important dimension—typically, to the context in which the group is located or the individual members who make up the group.

If we go directly to people's experience and ask them what it is like to belong to a particular group, individuals *do* talk about the exhilaration of work in groups, but their comments are usually focused on the problematic experiences: "It's very *frustrating*—I have so many things on my mind, but I never seem able to say them." "Sometimes we work well together; at other times it is impossible, because there's so much *tension*." "Everyone seems so *ambivalent* about everything—it's overwhelming." "It's so *paradoxical*—we all like each other, but we never seem to connect." As a starting point, we suggest that it might be useful to examine the words *frustration, tension, ambivalence,* and *paradox* and what is being communicated when people choose such terms to describe their experiences in groups. *Webster's New Collegiate Dictionary* (1975) and the *American College Dictionary* (1960) define these words as follows: *frustration*—"a deep chronic sense or state of insecurity and dissatisfaction arising from unresolved problems or unfulfilled needs" (Webster's); *tension*—"a state of being stressed or strained, mental or emotional strain, strong intellectual effort, intense suppressed excitement" (American); "a balance maintained in an artistic work between opposing forces or elements" (Webster's); *ambivalence*—"co-existence of opposite and conflicting feelings about the same person, object or action" (American); and *paradox*—"a statement or proposition, seemingly self-contradictory or absurd, and yet explicable as expressing a truth" (American). If we search for a common thread in the formal definitions of these terms, we notice that at the core of each concept is a struggle with opposites, especially the attempt to create meaning and coherence out of what seems to lack them. It seems that a great deal of group energy is poured into dealing with these opposites but that each method for "disposing" of the conflict becomes a stimulus for a new set of group tensions, with sides often being taken over whether the discord itself should be confronted or ignored. As group members describe their efforts to conquer conflict, they seem to tell a story of being conquered by it.

This suggests a place to start our exploration. What is it about groups that stirs actions, thoughts, and feelings in members that they experience as contradictory? How are those apparent contradictions managed, both by the group as a whole and by individual members? How do our systems of understanding influence how we experience these contradictions?

Creating a Frame

On turning to the literature of group dynamics for guidance on these questions, we are struck by two features. One is the paucity of reference to conflict in theories about internal group processes. The other is that, in discussing group development and the phases that groups pass through, writers point to tensions that need to be "worked through" when transition points are encountered. What is actually involved in the process of "working through" is often unaddressed. Both of these issues will be addressed later in this book. For the moment, however, our concern is to indicate that there has been very little theory offered about how to understand internal group conflict. The attention of most of those who do address the topic is focused on conflict resolution or avoidance. One possible explanation for this is that conflict is usually described in terms of different interests, different values, different goals, and so on, with very little consideration to how the *experience of conflict* is created by the ways that groups and their members interpret the experience of group life.

While it is often said that conflict can be constructive and productive for a group, our observation is that group members do not "experience" conflict this way. In the presence of hostile and angry emotions, group members seem afraid that the conflict will engulf them and destroy the fragile fabric holding them together—the conflict heightens the group's awareness of its potential fragility. When there is no conflict, members feel that their group is less fragile, whether this is "true" or not. The

fear that the group would be destroyed by the conflicts it generates encourages members to deny or suppress those conflicts or
to seek their resolution when they emerge.

In this book, we seek to change frame from the predomi-
nant treatments of group conflict by exploring the thesis that
group life is inherently paradoxical. We argue that it is impossible to have a group without certain types of conflict and that
the wish to have those conflicts "resolved" stems from an imperfect understanding of the meaning that conflict has in the life
of the group. We acknowledge that conflict often becomes paralyzing for the group and often drives members to the brink of
withdrawal, but we also suggest that the role of conflict in
groups is a complex one.

What Is Paradox?

"All Cretans are liars!" These words, spoken in obvious
exasperation by a Cretan named Epimenides, made him famous.
Across the years, his singular outburst has been elevated to im-
mortal levels as the quintessential paradox, simplified over time
into forms such as "I am lying" or "This statement is false."
The key to the paradox is that the listener is invited into a true-
or-false frame; yet, if you think that the statement is true, it
immediately backfires on you and appears false, and if you
think it is false, it suddenly becomes true. This sets off a vicious
cycle that Hofstadter (1979) labels a "strange loop."

The clearest illustration of a strange loop is what happens
when one moves upward (or downward) through the levels of
some hierarchical system only to find oneself right back at the
starting point. The lithograph *Waterfall,* by Escher, highlights
what Hofstadter is referring to. This is a painting of a medieval
water construction, such as one might find on the side of a
stream. There are staircases, little buildings, and a man-made
waterfall descending from the top level of two towers. The
viewer is immediately drawn to the question of how the water
gets to the peak to make the waterfall possible. At first, you assume that there must be a mechanical pump, but as you look
for such a mechanism, your eyes are pulled into the flow of wa-

ter in a downward direction, obviously propelled by gravity. As your eyes follow the *downward* flow through a series of constructed contours, you suddenly find yourself at the top of the construction, poised at the peak of the waterfall. While repetitively moving downward, you were simultaneously, but unknowingly, going up—a strange loop.

Hughes and Brecht (1975) provide a formal definition of paradox: a statement or set of statements that are self-referential and contradictory and that trigger a vicious circle. All three aspects, self-reference, contradiction, and the vicious circle, are necessary for paradox. There are many propositions that are self-referential but not paradoxical; for example, "This is a sentence." There are also statements that are self-referential *and* contradictory yet still not paradoxical; for example, "This sentence is written in Chinese." There are even statements that are self-referential, contradictory, and mildly circular, such as "It is forbidden to forbid" or "never say never," but that do not sustain one in an intensely vicious circle. It is only when we get to the "I am lying" or "Please ignore this statement" level that the vicious circle is deeply engaging. Then we have all the necessary conditions for paradox.

Throughout the twentieth century, numerous philosophers and mathematicians have toyed with paradox. For some, such as Russell, Whitehead, and Gödel, it was serious work; for others, it was for the purpose of humor. In 1908, for example, the mathematician Kurt Grelling created the paradox now known as "heterologicality." Some adjectives, such as *short* and *English,* apply to themselves; others, such as *long* and *French,* do not. If we call the first group *autological* an^r the second group *heterological,* then we confront the question of whether the adjective *heterological* is itself heterological. If it is, by definition it does not apply to itself, and hence it cannot be heterological. If it is not, then by definition it does apply to itself, and so it must be heterological (Hughes and Brecht, 1975).

Jourdain (1913) suggested printing on one side of a card the words "The statement on the other side of this card is true" and on the opposite side "The statement on the other side of this card is false." In this case, the paradox may be found not within the statement, as in the "I am lying" case, but in the relationship between the sentences on the two sides of the card. A modern, more simplified version of Jourdain's paradox is as follows:

> The following sentence is false.
> The preceding sentence is true.

Neither of these statements, taken separately, is problematic. It is only when they are taken together that paradox is created. When the second sentence is *framed* by the first, we suddenly find that the first is framed by the second. In trying to sort out which is true and which is false, we get tangled in a strange loop, a jumbled hierarchy that exists in the area *between* the two explicit statements. To find the location of the paradox, we cannot fixate our eyes on the concrete, as in the "I am lying" example. Rather, we must look into the empty space between the sentences. In other words, we cannot simply look at the text to find the paradox. We must look at what is implicitly written between the lines, in the con-text or the sub-text, if you will. There the paradox lies, ready to grab us as we focus our attention on the formal text.

The work of Whitehead and Russell (1910–1913) embodied in *Principia Mathematica* laid much of the foundation for the twentieth-century mathematical struggle with paradox. As Hofstadter (1979) expressed it, "They set out with the purpose of banishing strange loops from mathematics" as a commitment to creating a pure form of reasoning. But their endeavors exposed numerous strange loops, showing that while we can think using one set of symbols, if we use these same symbols for thinking about our thinking, we find ourselves caught in a tangled hierarchy that creates remarkable confusion.

Gödel, with his now-famous incompleteness theorem, provided another level of understanding about paradox by drawing a distinction between a statement of number theory and statements about statements of number theory, what we now readily recognize as statements and metastatements. He demonstrated that it is possible to make true statements within a particular system that cannot be proved by the exclusive use of the elements and logic of that system. In so doing, he highlighted the limitation of any reasoning that depends upon itself for the basis of self-reflection.

The Central Thesis

The paradoxical perspective that forms the theoretical base of this book is concerned with the observation that groups are pervaded by a wide range of emotions, thoughts, and actions that their members experience as contradictory, and that the attempts to unravel these contradictory forces create a circular process that is paralyzing to groups. The more that members seek to pull the contradictions apart, to separate them so that they will not be experienced as contradictory, the more enmeshed they become in the self-referential binds of paradox. It is precisely because the contradictions *are* bound together that the circularity exists. To illustrate, a paradox such as "All rules are meant to be broken, including this one" contains a "truth" that is expressed via the juxtaposition of the paradox's contradictory elements. If we examine the statement, what emerges is that the establishment of rules and the breaking of them are inextricably linked. The idea of breaking a rule is grounded in the notion of the rule itself, and vice versa. In our examination of the role of paradox in groups, this link between contradictory and opposing forces will emerge as a central feature, but one that is often overlooked.

In presenting a paradoxical view, we want to emphasize that the contradictory aspects of group life have both experiential and reflective parts to them. Contradictions can exist in both *what* people experience as actually happening to them in the group and *how* these experiences are thought about, or "framed." We are as concerned with the issue of framing as we are with the "reality" of the experience itself, since framing substantially affects "reality" in the world of interactions.

Given that groups bring to the surface powerful contradictions in their membership, a major task of the group then becomes the "containment," or management, of these contradictions and their effects. The successful management of these tensions can provide members with a connection both among themselves and with the group. This connection can help bring into alignment the work involved in developing a group's collective life and the development of individuals upon whose energies the group depends. When a group fails to "hold" these contradictions and works to have them expelled from its midst or carried burdensomely by one particular member or subgroup, then the preconditions for "stuckness" have been created.

Our central thesis is that group life is inherently paradoxical. In using the term *inherently,* we do not mean that group life is not "inherently" other things as well—just as someone's being inherently intelligent does not preclude that person from being inherently attractive or inherently athletic as well. Were it not for the disorienting aspects of language, we may have stated the proposition as an exploration of the inherently paradoxical side or dimensions of group life. But this implies that the paradoxical is something to be compared with whatever represents the other side or dimensions. In saying that a group is inherently paradoxical, we mean that paradox is contained within the very core of the conception of a group, and that a group's paradoxical nature needs to be understood along with all other aspects of group life.

In referring to the inherently paradoxical nature of group life, we mean that individual members experience the group as being filled with contradictory and opposing emotions, thoughts, and actions that *coexist* inside the group. As group members struggle to manage the tensions generated by these contradictory and opposing forces, the essential process dynamics of group life are created. These forces derive from individual and collective reactions to the interdependence of members in groups and of groups in their social environment. Membership in groups simultaneously creates fear and hope—fear that the group will be either overwhelming or isolating and hope that participation will be both personally and collectively enhancing—both of which come from the power of the collective and the associated potential strength that emanates from the mutual interdependencies of members. As individuals come together to form groups, their differences allow for the simultaneous expression of both hopes and fears, and even the opposing varia-

tions within each category. The simultaneous expression of
these contradictory reactions actually makes the group a safer
place, albeit a place full of opposing forces. The coexistence of
these opposing forces is as necessary as it is disquieting, for their
presence in the group allows individuals to participate, in spite
of the ambivalence that they bring to collective endeavors. It is
in this sense that paradox is an essential and inherent characteristic of group life.

One question that might be asked is whether anything in
groups is not paradoxical, and, if so, what we make of the ideas
about groups that have been developed without using a paradoxical frame. Our "answer" to this question has four elements:
(1) We are not attempting to invalidate previously established
concepts. Rather, we are asking what additional dimensions can
be brought to our understanding by the incorporation of a paradoxical frame, much as the second eye enables us to see depth
in the vistas that we can see only as flat when we are restricted
to vision with one eye. (2) We do see contradiction and the attempt to have it experienced as "not contradiction" to be at the
core of what it means for people "to group together," hence
our use of the phrase "inherently paradoxical." However, we
do not see groups as inevitably enslaved to an existence bound
up with paradox. The dynamic of liberation is as much a feature
of a paradoxical frame as is enmeshment. (3) We argue that
group processes can be unknowingly embroiled in the web of
paradox merely through how they are framed. *Frame contradiction differently* and the self-referential, self-renunciating circularity may well be broken. (4) Groups, as all human constructions, must be understood in terms of constructivist principles.
By this we mean that "social reality" and our ways of "conceiv-
ing of reality" are one and the same process. Hence, any concern with what is "really the case" is an exploration of the human and social processes of "reality construction."

This conceptualization of group dynamics has a number
of characteristics. First, it is clearly about *group dynamics,* the
study of the behavior of groups and people in group settings
(Homans, 1950; Mills, 1964; Bradford, Gibb, and Benne, 1964;
Cartwright and Zander, 1968; Bales, 1970; Luft, 1970). It is

concerned with the kinds of groups we find naturally occurring in everyday organizational life, such as groups in the workplace, groups in social settings, and classroom groups in educational environments. We also consider those groupings that exist as a consequence of historical and social forces, such as ethnicity, race, gender, and age, as they are expressed in the behavior and unconscious lives of these organizational groups. We do not consider "temporary groups," such as those created by researchers for the purpose of controlled experimentation. In our view, these clusterings of individuals in a "grouped environment" have an insufficient "life of their own" to develop the dynamics that we are interested in exploring here. We do consider as relevant, however, therapy groups, experiential groups developed for educational purposes or for the personal growth of members, and groups in simulated settings, as long as the groups exist over an extended period of time.

Second, this conceptualization focuses on *underlying group processes,* those emotional and psychological processes that exist when the influence of group task has been taken out. Put another way, we are concerned with those processes that are themselves shaped by the specific behavioral tasks that bring many groups together but are neither created nor destroyed by the character of these tasks. The rich and thoughtful tradition of research on these underlying group processes (Le Bon, 1895; Freud, 1949; Bennis and Shepard, 1956; Bion, 1961; Slater, 1966; Schutz, 1958; Tuckman, 1965; Whitaker and Lieberman, 1964; Bales, 1970; Gibbard, Hartman, and Mann, 1974; Coleman and Bexton, 1975; Rice, 1965) provides an intellectual point of departure for this paradoxical conceptualization.

Third, an exploration of this central thesis requires examination of both *conscious* as well as *unconscious dynamics* at both the individual and collective levels. By definition, these latter dynamics must be inferred from the behavior of individuals and groups, since they are "out of awareness" unless systematically attended to. It is not our purpose here to "prove" or "disprove" the existence of unconscious reactions and emotions; their existence is axiomatic in our conceptualization of group dynamics.

Fourth, in order to understand what happens in groups and why, it is necessary to examine both *internal group* and *external* or *intergroup dynamics*. A study of internal dynamics looks at the events, dilemmas, issues, and processes that occur with regularity in most small groups and seeks to identify what they are and why they occur. The study of intergroup dynamics (Coser, 1956; Sherif and others, 1961; Alderfer, 1977, 1986) looks at the group as a unit embedded in a larger social context, connected to its surroundings through its members and through its activities with other groups. How is what happens in small groups influenced and shaped by the larger social context? Are there regularities in the ways in which groups reflect the culture in which they are embedded? Do small groups influence the culture in return? In our attempt to understand underlying group processes, we find it necessary to look at both internal and external dynamics.

Fifth, our conceptualization is derived from our observations and experiences in groups, coupled with previous theoretical and empirical research on group dynamics. In this sense, it is an attempt to develop a *descriptive conceptualization* that "best fits" what we and others have observed about groups. This work leads us to certain propositions about group behavior, and we find that, inevitably, there are prescriptive elements to the emerging theory. What follows is an elaboration and illustration of a paradoxical conceptualization of groups, not an empirical test of its validity. Similarly, the normative aspects of the theory are d rived from the conceptualization.

Finally, implicit in our description of the paradoxical nature of group life is *a theory about* how *movement* occurs. A theory of group movement seeks to understand the unfolding of behavior in groups. How do groups move from one phase or theme to another, if they do? Is this progress, and against what standard? We will attempt to explore the issue of movement, using a paradoxical perspective on group life.

2

Tracing the Roots
of Paradoxical Thought

In recent years, paradoxical thinking has had its greatest impact in the field of family therapy. But a paradoxical perspective has been present in the thought and practice of psychotherapists for most of the twentieth century. More generally, paradox and paradoxical thought have been part of social theory since people began to record their reflections on the human condition. Paradox has long been an explicit element in Eastern religion and philosophy and was written about in the West by Zeno of Elea in the fourth century B.C. (Hughes and Brecht, 1975).

While acknowledging the early roots of paradox, our purpose in this chapter is to illustrate the role of paradox in social theory and practice in this century. We will expand on the description of paradox presented in the previous chapter by examining the presence of paradox in two arenas, psychotherapeutic practice and the work on small groups in the behavioral sciences.

Paradox in Psychotherapeutic Practice

It could be argued that the phenomenon of resistance represents a fundamental paradox that is at the core of many individual, group, and family psychotherapeutic approaches. It is neither unusual nor mystifying to find individuals and groups who simultaneously want to change and do not want to change,

19

are desperate to get "well" and are deeply invested in staying "sick." As we shall see, what makes this contradiction paradoxical is the link between these apparently opposing forces. It is often the task of the therapist to help discover the framework that makes sense of both the desire for change and the resistance to it. The connection between these opposing forces often reveals a "truth" about the individual or the group.

The role of paradox, however, is not always apparent in an examination of psychotherapeutic theory and practice in the twentieth century. In this section, we will examine briefly the presence of a paradoxical perspective in the work of selected individual, group, and family therapists. It will be evident that each had some awareness of the paradoxical aspects of psychological disturbance and of the curative process. It will also be clear that there is a great deal of variation in the degree to which these therapists explicitly articulated a theory of paradox in their work.

Individual Psychotherapy

Alfred Adler. By the second decade of this century, Adler had begun to use paradox in his clinical work (Weeks and L'Abate, 1982). After observing that patients repeatedly tried to draw him into a power struggle, Adler (1956) came to recognize that the potential fight was stirred by the patient's resistances. Believing that it was necessary to uncover the internal meaning of the resistances, Adler refused to engage in the power struggle and instead adopted the disarming approach of actually encouraging the resistance. In his view, the patient was mistakenly understanding the presenting symptoms as the cause of the problem. Making obvious the "symptomness" of this behavior became the starting point of the therapeutic process for Adler. He would *prescribe the symptom*—that is, say to the patient that the way to get well was by getting more "ill"—working on the principle that acceptance of the resistance was a necessary prerequisite to uncovering what the patient was working so hard to defend against.

Adler (1956) developed numerous paradoxical interventions, several of which have become common in the lexicon of therapeutic activity, such as (1) giving the client permission to have a symptom, (2) encouraging the client to exaggerate the symptom, (3) refining and improving the symptom through practice, and (4) redefining the symptom so that it could be cast in a positive rather than a negative light (Mozdzierz, Macchitelli, and Lisiecki, 1976).

Adler was also one of the first to attend to the interpersonal dynamics involved in depression, and this he also treated paradoxically. For example, he would often tell a depressed patient that the problem resulted from doing things that he or she did not want to do. "Never do anything you don't like," would be Adler's instruction. To which the retort would often come, "But there is nothing I like doing." To this, Adler would reply, "Then refrain from doing anything you dislike," thereby paradoxically transferring back to the patient the responsibility that the patient was attempting to displace onto the therapist (Adler, 1956, pp. 346-367).

Victor Frankl. Frankl developed for the clinical tradition the concept of paradoxical injunction. This is the explicit directing of the patient to will the symptom to occur. Frankl started using this technique as early as 1925, although he did not describe it until 1939 (see Frankl, 1975; Weeks and L'Abate, 1982). The concept of paradoxical injunction had, in fact, been around since the late sixteenth century, embodied in Montaigne's ([1595] 1958) *Essays.* Each essay involved a central life paradox and the jarring of some familiar aspect of life out of the accepted categories of truth and falsehood by the injunction of some being that Montaigne called *Other* (Wilden, 1980).

Frankl (1965) starts with the premise that at the center of each person's existence there is a deep yearning for meaning. Those who are unable or unwilling to find or create meaning become overwhelmed by anxiety that has to be dealt with in some way. Familiar methods, suggests Frankl, are anxiety neuroses and phobic reactions where internal vicious cycles are manufactured to hide from (or remain blind to) the anxieties associated with a sense of meaninglessness. These vicious cycles are both loved and hated by the patient, loved because they provide a smokescreen to that which is threatening, and hated because they demand so much energy to maintain and are often debilitating in and of themselves.

The patient, who often seeks help at a time when it is getting difficult to maintain the balance of the vicious cycle, usually does so with the wish that the therapist will take on one side of the struggle (the aspect that the patient hates) and attempt to make the symptom go away. Should this happen, the patient could then become increasingly invested in the aspect of it that he or she loves, thereby strengthening his or her capacity to protect against the anxieties that catalyzed the symptoms in the first place. In other words, the patient tries to replace the internal vicious cycle that is falling apart with one that will be structured into the relationship with the therapist. By refusing to take on a symptom-relieving function, by reinforcing the value of the resistance (as did Adler), and by encouraging the intensification of the symptom, the therapist is assisting the patient in tipping the vicious cycle out of the contours in which it has been revolving. At the same time, the patient is being encouraged to take responsibility for his or her own life, which is important, since responsibility is what is being avoided in the efforts to escape from feelings of meaninglessness. For Frankl, this is the work of what he labels logotherapy, the seeking and creating of meaning.

Foerster (1985) quoted a story of a logotherapeutic encounter between Frankl and a distraught man in which the essence of Frankl's thinking about paradox is evident. A husband and wife incarcerated in separate Nazi concentration camps were amazed to discover, after the liberation, that they both had survived. They were ecstatic. Their joy, however, was short-lived, for the wife soon became ill and died, stricken by a disease that she had contracted while being imprisoned. The husband went into a depression so deep that life no longer seemed worth living for him. Victor Frankl's help was sought. Frankl listened for a long time to this agonized story. When he eventually got around to speaking, his comments were very simple: "Please answer me one question. If I could find you a woman who looked just like your wife, who knew you exactly as she did, who knew all your stories and laughed at all the same places, who loved you just as she did, would you want her?" The depressed man thought long and hard. After a considerable silence, he replied, "No." Frankl got up, shook him by the hand, wished him well, and said good-bye.

In this case, the power of Frankl's paradoxical intervention revolved around confronting the depressed man with two sets of realities that reframed the internal vicious cycles that were paralyzing him. The first was to confront him with his own ambivalences about his now-deceased wife—he did not feel only positive things about her when she was alive, but, now that she was dead, he had become fixated on the positive side. By resurfacing and supporting the historical ambivalence, Frankl was confronting the man with a way to break out of the grooves that entrapped him. The second facet of this intervention was that this man, as a consequence of his wife's death, had become someone other than who he was when she was alive. He had become a person who could not stand life without his wife. Before she died, he was not that person. By focusing on the characteristics of the man's wife, Frankl was paradoxically pointing out that the man had already begun to change significantly and that it was the resistance to letting the flow of these changes continue that was paralyzing him, leaving him in a depressed state. By focusing on the man's choices about his wife, using her as a fixed reference—fixed because she was now no longer changing in his experience of her—the depressed man was forced to confront the dynamic nature of his own life. (This interpretation was formulated by Larry Hirschhorn and Jim Krantz in a private conversation in 1985.)

Otto Rank. At the same time that Adler and Frankl were bringing life to psychotherapeutic paradoxical techniques, Otto Rank, one of the Freudian inner circle, was beginning to explore what could now be labeled Rank's paradox.

Each of us is inextricably engaged in the struggles of our two selves: our creatureliness, our appetite, our animal nature, on the one hand, and our ingenuity, our insight, our conscious-

ness, on the other (Becker, 1973, 1975). We are aware of life
and death. We know that only as we indulge our animal natures,
as we consume food, as we eat other organisms, can we live. Yet
we also know that the very living of our lives brings us closer to
death, to extinction. Our knowledge that death is the consequence of life confronts each of us with anxiety. Every piece of
living, every attempt to create something special, every act to
imbue experience with meaning is threatened by the reality of
extinction. The end is never ambiguous. It is always death. This
creates a central paradox for humans. While each of us wants to
persevere, we are "cursed" with the special burden of knowing
that our efforts to persevere simply bring us closer to the extinction (death) of what we cherish the most (life).

Rank (1936) used as the basis of this theoretical work the
twin burdens of the *fear of life* and the *fear of death*. In this
formulation, he was advancing what could be viewed as one of
Freud's greatest discoveries, that the cause of much psychological illness is the fear of knowledge of oneself and the parallel fear
of the outside world (Maslow, 1963). While Freud worked with
these observations in frames such as "wrecked by success" and
"death instinct," Rank, operating in tandem with the existential
philosophy of his day, presented the view that it was quite normal for human beings to feel overwhelmed by the anxieties of
existence and that culturally reinforced illusions were helpful in
that they enabled individuals to gain some relief from the bur-
densome anxiety that accompanied reality. However, it would
be a great mistake to believe that these illusions were *the* reality. While they provided a way to cope with reality, to believe
that they were *the* reality would be maladaptive. Rank's view
was that we need the illusions because we have not learned to
embrace the full power of the anxiety that the reality of existence brings.

In his work with neurosis, Rank (1936) managed to turn
certain assumptions of the day on their heads. He suggested that
because much cultural life is a lie created to protect individuals
from the pain of reality (Becker, 1973), one could look at the
neurotic as someone who is having the following problem: It
seems impossible to accept what society says is real; yet to re-

ject these social illusions means to be out of step with everyone else. Then the self seems unreal, and feeling unreal about oneself makes it increasingly difficult to sort out what is real about the outside world. The only option appears to be to follow an isolated/isolating path; yet in opting out of society's illusions, another subtle illusion becomes created, that human existence can be lived in isolation. Through this cycle, the neurotic deprives himself or herself of the natural therapy contained in the illusions about everyday life and becomes trapped instead in a personal illusion.

This, then, is the heart of Rank's paradox. It is easy to become overwhelmed by too much human awareness about both the creative possibilities of life and the meaninglessness of life in the light of death. To protect us, society has created cultural illusions that the neurotic refuses to accept; in rejecting these, the neurotic creates an illusion of his or her own and becomes blind to the illusory nature of his or her escape from the "truth about truth." In this regard, the neurotic's symptoms can be understood as a communication about truth.

Carl Jung. Of all the early psychoanalytical writers, it was Jung who most explicitly addressed the philosophical aspects of paradox and the nature of reality. Perhaps the most poignant of his contributions in this area is the concept of the shadow, which Jung described in archetypal terms. It first forced its way into his awareness via the dream that he recounted in his memoirs (Jung, 1965): "It was night in some unknown place, and I was making slow and painful headway against a mighty wind. I had my hands cupped around a tiny light which threatened to go out at any moment. Everything depended on my keeping this little light alive. Suddenly I had the feeling that something was coming up behind me. But at the same moment I was conscious, in spite of my terror, that I must keep my little light going regardless of all dangers."

Here, the shadowy dark is created by the light. While being the complement of the light, the dark is also necessary for there to be any experience of light. Without dark, everything would be light, and then there could be no knowledge of light.

It is only because of dark that light is knowable. Jung took the power of this metaphor of the light and the shadow to remarkable lengths, creating a literal scandal in the theological world with his work *Answer to Job* (Jung, 1958). Here, he reasoned that evil was in fact the shadowy side of God's luminescence. And man, created in God's image, then became burdened with both sides, good and evil. In watching humans struggle with the contradictory nature of experience, God comes to find out something about his own nature. That is, God sees in man some things about himself mirrored back. Elaborating further, Jung reasoned that the traditional view of Christ's work of redemption was too one-sided. For Jung, the atonement was not only a "payment of a human debt to God, but reparation for a wrong done by God to man" (Jung, 1958, p. 56).

Whether Jung is right or wrong about the intentions of the Almighty is beside the point. What is important for our purposes is to acknowledge the intensity of Jung's thinking in a paradoxical frame. He saw opposites as necessary for the articulation of unity, which he described as antinomy, the totality of inner opposites. That is, wholeness is possible only via the coexistence of opposites. He took the view that meaning was found (or created) in the paradox that resulted from the juxtaposition of opposites, each searching for its complementary side in the drive for unity. Jung worked to bring together the holistic philosophies of the East—Yin and Yang—with the dualistic approaches of Western thought.

Fritz Perls. By the late 1950s, Gestalt therapy, the creation of Fritz Perls, had become internationally established. Although the Gestaltists rarely use the term *paradox* (Seltzer, 1984) and in fact refuse to acknowledge that they have any place in the paradoxical tradition, there are three clear ways in which the Gestalt movement works in a paradoxical frame. The first is the Gestalt therapists' insistence on working in the present (what they refer to as the "here and now"). When clients come to therapy, they of course bring a history and invariably want to explain themselves in terms of past events; for example, "my father beat me as a child," "my mother died when I was eight years old." The problem with the "explanation" is that it is presented in such a way that there is nothing that can ever be done about it—the beatings cannot be undone, and mother cannot be brought back to life. The Gestalt approach, by staying in the here and now, confronts the client with the ways he or she is currently invested in avoiding the possibilities of the present through tenaciously remaining fixated on the past. This time reframing, kaleidoscoping past into present, puts the clients in a position of personal responsibility, where they come to see themselves as active agents of remaining emotionally stuck and as the only ones who can genuinely create any personal transformation (Polster and Polster, 1973).

The second paradoxical element of the Gestalt approach is that the therapist does not adopt the role of being a changer but rather helps the client to be both where and what he or she is. In this regard, the client coming to the therapy with the wish to be different encounters a therapist who paradoxically encourages the client not to change but rather to become what he or she is (Beisser, 1970). Seltzer (1984) explains this paradoxical element of Gestalt therapy with a number of examples. He suggests that Perls had an "implicit notion" that the more one stays the same, the more one is *then* able to change, because the change is grounded in an acceptance of self that has been resisted. This acceptance of "sameness," says Seltzer, represents a radically different *attitude* toward the self, or, in our words, a different way of framing the self. Seltzer also quotes Perls (1976)—"Any intention toward change will achieve the opposite"—and describes Perls's encouragement of clients to become more of what they were so as to foster the emergence of their own counterforce. It is the inclusion of this counterforce that stimulates change.

The third paradoxical element may be seen in a number of Gestalt techniques, such as the empty-chair role reversal. The client, torn apart by two internal sides of self, is invited by the therapist to sit in one chair facing an empty chair with the task of having a conversation with him- or herself. The client, in chair A, looks across at chair B and "sees" there a version of self different from the one in chair A. From position A, he or she speaks to the opposite part of self "located" in chair *B* and then physically moves to chair *B* to respond to what was said from chair *A*. In no time, the client is jumping from *A* to *B*, engaging in an intense internal dialogue between discordant inner selves. The paradoxical nature of this work is that the client is brought to the position of creating an internal way of containing that which is experienced as "opposites," thereby diffusing the tendency to create an oppositional relationship with some other in the interpersonal arena, which would normally facilitate a flight from that which is internally troublesome.

Group Psychotherapy

To illustrate the role of paradox in group psychotherapy, we have chosen to examine Freud's (1922) work on groups (work that spawned the practice of group therapy) and the more recent work of Whitaker and Lieberman (1964) on group psychotherapy. Neither of these traditions specifically spelled out a theory of paradox, although it is possible to look back, as several writers have done, and see that this work is punctuated with paradox.

Sigmund Freud. Freud's founding conceptualization of the importance of groups has some essential paradoxical aspects. He used as his starting point McDougall's description of the organized group (continuity of existence, knowledge by members of the nature, composition, functions, capacities of the group, the importance of a group's interacting with other groups partly similarly and partly differently, the presence of customs and habits, and structure that facilitated specialization and differentiation) (Sutherland, 1985). From this, Freud made a link to the individual, indicating that individual functioning depended upon each person carrying around inside him- or herself internal images of the organized group, based on the experiences of each person's initial group, the family of origin. If the person's earliest experiences were of a family group that was unorganized (that is, lacking the essential characteristics of McDougall's organized group), then it would be difficult for that individual to develop his or her own distinctiveness.

Freud's paradox was that a person striving for individuality is often trying to flee from the overwhelming impact of the unorganized family group being carried around in his or her internal images. However, to develop the distinctiveness necessary to cope with those "internal images," the individual has to learn how to create a new sense of internal organization of the primary (family) group that was unorganized (or underorganized) when it was being lived. Hence, from a Freudian perspective, to become fully individuated it is necessary to work on and deal with one's groupness; but it is the impairment of one's groupness that stirs the desire to be individuated in the first place. If it were possible to come to grips with the group, individuation would not be so important; once it is unimportant, individuation becomes realized (Sutherland, 1985).

Dorothy S. Whitaker and Morton Lieberman. Whitaker and Lieberman (1964) developed an approach to understanding group behavior called "focal conflict analysis." The centrality of conflict is apparent in their terminology. For Whitaker and Lieberman, the behavior of individuals in a group can be understood in terms of the focal conflict that such behavior addresses. "Successive individual behaviors are linked associatively and refer to a common underlying concern about the here-and-now situation. The sequence of diverse events which occur in a group can be conceptualized as a common, covert conflict (the group focal conflict) which consists of an impulse or wish (the disturbing motive) opposed by an associated fear (the reactive motive). Both aspects of the group focal conflict refer to the current setting. When confronted with a group focal conflict [group members] direct efforts toward establishing a solution which will reduce anxiety by alleviating the reactive fears and, at the same time, satisfy to the maximum possible degree the disturbing impulse" (Whitaker and Lieberman, 1964, pp. 18–19).

The rebellious hostility of one member of a group may, for example, be the group's solution to the conflict between the wish to express angry feelings toward its leader and the fear of retaliation by this same leader. Group life is a succession of focal conflicts, with the solution to one conflict providing the seeds for the next disturbing motive. These focal conflicts are related to the unconscious, emotional life of the group but are played out in the behavioral conflict among group members or group members and the leaders. The therapist's role is to help the group address both the wish and the fear as it searches for a solution that "enables" the group to work on its primary task.

Although on the surface Whitaker and Lieberman do not appear to be working with the concept of paradox at all, a closer look suggests that "focal conflict theory" is an assertion of the inherently contradictory nature of unconscious wishes and fear in groups *and* of the circularity (series of restrictive solutions) that occurs when one side or the other of these opposing forces dominates the unconscious life of the group. Group change is facilitated by acknowledging and confronting the demands on *both* sides of the conflict, by exploring and addressing the role of these opposing forces in the group.

Family Therapy

Paradoxical family therapy grew from the work done by the Palo Alto group on schizophrenia. They came to understand schizophrenia to be a result of repetitive and circuitous patterns of behavior that were caught in the binds generated by a conflict of meaning. Since meaning depends on the relationship between an event and its context, if there were only one context, then the meaning would be clear, and appropriate behavior would be easy to determine. But if perchance there were two contexts for the same event, then there could be two meaning and, hence, potentially two sets of implications. Consider Brown's (1986) example of a mother who embraces her young daughter, kissing "her hard on the cheek. The little girl says, 'Mommy, you're hurting me.' Mother responds, 'No, dear, Mommy loves you' " (p. 1). In this case, there are *two* contexts that arise from the *same* communication. The meaning of the message being received by the child would depend on which of the contexts, the kiss or the painful squeeze, she is responding to. If she accepts both simultaneously, everything is very confusing. Bateson (1972) labeled such a situation *double binding.* One way of coping with such dissonance is to keep the situation as undefined as possible. However, that ill definition can lead to a vacillation between the two communications, triggering a cycling, as it were, within the contours of the double bind. Keeping relationships undefined as a means of avoiding the pain of the double-binding communication is the pattern of the schizophrenic.

This difficulty does not exist only or even primarily in the internal life of the individual. It also exists in the relationships among people. This recognition led to the work with families some of whom could be described as being in schizophrenic transaction, as the Milan group (Selvini Palazzoli, Boscolo, Cecchin, and Prata, 1978) refers to it. When a family is caught in symmetrical patterns of interaction that are exasperating, members usually feel that they cannot talk about it together. What emerges is a symmetrical system where each person hates his or her own behavior but feels that there are no alternatives, given what everyone else is doing (Bowen, 1978). What gets created is a type of closed circuit based on each member's rejection of how everyone else defines the relationship. Each member of the family comes to feel rejected by every other member and then uses this experience of rejection as a justification to counterattack, which, of course, simply brings more rejection (Laing, 1969). While every member finds this way of interacting to be horrible, each continues to repeat his or her contribution to the awfulness as though there were no alternatives, very much like an addict. Although each experience in a family in schizophrenic transaction is self-defeating, family members stoically refuse to accept defeat and return repetitively to the battlefield to try but one more time. Failure is unbearable, and being willing to continue to fight seems to be treated as a demonstration that all is not yet lost. Withdrawal is also unacceptable, as is winning, so everyone becomes invested in keeping family relationships undefined or in the process of being defined.

One clear example of a family caught in schizophrenic transaction, described by Karpman (1968), is the familiar triangle bound up by the three roles of persecutor, rescuer, and victim. Typically, rules become developed in a family about how these roles are to be played out, even though different members of the family may occupy these various roles from time to time. The key issue, however, is that once the persecutor-rescuer-victim triangle is activated, there are implicitly agreed-upon rules by which all members play. And even though there may be very destructive consequences flowing from the triangular patterns, no player is allowed to leave the field of interaction until the whole pattern has been played out.

The triangle of persecutor-victim-rescuer can be understood in terms of power dynamics. The pattern is as follows: the rescuer gets to feel loved by the victim because of the dependency needs expressed; the persecutor gets to feel powerful and gains the opportunity to express sadistic feelings; the victim in turn gets to feel love from the rescuer and a sense of importance from the persecutor, because at least the persecutor is paying the victim some attention. Ultimately, though, what is actually in it for the victim is the chance to be really powerful. In fact, the victim's position can get to be quite tyrannical in that he or she can exert inordinate influence while charading as helplessly dependent.

In this type of family interaction, the therapist has the paradoxical task of exposing the power of the victim's powerlessness and making it possible for everyone involved in the triangle to begin to understand and use power differently. The beginning point is to have those who experience themselves as powerful to recognize how their behavior is being controlled and those who claim powerlessness to acknowledge just how controlling their behavior is. Typically, the therapist will intervene by congratulating the victim on the amount of power he or she has accumulated and his or her capacity to steal love from the others and by encouraging members of the triangle to escalate their behaviors so that the covert processes will be made obvious (Minuchin, 1974). For example, the therapist might say to the rescuer, "When you feel unloved, I want you to do something for (the victim)"; to the persecutor, "When you feel lacking in self-confidence, I want you to invent ways of blaming others for your shortcomings or mistakes"; and to the victim, "When you feel helpless or powerless, I want you to pretend to be even more helpless and get people to take care of you just like you were a child" (Weeks and L'Abate, 1982). These interventions are based on the principle that naturally self-corrective forces will be released in the family's relationships if the counterproductive, hidden rules of interaction are first made visible and then shattered by everyone stretching them beyond the limits of their capacity to constrain everyone's behavior (Haley, 1976).

Another paradoxical pattern that emerges in families involves the recognition that change is needed (Satir, 1967). If it is the family that is seeking help for the identified patient, the message is clearly "he or she needs to be changed." If it is the identified patient seeking help, the message is "they need to be changed, and I want you (therapist) to work out for me how to change them." No matter who approaches the therapist, the pattern is the same. The relationships are no longer tolerable, and change is necessary. The central question, though, is who has to change? Always it is the *other*. But what changes need to be made? If other behaves differently, is that sufficient? Never! Other has to cease *being* what other is! That is, each is saying that "only if you are not what you are can I be what I am not but what I should have been" (Selvini Palazzoli, Boscolo, Cecchin, and Prata, 1978, p. 36).

Despite the circularity of these family interactions, certain members of the family believe that they are capable of gaining unilateral control of the definition of the relationship, which, of course, is an illusion, for the very notion of circularity means that linear control is not possible. The battle for control becomes like a game of winning and losing where no sooner does one member believe that he or she has won than the discovery emerges that winning in fact meant losing—a double bind—creating the feeling of having won the battle and lost the war (Minuchin, 1974).

To work paradoxically with such a family, it is important not to operate simply in their communication system but to elevate the therapeutic work to the metacommunicative level (Haley, 1976). This is done by speaking within the system of the schizophrenic interaction but placing on the exchanges binds that make it possible neither to obey nor to rebel against what is being said. The idea is that this forces the family to relate in a way that gets out of the grooves that had kept them all going endlessly round in circles, creating a cycle of helpless interactions where everyone's efforts to make things better simply made the situation worse. The paradoxical approach is focused on creating definitions where definition had previously been avoided. Family therapists have created a large number of paradoxical techniques designed to catalyze the family's movement out of the double-binding situations that were created originally as a way of dealing with internal contradictions.

Reframing. This involves changing the emotional and conceptual contexts in which family events are experienced and placing them in different frames that, while fitting the same facts, give entirely new and revitalizing meanings to what was dragging the family down (Watzlawick, Weakland, and Fisch, 1974). For example, the threat to a family's internal stability posed by its teenager's desire to reach out beyond the bounds of behavior usually viewed as tolerable may be reframed as an opportunity to expand the family's resilience and capacity to adapt to changing external demands. In this situation, the frame has been shifted from the level of the relationships within the family to the relationships between the family and its environment (Jackson, 1968).

Relabeling. This is the changing of the label attached to a person, problem, or behavior without switching frames of reference, as in the above example (Haley, 1973). It usually involves placing a positive, adaptive, or normal connotation on that which is being viewed as negative, maladaptive, or abnormal. Hence, a young child's tantrums during the "terrible twos" may be seen not as tantrums but as the necessary learning of the concept of "no" so that he or she will mature into a being capable of having a real sense of what saying "yes" means.

Paradoxical Prescription. This technique focuses on making the rules of the family interaction visible by creating specific family rituals (Andolfi, 1974). For example, a family may be instructed as follows: On Tuesdays, Thursdays, and Saturdays, the father must decide alone what to do with the person called the identified patient. On other days, except Sunday, mother must decide, at her absolute discretion, what to do, acting as if father were not even there. On Sundays, everyone must behave spontaneously (Selvini Palazzoli, Boscolo, Cecchin, and Prata, 1978). This prescription makes visible the way that parents normally interfere with each other, it breaks up the normal triangles, and it makes visible how the parents compete with each other over who is more helpful for the child (Weeks and L'Abate, 1982).

Paradoxical Descriptions. The mere describing of an event involves giving it certain attributes. Family therapists can use this paradoxically by presenting what they see to be transpiring in merely descriptive terms, yet folding prescriptions into their descriptions (Stierlin, 1974). While this may seem sneaky, it has power. For example, telling a family that it has a real talent for creating rich symptoms, thereby avoiding the terrible problems a family not so clever might have to deal with, puts it in the paradoxical position of potentially feeling good about what it feels bad about. The message is that it is better for the family to experience the pain of the symptoms than to endure the pain of that which causes the symptoms; of course, ultimately this is recognized as being ridiculous.

Restraining. This refers to the actions of the therapist that inhibit or forbid change (Watzlawick, Weakland, and Fisch, 1974). Inhibiting usually means demanding that change occur at a slower pace than the family believes should be the case, while forbidding change is simply affirming that change (in the way it is occurring) will do no good. Typically, change is forbidden by encouraging the family members to simply give in to those feelings of helplessness that overwhelm them all and to accept that this is a family that is unchangeable (Minuchin, 1974). The intent behind this is to break the cycle created by the hubris of the members who are so into their own sense of control that they believe they can move mountains so long as they learn the right techniques and exert enough effort.

In each of these therapeutic interventions, the key is

bringing the family as a whole face to face with the contradictions involved in family life. The therapist works to uncover at least two activities occurring simultaneously: the family's attempt to create an illusion of good feeling and the pain and confusion of family members with regard to themselves and the family unit.

Paradox in Theory and Research on Groups

As difficult as it is to see the presence of a paradoxical perspective in group psychotherapy, it is even harder to find explicit reference to the role of paradox in small-group research. At the core of a paradoxical view of group dynamics, however, are the issue of opposites and the question of how the existence of oppositional and contradictory forces affect the behavior of groups. The centrality of opposition and contradiction in the definition of paradox provides us with a place to start in our search for the presence of paradox in current theory and research on small groups—namely, the topic of conflict. The fact that the description of conflict in groups often has a repetitive, circular quality similar to that of paradox also suggests that conflict in groups is an appropriate place to look for the presence of paradox.

Conflict is a familiar experience to anyone who has spent time working in groups. It can be defined simply as the clash of oppositional forces, including ideas, persons, interests, wishes, and drives. These oppositional forces are usually assumed to be antagonistic, incompatible, and contradictory as they are perceived by the people involved. Conflict in groups is not viewed as inherently constructive or destructive (Deutsch, 1973), and it has been suggested that small groups can actually realize significant benefit from the experience of conflict, including the reaffirmation of stability and the revitalization of group norms (Coser, 1956).

Since conflict in small groups is both common and emotionally powerful, one would expect to find substantial attention paid to the topic in the research literature on small groups. Interestingly, this is not the case. In McGrath and Altman's

(1966) review and classification of small-group research, conflict is not one of the thirty-one "substantive classes" the authors use to organize their sample of 250 studies on groups. The word *conflict* appears infrequently even under such categories as "influence and conformity pressures" or "patterns of interaction" and then only as a dependent variable, like group goal orientation or cohesiveness. If one wanted to find out about the role of conflict in groups or about the impact of conflict on member attitudes or group performance, it would be very difficult to pursue such issues using McGrath and Altman (1966) as a reference guide. More recently, Hare's (1976) *Handbook of Small Group Research,* an excellent summary of work in a variety of areas, does not even list *conflict* in the index, and Zander's (1977, 1982) two recent works on groups mention within-group conflict on exactly three pages, and then only in passing. Bales and Cohen (1979) too devote only a handful of pages to the topic of conflict, in spite of the fact (or perhaps because of it) that most of their book describes polarization in small groups. Even in the psychoanalytically oriented *Analysis of Groups* (Gibbard, Hartman, and Mann, 1974), only two of the sixteen articles address conflict as a substantive topic in its own right.

There are some notable exceptions to the general trend (for example, Deutsch, 1973; Bradford, Gibb, and Benne, 1964; Whitaker and Lieberman, 1964; Gustafson and others, 1981; Yalom, 1985), but one cannot help but be struck by the relative inattention to the phenomenon of conflict in groups. Even if one suspects that much of the research that has been done on small groups is relevant to the issue of conflict (for example, cohesiveness, effectiveness, "groupthink," and so on), it is still curious that few authors spend much time making these connections. When conflict *is* addressed in the literature on small groups, it is viewed as an inevitable feature of group life, born of the differences that individuals bring to groups (Deutsch, 1973; Sartre, 1976) or the "playing out" in an interpersonal setting of the intrapsychic conflicts within members (Klein, 1959; Wells, 1980). Although the view that conflict is inevitable in small groups is consistent with the contention that groups are inherently paradoxical because the observation about conflict suggests that opposing and contradictory forces are always present in groups, most of the research on conflict in small groups treats the opposing or contradictory forces as separate and distinct. As a result, conflict is treated as either a problem or a phase, and the critical work in groups with respect to conflict involves conflict resolution and compromise. The presence of paradox is hard to find in the literature.

It is understandable why many observers of small-group behavior (who are themselves participants in small groups) consider conflict to be a problem that needs to be and can be minimized or controlled. From the perspective of group effectiveness, for example, the clash of opposing forces and the hostility or anger that may accompany it represent potentially significant "process losses" (Hackman and Morris, 1975). Imperatives such as "let's keep emotions out of this," "let's not fight now," "can we do this in a rational, problem-solving way" all speak to the desire to keep strong, conflicting feelings out of the group's process. Disagreement is both acceptable and desirable in this view of group behavior but is distinguished from true conflict by the level and intensity of the emotions involved and, implicitly, by the group's ability to manage disagreement without losing control. Conflict represents a danger to effective group functioning, since it may take time, be irrelevant to the task at hand, or disrupt the interpersonal relationships needed for possible "process gains" (see Schwartzman, 1986, for a review of some research with this perspective).

Approaches to "solving" the problem of group conflict include (1) reducing the incidence of destructive conflict by creating conditions that promote cooperation and conflict resolution (Deutsch, 1973), (2) pre-empting conflict of any kind by "designing" the task of the group so as to minimize conflict, and (3) "decomposing" the group, as in the case of the Nominal Group Technique and Delphi approaches (Delbecq, Van de Ven, and Gustafson, 1975), in order to minimize and control group-level interaction (Schwartzman, 1986). Conflict resolution is the process of discovering and creating the conditions under which conflict can be minimized or transformed (Deutsch,

1973). These conditions range from those described by Deutsch (1973) as facilitating cooperation in conflict situations to those in which the group interaction is limited structurally.

Another perspective on small-group behavior views conflict as a phase during which some hostile emotion must be expressed or a set of differences must be reconciled. Gibbard, Hartman, and Mann (1974) describe two types of "phase" theories in the literature on group development, linear-progressive and life cycle. In a linear-progressive model, the phases of a group's life build toward a state of maturity or steady-state functioning. In a life-cycle model, the phases of group life are roughly analogous to the stages of growth and decline characteristic of a living system: birth, adolescence, maturation, adulthood, decline, and death. It is the end point and a group's awareness of this end point that distinguish linear-progressive from life-cycle theories of group development.

Many of the phase theories of group development include a phase that has conflict as a central theme. "Storming," Tuckman's (1965) second phase in the sequence forming-storming-norming-performing, is a stage in which hostility is directed toward other members or the leader as a way of expressing individuality and resistance to the formation of the group. Bennis and Shepard (1956) and Slater (1966) describe psychoanalytically based models of group development that include a phase in which the group rebels against and attacks the leader, and/or subgroups align themselves against each other over the resolution of a central conflict in the group. In each of these models, the inability to resolve the central conflicts in the group or to learn conflict-resolution skills is seen as forestalling movement toward the establishment of mature norms of interaction and work (Tuckman, 1965), interdependent working relationships (Bennis and Shepard, 1956), or the free expression of positive and negative emotions (Slater, 1966). Conflict is a necessary phase of group life. Without passing through this phase and successfully negotiating it, group progress is unlikely.

There are examples in the literature on groups of a third perspective on conflict, which views conflict as an attendant process to collective life, not merely one to be minimized or resolved and moved past. This perspective seems more compatible with a paradoxical view of group life, because the researchers in this area have acknowledged, either implicitly or explicitly, the connection between the opposing or contradictory forces as well as the connection between the ongoing presence of contradictory forces and the survival and growth of the group. We examine the work of Bion (1961) and the reflections that Benne (1964) made on the T-group movement as illustrations of this third perspective.

Wilfred Bion. In Bion's (1961) work with groups, he found struggle and conflict at both the conscious and unconscious levels. He described groups as having three emotional states (what he called basic assumptions): dependency, fight-flight, and pairing. In addition, he called the aspect of the group dedicated to the primary task the "work group."

> The dependency group perceives the leader as omnipotent and omniscient while considering themselves inadequate, immature and incompetent. This idealization of the leader is matched by desperate efforts to extract knowledge, power and goodness from him [*sic*] in a forever dissatisfied way. The failure of the leader to live up to such an ideal of perfection is first met with denial, and then with a rapid, complete devaluation ... and a search for substitute leadership ... members feel united by a common sense of needfulness, helplessness and fear of an outside world vaguely experienced as empty or frustrating.
>
> The fight-flight group is united against vaguely perceived external enemies, as well as to protect the group from any in-fighting. Any opposition to the "ideology" shared by the majority ... cannot be tolerated and the group easily splits into subgroups which fight each other. In short, splitting, projection of aggression and "productive identification" are predominant, and the search for nurture and dependency ... is here replaced by conflicts around

aggressive control, with suspiciousness, fight and
dread of annihilation prevailing.

The pairing assumption leads the group to
focus on two of its members—a couple (frequently
but not necessarily heterosexual) to symbolize the
group's hopeful expectation that the selected pair
will "reproduce" itself, thus preserving the group's
threatened identity and survival. . . . The pairing
group, in short, experiences generalized intimacy
and sexual developments as a potential protection
against the dangerous conflicts around dependency
and aggression [Kernberg, 1980, pp. 213-214].

For Bion, group process was the constantly changing
dominance of one or the other of the emotional states or work-
group conditions. Conflict is a central, recurring, and inevitable
part of Bion's theory in two ways. In its simplest form, one of
the three recurring emotional states (fight-flight) involves conflict explicitly. On a broader level, the work group is always in
conflict with the three emotional states. At both levels, the connection between the opposing forces is explicit. Both the fight
and the flight reactions (and subgroups) are a response to threat,
and both the work group and the basic-assumption groups are a
response to the ambivalences evoked by collective activity.

Schermer (1985) explicitly points to the place of paradox
in Bion's work. He illustrates using the fight-flight dynamic in a
group. When members begin to experience unmanageable internal tensions, intermember relations become threatened, producing the possibility of group chaos unless some method can be
developed to defend against the tensions. The group invariably
"manages" this situation by splitting into subgroups, which
then proceed to fight with each other. The group's managerial
focus is accordingly shifted to containing these warring subgroups. In the process, individually based tensions that had their
birth in paradox, the coexistence of feelings that were experienced as opposites, become expressed in a polarized way at the
group level. The larger paradox is that the complex management
of the polarized group relations is a substitute for the acceptance of an individual paradox that would vanish as an issue to

be attended to if there were a way to simply accept the existence of these seemingly contradictory emotions.

The paradoxical elements of Bion's work were made explicit by Newman (1974) in a chapter devoted to paradox. Her work, solidly in the tradition spawned by Bion's work, attempted to articulate the following types of paradoxes found in the unconscious life of groups and their members: (1) While individuals join together in groups primarily to do what seemed like an agreed-upon task, once they have assembled, the group spends a great deal of time defining what that task is. After the group has agreed to work on a task, it often spends more energy destroying the task than working toward its fulfillment. The group usually must run into its own resistance to doing the task and make that resistance visible to itself before it is ready to work constructively on the task that drew the individuals together in the first place. (2) People are often driven to join a group or stay in one to deal with their loneliness, yet the group experience often makes them feel more lonely. The bind for members of a group is that the group stirs their oceanic fears of being swallowed up, with the attendant possibility of losing their identity, their autonomy, their own personal boundaries. (3) An individual often joins a group to overcome a sense of personal inadequacy due to anxiety about being competent. Yet, in the group, a new collective anxiety is usually created at a level of intensity that makes members feel even more inadequate than they did before joining the group. Despite the fact that members in groups wish to gain something that they lack as individuals, belonging to a group in fact involves taking on roles that, while sustaining the collective needs of the group, often limit the options of the individuals who fill them. In addition to the individual doubts, fears, and frustrations that each person is feeling, those who are occupying particular roles in the group both take on and are expected to feel the special doubts, fears, and frustrations of those roles on behalf of others in the group.

Newman (1974) highlights a special point that has been central to the understanding of groups for several decades: that one can never really be free from the multiple group memberships each carries around. Even when we are most attuned to our own individuality, we all have groups in our heads, such as our internalized experiences of our own family dynamics and our images about the appropriate behavior for those who belong to our work group, profession, classroom, or whatever (Berg, 1978). Further, as Alderfer (1977) makes explicit, when we encounter others with different group memberships (such as race, age, gender, or socioeconomic standing), our own racial, gender, age, or socioeconomic group memberships become salient because those who are different from us see us in terms of our group identifications, just as we see them in terms of theirs. Hence, we are all engaged in the paradox (mentioned by numerous writers) that in order to be an individual we have to take on our groupness.

Kenneth Benne. Looking back on seventeen years of work in the National Training Laboratories, Benne (1964) adopted a paradoxical frame to reflect on the processes active in the T-group. His central thesis was that much could be gained in a group when naturally occurring polarizations or conflicts could be transformed into paradoxes. Three such transformations illustrate Benne's thinking.

The original goal of an experiential group, to study its own internal processes, creates many ambiguities for the unformed group. These ambiguities become so disorienting that members develop a secondary goal, to dispel the anxieties created by the original goal. The primary and secondary goals become embodied in the emergence of two subgroups, one of which focuses on producing something, presumably in the hope that production will take the anxieties away, while the other remains invested in feeling the intensity of the anxiety that the original goal created. The dilemma for the "producer" subgroup is that they cannot determine what appropriate production might be. Hence, the members of the "feeling" subgroup point out to them that the producers are *feeling* frustrated by their inability to produce and that it might be better to simply feel this frustration rather than beat on themselves to produce. On the other side, the producers retort that if the feeling subgroup were not so interested in distracting everyone by insisting on feeling everything, then the process of production might be possible and the destructive feelings would then disappear. At this point, the group is stuck, and members look to the leader (or facilitator) to set them free. However, each side believes that if the leader/facilitator would throw his or her weight behind its particular perspective, all would be well. Of course, to do this would only intensify the struggle and trigger each subgroup into another battle over whether the leader/facilitator is doing the right or wrong thing. Paradoxically, suggests Benne (1964), the function of the leader has to be giving support to both sides, thereby escalating the conflict that needed leadership in the first place; in the process, group members are confronted even more strongly with the realization that they alone can work out the issues for which they feel leadership is necessary.

Another paradox of Benne's is that members get split on the issue of whether the group exists for the individuals or the individuals for the group. This is manifest in a struggle over group maintenance versus self-maintenance. Of course, this bipolar position fades only when members accept their groupness and when the group accepts the importance of its individual members. Hence, the group gains its solidarity as individuality is legitimated, and individuality is established when the primacy of the group is affirmed.

A third example that Benne gives of the paradoxical polarizations in groups is that a great benefit of a group is that it enables alternatives to be generated that are not possible for individuals alone. The problem is that, for a group to choose, it must make judgments. To make these judgments, however, standards of intermember interactions must be established. But the establishment of these standards depends on judgments. To break out of this cycle, a group must be willing to do what seems impossible: to make judgments without first establishing standards and to set standards through the process of making judgments. This is a paradox. By making judgments, a group creates the standards that it needed in order to make the judgments.

Paradox and Conflict

When we look at the examples we have chosen in the fields of individual and group psychotherapy, family therapy, and small-group research, we see a pattern that takes us a step toward understanding the relationship between paradox and conflict. In those cases where a paradoxical presence can be discerned (by us or by the researchers and practitioners themselves), there are three important elements. First is an awareness of the presence of opposing or contradictory forces. Second is an acknowledgment and understanding that these are natural and inevitable forces that attend individual and collective life. Third is an assertion, often but not always tacit, that these contradictory forces are somehow linked or connected. It is this link, the idea that the contradictory or opposing forces spring from a common source, that differentiates conflict from paradox. The contradiction of *paradox* asserts that there *is* a frame that, when applied, makes sense of the apparent contradiction. This framework gives meaning to the coexisting opposites. In much of the work of the individual psychotherapists and in the work of Whitaker and Lieberman (1964), Bion (1961), and Benne (1964), a paradoxical perspective is present in the articulation not just of the opposing forces inside individuals and groups but also of the "underlying issue," framework, or theme that connects these forces.

But what exactly *is* the connection? How do these contradictory forces come to be linked? What individual and collective processes give rise to coexisting but opposing forces linked to each other so tightly that it seems almost impossible to escape from the circularity their juxtaposition creates? What is it that makes the special circumstance where conflict takes on a paradoxical quality? Answering these questions requires us to explore two additional conceptual domains. First, we will briefly discuss the epistemological area circumscribed by the issues of negation, self-reference, and double bind. Chapter Three will examine the connections between seemingly contradictory forces and will illustrate some of the forces of circularity embedded in these connections. Second, in Chapter Four we will look at the psychological processes of splitting and projection that occur at individual, group, and intergroup levels. These processes describe how contradictory, self-referential experiences are created in groups.

3

Understanding
Paradoxical Processes:
Negation, Self-Reference,
and Double Bind

In the last chapter, we reviewed the presence of paradox in the work of twentieth-century social theory in the areas of psychotherapy and small-group research. It was evident that many theoreticians and practitioners understood the essential nature of the paradoxical dynamic and its force in individual and collective life. People who studied and worked with individuals and groups found them struggling to make sense out of tensions and conflicts that were experienced as contradictory. These researchers also noticed that the contradictions were connected somehow, usually by an overarching concept that was able to frame a relationship between the opposing forces. Our purpose in this chapter is to explore how our ways of knowing about and understanding the social world contribute to our experience of contradiction. In describing how we often create the experience of contradiction, we will also discover the links between the contradictions and some of the reasons why it is so difficult to see these links.

People, groups, and organizations are social entities that not only act but reflect upon their actions. When we observe these reflective processes, patterns emerge. For example, how a group thinks about its experiences of conflict both gives that conflict its meaning and sets the parameters for possible courses of action. Consider a group that is committed to a particular direction but some of whose members are uncertain about the wisdom of the path being taken. It is commonplace for this to be dealt with in a way that generates two subgroups, aligned along the dimensions of commitment and noncommitment. If the "committed" members see the opposition as an attempt to thwart the group's progress, they may treat those taking a different perspective as an enemy to be overcome, thereby creating an internal conflict. On the other hand, if the opposition is seen as a natural part of the very concept of commitment, the same committed subgroup may embrace those who are different as being part of itself, thereby enriching everyone's understanding of what commitment means.

In the human arena, something that is not conflictual in its essence can be made so simply by how those involved elect to think about it. That is, the actual domain of conflict may be in the system of thinking of those engaged in the event rather than in the event itself. This means that when experiences of conflict are an expression of our thinking patterns, the process of transforming conflict of necessity involves a shift in our modes of thinking. It is therefore very important that we examine how human consciousness engages in reflecting on itself.

We begin by stating the philosophical heritage of the *existential paradox* as it was understood at the turn of the century when the psychoanalytical tradition was being formed. The existential paradox introduces the concept of *negation*, which in turn provides the foundation for reflective self-consciousness in groups. We then move to a discussion of the problem of *logical types*, or multiple frames. Concepts that have meaning at one level of understanding get mixed up with the meanings these concepts have at another level. The result is a conflict of "logics" that creates activities that appear to be contradictory and unresolvable. We will then address the attendant problem of *double bind.* Each event derives its meaning from the relationship of that event to the context in which it is framed.

Sometimes the same event may be framed by two or more contexts that create multiple and contradictory meanings. If the situation demands that some action be taken, it may prove to be overwhelming because the choices suggested by one framing are antithetical to those implied by another. And it may turn out that there are no cues as to which framing is more appropriate. Such a situation is ultimately double binding. The last theme is that of *self-reference*. When a social entity uses itself as a mirror through which it judges what it is like, it often sees only the parts of itself that confirm what it wants to know; that is, that will enable it to remain basically as it wants to be. Systems that are primarily self-referential create binds for themselves that are difficult to get out of. Each of these epistemological themes makes a contribution to our understanding of the circular nature of contradiction in paradox.

The Existential Paradox

Kierkegaard ([1844] 1957) introduced what has now become referred to as the existential paradox. The foundation for Kierkegaard's view of humanity may be found in his interpretation of the myth of Adam and Eve and their ejection from the Garden of Eden. Kierkegaard suggested that this myth deals with the dawning of consciousness symbolized as a descent from innocence, a *fall* into self-consciousness as it were, an awakening from a comfortable ignorance. What happened to humanity was that we became capable of reflecting on our condition, which brought an awareness of our dual natures: our creatureliness and our partial divinity, the mortality of our bodies and the capacity to project ourselves beyond the limits dictated by death. With this realization came existential anxiety, that sense of dread that accompanies ambiguity. For some, this triggers the desire to retreat to an earlier state of ignorance where ambiguity does not exist. Others wish that someone, some Other, Yahweh, would provide a way out, an unambiguous resolution. But for all, the Adam and Eve myth makes clear that each must be responsible and learn how to live with the judgment that accompanies responsibility. In particular, as God told Adam, eat of the fruit of the tree of knowledge and "thou shalt surely die"—or, saying it with slightly different emphasis, "if you taste of knowledge, it will bring to you an awareness of your own mortality." Hence, suggested Kierkegaard, the meaning of the Garden of Eden myth is that we are born into the dilemma of having to unify, within our beings, the ultimate opposites of life and death. With this awakening, the existential paradox had its birth.

Rollo May (1975) suggests that the myth of Adam is re-enacted in every infant, beginning a few months after birth, reaching a peak at age two or three, when concepts such as right and wrong and yes and no come to life, and then continuing in various forms through all phases of development and maturation. In particular, we each have to work out our own individual way of dealing with the tensions created by the dual natures of our creatureliness and our self-reflectiveness. One option is to feel overwhelmed and depressed. Another is to rail against God for making it this way. Another is to rebel, to struggle against death, to attempt to immortalize ourselves. And in the attempt to reject or deny the realities of death, we provide an added dimension to our living, punctuating it with the artifacts we create. Thus, in the face of the knowledge of mortality, some generate the courage to live life with more intensity than would be the case were there no knowledge of death. This in turn makes the reality of death more devastating, because it represents an end to an even bigger sense of living. In May's view, the reality of death is the major stimulus for human creativity.

Working with this realization, Brown (1959) and Becker (1973) brought a whole new dimension to what has been classically referred to in psychoanalytical thought as the Oedipus complex. Rather than this human theme being treated in the narrow confines of sexual lust and competitiveness with the father, it could be viewed as a metaphor for the child's struggle over whether he or she "will be a passive object of fate, an appendage of others, a plaything of the world, or whether he or she will be an active center within him/herself" (Becker, 1973, pp. 35, 36). With a little reframing, the oedipal complex could be understood as the oedipal project, the child's movement from passivity, from obliteration, from dependency, in a struggle to become the *father of him- or herself*, the creator and sustainer of his or her own life. The project that gets taken on is a way to affirm one's own life, together with all the attendant pitfalls; but it also contains within it the wish to flee from death.

Stated in theoretical terms, the oedipal project highlights that the affirmation contains the negation within it, that the tensions between affirmation and negation are essentially paradoxical. Any attempt to transcend this conflict involves the "fathering" of a new way of being and the affirming at a meta-level of the link between affirmation and negation at the lower level. This meta-affirmation, although rarely recognized, also has its own metanegation embedded within it. Borrowing from Jung's metaphor of the light and the shadow, this means that every attempt to throw additional light on the dark so that the dark can be seen to be a part of the light actually creates a larger darkness, since there cannot be an expanded light without an expanded darkness. This growth in the dark is a complementary and necessary companion to the light's increased luminescence.

The Role of Negation

While an understanding of affirmation-negation and life-death dynamics was developing within the existential psychotherapies, the communication theorists, led by Bateson (1972), were building an epistemological base for understanding the larger issue of which the existential paradox is a part. The key to understanding their work may be found in the distinction between digital and analogical systems of thought, familiar these days because of the presence of analogue and digital computers but also commonly referred to as the left brain–right brain phenomenon. For the person who is right-handed, the left brain operates on digital principles and is the seat of logical reasoning. The right brain is analogical—it has no concept of "no," does not create order in terms of sequences, and is the seat of the expressive and artistic sides of human intellectual functioning. Our dream life is analogical. There is no "no" in the unconscious.

For this reason, when we wake and want to tell someone our dreams, it is impossible to know where to start. We invariably begin at some point, then discover partway through the telling that we have to begin somewhere else in the dream in order to make sense out of what we are describing. What we are encountering is the frustration of representing in digital form that which is essentially analogical.

The analogue and the digital operate on two radically different systems. The analogue is based on the principle of more/less and both/and, whereas the digital uses either/or and on/off mechanisms. It is very difficult in the analogical frame to represent negation, for in this system there is no true zero. At the zero point everything is off. Not so with the digital, which combines a large number of on/off switches and is capable of representing both positives and negatives (Wilden, 1980).

A particular dilemma for the analogical system is the difficulty of representing "no-thing" or saying "I'm not doing anything." In his theory of play, Bateson (1955) highlights this problem for animals whose brains are structured in such a way that they can communicate only analogically. Bateson suggests that if an animal wants to say "I don't want to fight," it can communicate this behaviorally by merely refusing to fight. However, for the animal to say "I'm not fighting," what it does is fight and then stop. In the process, it is saying, "it's fighting I'm now not doing." In this sense, the animal who has had to fight to say it is not fighting has said the opposite of what it meant in order to mean the opposite of what it said (Bateson, Jackson, Haley, and Weakland, 1956). In the analogical system, to communicate "not," the animal has to make two contradictory statements.

Bateson elaborates the complexity of this theme in his analysis of play in animals where the playful nip stands for a bite, something it is not. Whereas the bite is what it is, the nip is not. The nip signifies both the absence *and* the presence of the bite. In this sense, it is a metacommunication. It contains a positive statement, a negative statement, *and* an implicit negative metastatement folded inside it (Bateson, 1955). The playful "nip" is a phenomenon in which the actions of "play" are used to denote actions other than what they are—namely, "non-play." Hence, "nip" is a metaphor. It stands for something concrete and something abstract at the same time. Concretely, it says "this is a nip." Here the symbol "nip" stands for what it denotes. However, it also says "this is not a bite." It has been made into a second-level metaphor and in this sense is a meta-communication. Hence, the "nip" in its concrete form is a direct communication, and, in its abstract form of standing for "this is not a bite," it is a metacommunication.

The distinction between a statement and a metastatement is complex, but it is important to understand, for it links deeply to the strange loop that is at the heart of paradox. Consider a drawing of a pipe that has printed underneath it the words "This is not a pipe." Now clearly it is a pipe. So what is meant by the words "This is not a pipe"? Well, at the level of a metastatement, it really is a drawing of a pipe. In that sense, it is not a pipe but a representation of a pipe. So the "not a pipe" statement was not really focused on the pipe; it was trying to say something about the representation of the pipe. That is, the drawing of the pipe is not a pipe, it is a drawing. In this regard, the word *not* ends up becoming very tricky, because it can be a word used at a metastatement level that, if it gets applied at the statement level (or vice versa), can create remarkably tangled hierarchies.

This can be "seen" in the classic statement by Alice (in Wonderland), "I see nobody on the road," bringing the retort, "You must have incredibly powerful eyes to be able to see nobody." Of course, the real statement is "I do not see anybody." The *not* is intended as a negation on the operation of seeing rather than on the object (body). The displacement of the *not* creates a strange, tangled communication.

A problem with *not* is that it can be used in two totally different ways. There is a logical difference between the syntactical *not* of negation and the commonsense way that we use *not* to mean the absence (nonpresence) of something. In saying "*A* is not present," we use *not* differently than we do when we assert that *A* is *not* not *A*. In the latter case, *A* and not *A* are in a structural relationship of negation with each other.

To say that A is not present (absent) in the particular context is describing a relationship of exclusion rather than negation. "Houseness" is simply not present in the context of "tree." "Houseness" is absent from "treeness." It does not belong there. However, the light and the shadow, as per the Jungian dream discussed earlier, exist in a relationship of negation with each other. Negate light and you have shadow. Negate tree and you do not have house. You get "nontreeness." House may belong to the class of "nontreeness," but it does not assist in defining "nontreeness."

We can very often travel from A to B via the "path of not" yet be unable to return from B to A via the same "not path." Consider, for example, the conditions of *happy, unhappy, not happy,* and *not unhappy. Happy* and *not happy* are in a relation of negation with each other. *Unhappy* and *not unhappy* are not, however. *Not* in this case is a statement of absence. Unhappiness is not in my current experience. This does not mean that happiness is. If I am happy, it is possible to negate happiness and become unhappy. If, however, I am unhappy, negating unhappiness does not lead to happiness. It will probably produce depression or something worse than the original unhappiness. What one can see fairly easily here is that we have the problem of the double negative. In communication systems, the operation of negation is quite different from what it is in algebra. In mathematics, multiply positive by negative and the result is negative; multiply negative by negative and you get positive. Not so in communication systems. Negative multiplied by negative does not bring us back to the positive position. It will create something like negativism, as the existentialists would refer to it.

The special importance about *not* for our deliberation here is twofold: (1) it highlights how consciousness changed once the digital developed and was added to the analogical system of communication; and (2) it made possible the concept of different logical types, the heart of the problem of paradox that we will discuss below.

For any entity to be able to think about itself, it must be able to digitalize: that is, make the distinction between what it is and what it is not. Entities may relate analogically, but in order to *talk about or be aware of that relating,* they require the capacity to digitalize. To comprehend the analogue as analogue, we must be able to digitalize, to separate the analogue from what it is not. The analogue cannot do this for itself, because it does not possess a "not" system within it. In other words, to be able to talk about relations (analogue), we must be able to digitalize. We can relate analogically, but we cannot relate to our relations analogically. We cannot metacommunicate analogically; for that, we need to be able to digitalize. Were it not for "not," we could not talk about "not." In fact, we could not make distinctions between a part and its whole, and therefore metacommunication would be impossible. We could not talk *about* anything. We could talk (relate), but we could not talk about (metarelate). In this sense, "not" is a metacommunicative boundary and constitutes a necessary precondition for an entity's having both consciousness of self and consciousness of other. In other words, it is the ability to digitalize that allows an awareness of contradiction and simultaneously (at a metalevel) of the conditions or context out of which the contradiction arises (Smith 1982b).

Logical Types and Multiple Frames

The central concern of the theory of logical types may be stated as follows: "To describe a class of objects or events we require a concept (or set of concepts) that operate(s) at a different level of abstraction than the concepts appropriate for describing one of the objects or events of which the class is constituted" (Bateson, Jackson, Haley, and Weakland, 1956). Thus, to describe the behavior of a group, for example, we need concepts structured at a different level of operation than those relevant for describing the behavior of the individuals who make up the group. It is not that the group behaves or exists independent of its individual members, or vice versa, but that the group and its individual members are not the same thing. This is captured partially in the concept of the whole being more than the sum of its parts. However, the logical typing issue goes beyond what is implied by this cliché.

To illustrate what is meant by different levels of abstraction, we will consider an event that occurred in the late 1970s. A group of physicians came together to discuss how they, as medical practitioners, would deal with the role expected of them should a nuclear war occur. Observers of this group's initial meetings have provided a wide range of commentaries to capture what transpired, a sample of which follows: (1) The members shared their *personal* anxieties over the realization of their own mortality in the light of possible nuclear war; (2) the *group* gave expression to a widely held *national* feeling of total helplessness about the possibility of survival in a nuclear era; (3) the group took a hard look at the role *government* expected its members to play as part of the *national* civil defense program; (4) the *group* gave birth to an *organization* composed of many thousands of medical practitioners.

While the list of descriptions is large, in reality each of these "explanations" is a commentary on the *same* behaviors. It is not as though the commentators were observing different interactions. They were all at the same meetings. Rather, each "explanation" is aimed at a different level of abstraction. The reports of the meeting are framed in different ways, and each statement may be viewed as an appropriate reality in light of the frame used to represent it.

In this example, it is clear that this group event has a different meaning depending on how it is framed and that each of the frames comes from a radically different "system of thought." This is what is meant by the concept of different logical types. The meaning systems created by the concepts at one level are different from those at another level. One way to understand the logical typing issue is to try to make the link between the explanation of "sharing their personal anxieties over their own mortality" and that of "giving birth to a new organization." There is no self-evident way to do this. Such a movement requires a journey across conceptual terrain that is discontinuous. In fact, were there no descriptive events to which each of these frames is attached, the statements about "sharing personal anxieties" and "giving birth to a new organization" would be so unrelated that it is unlikely that one would even attempt to make a translation from one to the other.

Let us imagine that a decade later this same group of physicians were to sit around and discuss what really happened during their inaugural meeting. There might be a wide range of interpretations among the members, similar in scope to the variations offered by the initial commentators. Should someone say "but what really happened?" implying that there was one dominant truth, those who carried or expressed, on behalf of the group, the various framings of the event might become locked into a battle about whose views were more correct. Given that the multiple frames used created different logical conceptions, there could be no adequate resolution to this debate. The argument would subside only when members could accept that the event had multiple meanings and that members carried these various interpretations on behalf of the group as a whole. That is, each member stored a part of the collective experience in his or her individual memory, and when the members reassembled, the collective memory of the group was brought back together again with all its disparate and clashing parts.

All groups have experiences that can be framed in multiple ways. And when two or more parts of a group frame these experiences in different ways, they are using more than one system of logical typing for the purposes of storing their shared memory. Group members may well find themselves in conflict as a consequence of the presence in their exchanges with each other of these multiple, often contradictory, discontinuous systems of logical typing.

Double Bind

Using the concept of logical typing, Bateson (1972) showed that a social entity such as a group can find itself in an impossible situation (which he called double binding) as a consequence of the contradictory meanings and of the injunctions for simultaneous contradictory behaviors emanating from two or more contexts in which the entity's actions are embedded. By *contexts*, we mean the frames of reference, as in our earlier example of the group of physicians for social responsibility. This is especially important because in human consciousness, be it individual or shared, meaning lies not simply in the act or the symbol but in the relationship between the act or symbol and the context by which it is framed (Jaynes, 1976).

When the meaning system developed by a framing in one logical system suggests actions contradictory to those implied by the framing in another system, we have the essential ingredients of the double bind. Then the group, acting according to the logic that comes from the first framing, bangs into the "brick walls" provided by the logic of the second framing, and vice versa. At the level of interaction of individuals in human systems, this experience is sufficiently familiar to hardly need illustration. The clearest example is that of a junior officer in the military receiving a directive from his or her superior officer that at one level of framing makes no sense. To act according to the instruction will obviously produce a disaster, but to refuse to accept the order may mean being court-martialed for disobeying the authority's directions. Framed in this light and with the options that the junior officer experiences as open to him or her, the interaction is paradoxical and double binding.

Such situations are likely to create paralysis, because actions in either direction seem equally problematic. There seems no way to successfully do both. Hence, the social entity caught in such a situation engages in a logic that reinforces the problem. From the inside, the primary choices appear to be (1) exert effort to get out of the double-binding situation or (2) do nothing. Both alternatives lead to the same outcome, stuckness. From the inside perspective, the alternative of being obedient to one set of injunctions while rebelling against another is equally impossible, because it is so hard to determine which to rebel against and which to comply with. This path leads to an inevitable oscillation that, in essence, is another form of stuckness.

When someone is in a double bind, it sometimes dawns on that person that the whole situation needs to be redefined. But this brings with it another dilemma. That is, the need to *redefine* occurs only *after a clear definition* has been formed. Then, since redefining usually takes place in terms of what has already been defined (Weeks and L'Abate, 1982), the entity may get thrown into the even more complex problems of self-reference.

Self-Reference

One major difficulty for any social entity that exists in a condition that has been defined is the tendency to use this definition as the exclusive basis for reflecting on what needs to be redefined. The concern is that any self-reflecting social entity engaged in a pattern of interactions will be prone to use these patterns and the often unconscious rules that regulate them as the vehicle for understanding those patterns (Smith, 1985). This has been labeled the problem of self-reference.

Generally, we find self-reference appearing in two forms: tautology and paradox. Both generate a system of circularity and symmetry. Tautology operates on the same entity and involves the process of confirmation, which, when reduced to basics, produces banalities of the form "if P is true, then P is true!" Paradox operates within entities (for example, "Rule #1: All rules are made to be broken"), across entities within the same framework or logical type (for example, "the following statement is false; the preceding statement is true"), and across logical types (for example, the picture of a pipe labeled as not a pipe). Paradox also involves disconfirmation or contradiction, in the creation of not a banality but a vicious cycle.

To understand the importance of this issue in human consciousness, we must appreciate that some concepts come into being as a consequence of the definition of other concepts. This is a critical element in the self-referential problem. For example, the term *hopeless* has meaning only in reference to the concept of *hope*. In fact, by defining *hope*, we define *hopeless*. If we experience hopelessness and want to change, a typical solution would be to develop more hope. A paradoxical view would argue that the larger the category of hope, the larger the possibilities of hopelessness. To diminish hopelessness, the paradoxical way is to give up hope. By having less or no hope, we diminish or eliminate the concept of hopelessness and create the potential for a fresh start on those issues that became defined as hopeless. Consider the following analogy. If we notice that water is wet and decide that its wetness is a problem, we may seek a "solution" by attempting to eliminate the wetness of water. No matter how hard we try, that approach is hopeless. By giving up the hope of changing the wetness of water, we no longer become embroiled in the hopelessness of that task and see other alternatives to trying to change what is unchangeable.

The philosophical base of this idea deserves some explanation. A starting point is to recognize that the moment we define something as A, we delineate what is not A. However, not A is a part of A, for without A, there can be no not A (Wilden, 1980). Let us personalize this process. By saying I am "me," I am also saying what is "not me." Raising this issue to the level of the group, by affirming "this is what this group is," we are also formulating what "it is not." In other words, the negation, "nongroup," is contained within the affirmation of "group."

If we keep in mind this idea of affirmation, there is a chance that we will not get tangled up, but there is a common critical error. We tend to view "this is our group" or "this is me" in clear, affirmative terms but to view the negation "that is nongroup" or "that is not me" as being "other." This is the dilemma, for the moment we treat our "nongroup" ("not me") as "other," as "part of the environment," as "beyond us," as "context," as "them," we fall into the trap of using it as a system of reference. For example, we may affirm that our group is powerful, attribute the condition of powerlessness to "not us" (them), and then use *our* view of *their* powerlessness as a frame to understand our own power. In so doing, we, as a group, have used a part of us, albeit what we called "other," as the frame for understanding us. Then we have unwittingly created for ourselves a self-referential system with all the possibilities of contradiction and circular stuckness. Consider again the example of our group, discussed earlier, that is deeply committed to some course of action. This very commitment creates the experience of noncommitment. When the part of the group that falls into this negative side of the definition of commitment is experienced as resistant, the resistance is seen not as a part of the group, but as "other" that must be overcome if the committed side is to succeed. Thus, the resisting side of the group becomes viewed as "nongroup" and is placed in this position by the way in which the committed side elects to define itself. The committed side is doing what the resisting (noncommitted side) is not doing, and so on. The moment this epistemological switch has been thrown, we have the perfect condition for the two sides to become locked into an oppositional relationship. What may have started as a consequence of a paradoxical, self-referential phenomenon is turned into a conflict shrouded in either/ or, right/wrong, strong/weak systems of thought and action. The connection rooted in the process of self-definition is lost, and paradoxical tension becomes nonparadoxical conflict.

In summary, paradox can be seen to occur in entities that are reflecting on themselves when they get tangled up with what is "self" and what is not "self" or what is "not self." If an entity confuses the logical types of "not" in the sense of absence versus negation, it may well come to treat "not self" as other and then use other as a basis for understanding self. Should it do this, the entity will have created a self-referential system. To make matters more complex, it will be prone to attribute to "nonself" (other) the parts of self that it is negating, the parts that would create contradictions with its affirmative side. Hence, it takes internal contradictions and transposes the negative to the outside and then engages in an external struggle as a way to maintain an affirmative sense of self. In so doing, the entity creates the vicious cycle, predicated on self-reference and contradiction, which is the heart of paradox.

Paradoxical Experience

In this chapter, we have discussed how the processes of knowing about social reality contributed to an experience of contradiction *and* paradox in the world around us. The role that negation, self-reference, and logical typing play in defining and understanding collective life creates the experience of contradiction and opposition. These same processes of knowing also contribute to our experience of paradox, since the contradictions clearly emanate from a common source or express, through their connection, an underlying theme about individuals, subgroups, or groups that stand in opposition to each other. Because of the connection between negation and affirmation, between the identity of "self" and the identity of "other," and among the multiple frames that can be and are applied to any social event, our experience of contradiction is often an experience of paradox. When we experience *both* the contradictory, opposing forces and the connection between them, the simultaneous experience traps us in the circularity of paradox. Since the contradictions are a more salient feature of the knowing processes than are the connections, our response to the frustration of paradoxical experience is to sever the connections, thereby splitting the contradictory forces. This splitting frees us from the paradoxical experience but transforms paradox into conflict, leaving us in the position where we endlessly discuss the issues associated with the conflict without ever getting to the dynamics underlying the conflict. Our efforts to free ourselves can have the effect of pushing us further into the experience of an intractable conflict. It is to this process of splitting that we now turn.

4

❦❦❦❦❦❦❦❦❦❦❦❦❦❦❦

The Sources of Paradox
in Group Dynamics

In this chapter, we elaborate the central thesis of the book, that group life is inherently paradoxical. As indicated in the first chapter, we do not mean by this that groups are not other things as well. We are concerned, however, with the observation that groups are filled with a wide range of emotions, thoughts, and actions that are experienced as contradictory and that these contradictory forces create a circular process that can be paralyzing for groups. The simultaneous presence of opposite and contradictory forces and the repetitious "stuckness" that often accompanied these forces led us to consider that what we were observing was the expression of the paradoxical nature of group life.

Our description of a paradoxical conceptualization of group dynamics will attempt to answer the following questions: What are the sources of contradictory and oppositional forces in groups? What are the processes that define and often entrench these forces? Why is there often a circular and repetitive quality to the group dynamics that attend the coexistence of these forces? What would it mean to understand these opposites from a paradoxical perspective? We begin with a brief description of what we mean by "group as a whole" and then proceed to address these questions.

The Group as a Whole

What do we mean by the "group"? We often make reference to the behavior of a group as a whole. In so doing, we raise
several epistemological concerns. First, can a group "behave"?
Or is it just the elements, that is, its members, who behave?
While psychology has tended to look at behavior in individual
terms, we think that when talking about an individual's behavior in a group, it is both important and possible to distinguish
between that which expresses the life of the group as a whole
and that which expresses merely the needs and reactions of the
individual member.

In discussing the behavior of groups, we view the group
as a social entity capable of acting as a whole and of expressing
feelings and thoughts over and beyond those of its members.
Of course, at one level, it is nonsensical to talk about a group
feeling something, for the feelings reside in and are actually felt
by the members of the group. However, there are certain feelings that group members have that are quite different from
those that they experience in isolation or in some other context. These may be thought of as group-based feelings. We mean
this in a way different from the perspective that views such a
feeling as an individual response to a stimulus called "the
group." Must all group members feel the same in order for a
member's feelings to be labeled a group feeling? The answer is
"no," for it is possible for an individual to express a feeling on
behalf of all the members of the group; since that member has
expressed it, others are free to have different feelings (Gibbard,
Hartman, and Mann, 1974). Of course, group feelings can also
be expressed by an individual's statement that stands as a symbol of the whole. When Winston Churchill said, "We'll fight
them on the beaches . . . ," the world knew that Great Britain
as a whole felt this way, even though in reality there were some
individuals in Great Britain who were not willing to fight at all.

We consider it appropriate to talk about a group as a
whole when three conditions are met: (1) when the relations
among the group members on the critical issues being examined

are different from the relations between those group members and members of another group with which it interacts (this is like the similarity definition of Campbell, 1958); (2) when other groups in the environment hold the group as a whole accountable for the actions of its members; and (3) when the actions of the group members may be meaningfully attributed to the patterns of relationships within the group and not to the unique characteristics of the members themselves. To illustrate what is meant by this last dimension, if we replace individuals in a group with other individuals that have very different characteristics and they end up behaving just like those who were replaced, then the behaviors of both the replaced and replacing people may be viewed as expressing the character of the group as a whole and not merely the character of the members displaying the behavior.

The "group-as-a-whole" concept also helps sharpen the issue of framing. It is now possible to understand the same behavior or experience in groups using different conceptual "frame-works." Consider, for example, the individual who seems always out of step with the other group members and who draws a great deal of hostility for his or her apparent deviance. At the individual and interpersonal levels, the pain and anger inside the "deviant" member as well as the disdain, hostility, and smugness inside the other individuals point to the tension and polarization in the interpersonal relationships in the group. By changing frame and moving to the group-as-a-whole level of analysis, these same observations may suggest a sense of relief based on the shared belief that the painful (and conflictful) feelings in the group are located in only one person and will disappear once the person leaves. The group-as-a-whole phenomenon of scapegoating points out that what may be experienced as painful and tension filled at the personal and interpersonal levels may be deeply comforting for the entire group. The example further illustrates that the contradictory and oppositional forces in groups may exist *within* a level (between or among individuals) or *across* levels (between the interpersonal and the group as a whole) of group life.

For us, the starting point in elaborating a paradoxical theory of group relations is to look at what is stirred inside individuals as they join a group. We will then examine what occurs in the group as a whole as it struggles to be a unit in the light of the processes operative in its parts. Following this, we will turn to how the group as a whole deals with its relationships with other groups and the impact that this has on the creation, management, or avoidance of internal unity or fragmentation.

Individual Ambivalences

Membership and participation in a group evoke a variety of reactions in group members. Some of those reactions contribute to the experience of contradiction and conflict in the group as a whole. The literature of group dynamics suggests three internal, psychological sources of conflict: (1) the bringing together of individuals with different skills, interests, and values for the purpose of fulfilling group tasks that demand a level of variety not available in any single individual; (2) the perceptual tendency of individuals and groups toward polarization as a means of ordering and defining reality; and (3) the ambivalence of group members toward group-as-a-whole phenomena and the associated playing out of intrapsychic conflicts in interpersonal ways.

A group often needs people who are *different* to fulfill its primary task. This means that differences must be brought into the group and then integrated in a way that provides unity while preserving difference. Difference alone is enough to provide a platform for conflict, but the need to unify in light of the differences makes it almost inevitable that conflict will occur (Deutsch, 1973). Under these circumstances, the very fact that individuals contribute differences makes it possible for the group to be effective, yet these same differences threaten the group's capacity to function.

Bales and Cohen (1979) have observed that people in groups tend to differentiate others along three bipolar dimensions, which they label dominant-submissive, friendly-unfriendly, and instrumentally controlled–emotionally expressive. Bales and Cohen describe this as being a result of "an ubiquitous tendency of individuals to polarize image fields in their minds." If it is correct that there is a perceptually based propensity to polarize anything that is observed, then it follows that the life of a group will be filled with "oppositional forces" that exist as an artifact of members' perceptual processes. This means that individuals in groups and groups as a whole will always be managing differences even as they are seeking a certain level of homogeneity.

The most basic dilemma for individuals in groups is connected to the inner ambivalences generated by group membership. Each individual, on joining a group, experiences some ambivalence that stems from the *simultaneous* wish to be both "a part" of the group and "apart" from the group (Tillich, 1952). The simultaneous desire for inclusion and fusion triggers the fear of consumption, absorption, and deindividuation, while the desire to be independent triggers the fear of exclusion, aloneness, and isolation (Smith, 1982a). The psychodynamic literature suggests that this ambivalence is very much like, and in fact rooted in, the processes that individuals engage in during infancy, especially in relationship to mother (Wells, 1980). The desire to be separate *and* connected, coupled with the fear that only abandonment *or* fusion is possible, creates a sense of existential anxiety for all of us at primitive levels of awareness.

While the nature of the fusion-abandonment tension may not be self-evident to the individual in the group setting, the anxiety that emanates from it usually is. The experience for the individual joining a group is primarily one of a low-grade anxiety that surfaces as an amalgam of forces such as excitement over the possibilities represented in group membership, uncertainty about how he or she will fit in, fear that he or she will be less competent than when acting alone, and frustration over earlier group experiences. When such anxiety is stirred, the individual usually becomes preoccupied by a secondary fear, that this anxiety may escalate and get out of hand. An initial goal for the individual in the group is to keep a lid on this anxiety by pretending that it does not exist or by replacing it with behaviors that seem acceptable to others in the group. While the individual may be aware of the anxious feelings, the underlying roots of that anxiety are rarely recognized. As a result, the methods used to manage it can very often be self-defeating, as in the following scenario.

With the ambivalence that emanates from the twin desires to be connected and to remain individuated, the individual may seek either a path that enables connections to be made or one that involves holding back until the lay of the land is clear. Either path stirs even further the turbulent waters of the fusion-abandonment dynamic, because to do more of one or the other increases rather than reduces the imbalance in the relationship between them. As a result, anxiety is heightened rather than diminished if one or the other is selected as a solution, creating, in turn, an even greater need for anxiety management. Since anxiety seems to increase as a result of the path chosen, the individual concerned may suddenly conclude that the alternative is more attractive. One behavior often observed at this point is that the individual who moved to connect then retreats into self, or the person who initially held back may act to connect. Either choice sets up an inner oscillation.

When it is found that the actions taken to reduce anxiety are not working, another option is to engage in those behaviors more intensely, with the belief that the original choice was correct but that more of the behavior is necessary to get over an imaginary threshold. In such cases, individuals do the metaphoric equivalent of the person who encounters a foreigner unable to understand what is being said and proceeds to shout, as though the original problem were deafness and the solution, more decibels.

Since the experience of anxiety on joining a group is seated in ambivalences not readily accessible to consciousness, when the anxiety is handled in a way that increases it, ambivalences about the danger of either joining or not joining in the group are aroused, activating another oscillating process in the deep structure of the individual: if one invests oneself in the group, it might get really dangerous; on the other hand, if one does not get in there and gain some influence over the group, then everything will always seem out of control. This response increases ambivalence further but brings with it a subtle and sig-

nificant switch. At the unconscious level, the individual has begun to move the underlying focus from his or her own feelings—
that is, processes rooted within—to the emerging judgments
about what the group is like. This switch from managing self-
processes to making judgments about the group as individual
anxiety increases is a pervasive and significant human process.
In both the psychological and anthropological literature, it is
called splitting; and, since it is central to the existence of contradiction and opposition in groups, it deserves special attention.

Splitting

Formally, the term *splitting* is defined as the partitioning
of a set into two subsets (Laing, 1969). The most straightforward illustration in the clinical literature on the process of splitting is seen in the actions of an infant as it struggles with the
early ambivalence surrounding the desire to be fused with the
mother and the wish to be separated from her. This ambivalence
creates strong love-hate reactions toward the mother. To maintain a sense of psychological equilibrium, the infant splits the
feelings of good and bad and projects them onto different objects—for example, good mommy and bad daddy (Wells, 1980).
In infantile splitting, we also see the psychological dynamics of
projection and introjection at play. *Projection* occurs when I
take what is inside and map it onto outside (Laing, 1969). I feel
not OK—I see you as not OK. *Introjection* is the mapping of
outside onto inside (Laing, 1969). You think that I did something wrong—I must be a bad person. Projection and introjection are forms of displacement, where some dynamic that belongs in one place is moved to another.

Splitting may occur in such a way that someone else
takes on the characteristics of the self that the self unconsciously wants to dispose of or disown. The disowned parts of self are
projected onto another in such a way that the other begins to
act toward the person doing the projecting in a manner congruent with the projection. But the self engaging in the projection
now feels a strong identification with the other, because the

other embodies an aspect of the self on the self's behalf. This identification helps the self to maintain the full complement of feelings but with less anxiety. Consider, for example, an individual who has ambivalent feelings of both love and contempt toward him- or herself. If he or she consciously wants to feel only self-love, a typical action is to disown the contempt and unconsciously project it onto another. Then, through various interpersonal processes, the projecting individual manipulates the other into taking on the projection and behaving contemptuously (Bion, 1961). The individual is able to experience the other as contemptuous but at the same time feel an identification with the contemptuous behavior because it is an embodiment or enactment of a part of him- or herself that he or she is trying to disown and displace. This process is referred to in the clinical literature as projective identification. (See Klein, 1975; Ogden, 1979, 1982; Horwitz, 1983; Wells, 1980, for fuller accounts of the clinical view of projective identification.)

Jaques (1955) suggests that many of the dynamics operative in groups and organizations may be understood in terms of splitting and projective identification. For example, when soldiers adopt a position of full obedience toward their commander, they effectively split off a part of themselves and put it into the leader. It is as though a part of their egos is relocated in the external leader and they intensely identify with him because he is carrying a part of them around with him. When many soldiers surrender their obedience to the same leader, that leader ends up occupying this very special place for all of them. They all have a shared kind of projective identification, which in turn makes it possible to identify with each other (Redl, 1942). Jaques indicates that this can be good and bad. On the one hand, it enables cohesion to develop; on the other, it can create weird dynamics, such as in the famous case when the Assyrian soldiers became totally confused and incompetent on learning that their leader's head had been cut off (Freud, 1922). With the loss of the leader's head, it was as though each soldier had lost his own individual head, because each had placed part of himself into the leader via projective identification (Wells, 1980).

One of the key consequences of splitting for collective life is that certain individuals or subgroups can come to carry particular emotions or positions on behalf of others. As we have already noted, a leader may become the repository of the split-off parts of the followers that they elect to put into him or her. He or she then carries the leadership on the followers' behalf, leaving them free to disown or disengage their own leadership sides. But there are other types of splitting and disowning that can generate a variety of special roles where individuals or subgroups carry the "baggage" for others. A powerful example is when one individual in a group is made into a scapegoat by becoming the repository of the bad feelings of other group members, thereby enabling all but the scapegoat to feel good about themselves. These are very tenuous "good feelings," however, because they can be maintained only while that individual continues to carry the bad on behalf of them all. Should the "bad" member become "good," this poses an enormous threat to those experiencing themselves as good, because of the loss of the repository for the projected bad feelings. The "good" members may beat on the "bad" person for being "bad" but then vehemently resist his or her attempts to become good, because the others will then have no convenient repository for the displacement of their own bad feelings, a repository that seems so necessary for maintaining a sense of their own "goodness." Movement from the "bad" position by the scapegoat may be experienced by other group members as a threat that must be resisted.

Splitting as an Interactive Process. We started talking about the psychodynamic concept of splitting as a process that takes place within an individual. Yet we are now discussing it as though it were an operation occurring at the supraindividual level. This switch makes sense if it is appreciated that splitting, disowning, and projection, while being initially intrapersonal dynamics, occur in social interactions. They thus become elements of shared behavior, not merely isolated acts. In addition, it is rare that only one person is engaged in such processes in social interactions. Those being projected upon are usually doing their own fair share of splitting and projecting. Across time, interactions among people can be filled with the processes of splitting, projection, and introjection such that reciprocal patterns emerge. For example, two people may hate each other and feel good about themselves as a result, in large part because they mutually cooperate in providing a place where hatred can be relocated from self to other. Or two individuals may move to positions of submission and dominance such that the inept feelings of one are reinforced while the arrogant side of the other is gratified. By understanding these processes as operating at *both* the personal and interactive levels, it is possible to understand the idea that dynamics at one level (such as within the individual) can become enfolded into dynamics at another level (such as in the interpersonal relations within a group).

Having discussed how these internal splits become incorporated and expressed in interactive forms, our next step is to look at the patterns evoked in the group as a whole as an expression or a playing out of these dynamics. This leads us into the topics of role specialization and division into subgroups.

Role Specialization. Role specialization occurs when one individual, such as in the examples of leadership and scapegoating discussed earlier, takes on the projected material from several or all group members. When that individual acts, it is as though everyone has acted, because the part of each member projected onto that person has been given expression. The circumstances likely to provoke role specialization may emanate from sources inside or outside the group. For example, a group of teenagers sitting around feeling bored might engage vigorously in the initiatives of one member who stimulates some creative activity. On the other hand, this same group, suddenly threatened by a street gang, might rally around the heroic member most willing to organize so that they can take on the fight. Or, if the odds are too overwhelming, they may turn to the one who adopts a mediating posture and work to bolster his or her peacemaking skills.

The group literature is filled with both descriptions and theory about the various roles created in groups. In all cases,

however, a role has meaning only when others accept that role
as fulfilling these functions on their behalf, so that they do not
have to do it themselves or so that others may be free to take
on other roles. Role acceptance involves the notion that the person in the role is acting as others would if they were in that
position. Successful entry into the role means that other group
members are willing to let go of the parts of themselves that
want to fulfill this function and to adopt as their own what the
role occupier is doing because it seems to be a good or at least
adequate representation of the investments they have in these
activities. Members are projectively identified with such a role
in the sense that they feel responsible for and/or invested in the
consequences that flow from this role enactment.

   Subgroup Formation. The splitting associated with role
specialization can be thought of as complementary in that what
is taken on by the role enacter dovetails with the investments
represented by what is projected by others. Groups also use unconscious splitting processes to express the oppositional but
symmetrical sides of a difficult emotional issue. The clearest
example of this can be seen in the formation of subgroups
pitted against each other.
   Splitting associated with partitioning of the group as a
whole into subgroups can be identified and illustrated most
clearly in groups that have to make decisions on behalf of a con-
stituency. Consider the example of a seven-person board of
trustees of a local community agency, mandated to provide
emergency assistance for the needy and to invest resources in
the economic development of the community so that emergency assistance becomes unnecessary. These individuals were
chosen as enlightened members of the community because they
visibly possessed a mixture of both intellectual commitment to
economic development that fosters self-help and humanitarian
compassion to feed the starving and clothe the naked. When
they confronted the formal task of allocating dollars to a variety of activities, some members advocated the extreme positions: handouts, on one hand, and long-term community investment, on the other. But many fell in between these two poles,

vacillating between a decision to (a) feed ten hungry people today or (b) invest so that one hundred potentially hungry people tomorrow will never slip into that condition. Board members initially seemed uncertain, and an observer could sense each struggling with how to act in light of the mixture of feelings each carried inside.

One person, thinking out loud, indicated a leaning to position (b) but said that she could be swayed the other way. A second person expressed a minor preference for (a). A vacuum was being created that was calling for a voice to express support for option (b) so that the overall equilibrium—that is, room for a "gray-area" solution—could be preserved. The next person to speak came out clearly for (b), and there was a burst of applause from community members sitting, supposedly as silent observers, in the public gallery. After six board members had spoken, the votes were three for each side. Three men on the board had gone for (b), and three women had opted for (a). The last to speak was a man. He seemed paralyzed. There was an air of expectancy in the room. As he began, he noted that those for (a) were the women and those for (b) were the men, so at some level he felt pressure to vote with the men. He suggested that the problem for him was not wanting to feel hardhearted by voting against giving to the needy. That statement, especially the choice of the term *hard,* implied for some people that he would have characterized the welfare option as soft.

One of the women interrupted at this point with an objection to the sexist slur that women are soft, something that this man had not said but that might have been inferred, since it was the women who had tipped the balance of their ambivalences toward the welfare option. The board erupted into a fifteen-minute tangential debate over whether this statement had been sexist. When it was over, the three women had banded together as a bloc and were taking a much more rigid approach to the welfare option than they had previously. The man whose vacillations had started this detour continued to explore them, expressing for the first time the part of him that preferred the welfare option in this case. One of the female board members made an aside about his attempt to curry favor with the wom-

en. He got upset, turned to the chairperson, and said in exasperation, "I'm in a lose-lose position; I abstain."

The board was deadlocked with a three-three vote. The
chairperson was put in the position of having to cast a tie break-
er. At this moment he "carried" not only his own original ambivalence but what had become the collective ambivalence of this
group as a whole. To make the situation even more complex, he
was clearly feeling the pressure to manage the problems that
seemed likely if the board systematically divided along male-
female lines. He chose to take the heat off himself by suggesting
that the board needed to develop some policy guidelines so it
could know how to handle situations like this, and he proposed
that this be placed on the agenda for the next meeting and that
the current debate be postponed until those guidelines were
formulated.

This account illustrates how ambivalences that exist in individuals can become expressed in a group when it divides into
subgroups. The splitting, projective-identification explanation
for such a situation might look like this: The ambivalences experienced in each individual that we will call a and b become re-
aligned when subgroups form, each rallying around what we will
call A and B, respectively. Then, those in the subgroup taking
the B perspective carry this not only for themselves but on behalf of those who are taking the A position. This leaves those in
the A camp free to carry this torch without ambivalence, for
they are doing so not only for themselves but for the others as
well. Each subgroup can be said to be projectively identified
with, and hence deeply invested in, the position opposite to the
one it is taking. Should anything threaten the *other* subgroup's
position, each will act to re-establish it. In a sense, the collective
ambivalence in the group as a whole expressed in the opposition
of the subgroups may be viewed as a mirroring of the individually based ambivalences that the members are free to no longer
carry around inside themselves because the group is doing it on
their behalf. This example has an extra complexity in it as a result of the male-female split, a topic we will pick up later in this
book.

The splitting that occurs in subgroup formation such as

the above generates a symmetrical pattern, because the two parts created in the partitioning are each simultaneously seeking to dominate the other while remaining invested in keeping the rival a worthy and formidable opponent. From a projective-identification perspective, if each subgroup is not kept strong by the group as a whole, the factions might have to deal with the parts they have split off, recreating the original internal ambivalence that was excruciatingly difficult to handle in the first place.

In our discussion of splitting thus far, we have traced examples of how ambivalences residing within individuals may be handled in an interactive as opposed to a merely intrapersonal way. In this regard, the group offers to its members a unique opportunity to avoid always having to manage ambivalence alone. The group provides a shared mechanism that may make individuals hate the group but at the same time give them a chance to express the side that loves to hate.

Splitting from a Collective Perspective. We started our examination of splitting by discussing it as an individual process and then traced how it can become a collective-level process as well. The anthropological literature also discusses splitting and the idea that certain subsets "take on" a particular perspective or set of attributes on behalf of others. Bateson (1936) described splitting as an operation occurring at the collective level (as opposed to the psychodynamic approach, which makes the individual the central focus). He noted that social units, such as tribes, would engage in ritual activities such as dancing in a way that partitioned the whole into two parts, dancers and observers, usually male and female, respectively. Once such subgroups formed, the actions of each part helped to heighten the differentiation between them. For example, in tribal dances, the women's watching of the men's performance reinforced the men's exhibitionism. Conversely, the increased exhibitionism of the men would draw the women into more intense levels of spectatorship. The men exaggerated their exhibitionism in response to women's spectatorship, and vice versa (Lipset, 1980). Bateson described this as an oscillating and vibrating process through which role differentiation and intensification occurred. He coined the term "schismogenesis" (the creation of schisms) to describe this pattern, which he argued became manifest in two forms, one *complementary,* the other *symmetrical.*

In the complementary split, the parts take on different roles that together make a whole, as in dominance-submission, exhibitionism-spectatorship, master-apprentice. If one side is not adopted, the other side also fades. Once the complementary circuit is begun, intensification follows until both parts fully embody the pattern. For example, as the submissive becomes more passive, the dominant becomes more assertive, and vice versa. Through this process, a clear pattern of splitting occurs by which the whole is partitioned into two clearly distinguishable parts.

A symmetrical split is the pattern that emerges when the parts compete for the same or similar locations within the whole, such as in boasting, arms races, and wars. Here each part reacts identically, which increases the degree of reaction (Lipset, 1980). Bateson (1936) illustrated the symmetrical by his observations of the initiation rites of the Iatmul tribe, where two rival factions of men in the tribe taunted each other by bullying the novices. Thus, one subgroup's act of bullying the novices was viewed as a way of attacking the rival faction, which reciprocated by bullying the same novices more ferociously.

Bateson (1936) suggested that the distinction between complementary and symmetrical splitting is analogous to the difference between schism and heresy. Heresy is used to describe the partitioning of a religious sect where two subgroups develop doctrines opposed to one another, with the tendency of the minor group to be pushed out of the dominant setting, creating separate but linked parent and divergent groups. Schism, on the other hand, is the term for the splitting of a sect where two subgroups end up having doctrinal similarities but competing politics (Bateson, 1936). In the case of heresy, the political dynamics become externally focused as debates rage about whether the split-off segment can claim any literal or symbolic link to the parent group from which it emerged. In the case of schism, the political struggles are internally focused as the respective groups jostle for position and influence. Heresy is like complementary splitting, while schism resembles the symmetrical form.

Ethnocentrism and Splitting. The organizational literature has provided us with a rich description of the ethnocentric dynamic where interacting groups become embroiled in what could be referred to as the "we-they" process (see Levine and Campbell, 1972, and Alderfer, 1977, for overviews). When a group as a whole engages in ethnocentric interactions, it is very easy to see the dynamics of splitting and projective identification in operation. They are most visible under conditions of severe conflict, when each group sees itself as good and its adversary as bad and uses this justification for being oppositional, applying logic such as "only when they are eliminated will badness disappear." Since each group takes the same position, the conflict escalates to the point where both are behaving self-righteously, wholeheartedly denying that the accusations of the opponent have *any* validity. That is, each group, caught in ethnocentrism, is quite unable to acknowledge that it has negative characteristics of its own or that the other has any good in it.

The splitting and projective identification of ethnocentrism can be seen when a group operating in isolation divides into two opposing subgroups whose incessant clashes make group cohesion and collective action impossible. Such a group can be quite paralyzed as each part claims that it is right and the other is wrong, using this as a rationale for not cooperating with the interests of others. Coser (1956) reports that very often such divisions superficially disappear almost instantly on the encountering of another that can be made into an enemy. Then the group previously split into warring internal factions finds a way to put its differences aside in the service of unified action to deal with the new external opponent.

When the group is alone, the internal factions are more attuned to their differences than to their similarities. Although the parts continue to possess key similarities that are the basis of their belonging to the whole, these similarities fade into the background as their differences become dominant. And then, with the differences in sharp focus, each side struggles to assert its interests, engaging in the type of subgroup splitting and projective identification we discussed earlier where attempts are made to displace that which is bad, wrong, and ugly onto other while claiming good, right, and beauty for self. With the arrival of another, external group, this internal suppression of similarities and heightened differences reverses itself, and the differences *between* the groups become central. The original internal differences, which had been the seat of such conflict, fade in importance as they are driven out of the field of group vision, setting the stage for their suppression and potential displacement onto the external group. The aspects that a group hates most about another group are those it was having most difficulty accepting about itself while it was operating in isolation. When the external group leaves, the original group returns to those same internal splits that had been so dominant previously.

Social Paradox

Our discussion thus far in this chapter has highlighted that splitting is a process that occurs within social entities at many different levels. It can be found operating within individuals, in interpersonal relationships, in the development of subgroups, and in the interactions between groups. When a social entity is involved in splitting and projective identification, we have the precondition for the unfolding of social paradox. It is to this that we now turn.

To discuss this at a theoretical level, we will talk about subgroup A and subgroup B, but these entities could also be individuals or groups. As we discuss these patterns, the term *subgroups* could be replaced by "individuals A and B" or "groups A and B," and the dynamic would be the same. Three summarizing comments are important. First, when subgroup B voluntarily or unknowingly introjects parts of A, it does so because these internalizations fit into, are congruent with, make more complete, or help modify some already existing internal situation. Second, when subgroup A projects part of itself onto

B, it does so as an act of extruding something that is disquieting to *A*'s inner situation or whose elimination will enable that situation to be modified in a desired way. Third, when *A* gets *B* to carry and express its displaced parts, *A* will be invested in remaining in the vicinity of *B* to obtain vicarious gratification as the disowned parts of itself are enacted and to maintain the strength of the subgroup that carries these disowned parts.

   If subgroup *A* splits off a part of itself that it disowns, then it is saying that this is not *A*. It does not belong here. If *A* transposes those parts to *B* and *B* takes on (introjects) even a portion of the displaced not *A*, then we are embroiled in the self-referential dynamic discussed in the last chapter. In addition, although subgroup *A* may see subgroup *B* as an autonomous unit and independent of *A*, *A* will also consider *B* to be not *A*, that is, the absence or opposite of that which *A* is. In so doing, subgroup *A* has come to define subgroup *B* in *A*-based terms. Subgroup *A* will not consciously think of *B* as not *A* but rather refer to *B* as "other." Yet *B*'s "otherness" for *A* will, at least in part, be a result of its not-*A* quality.

   This issue is important because an entity's self-knowledge is deeply rooted in a process of social comparison (see Cooley, 1922; Goodman, 1977; Smith, 1983). Stated simply, the only way that subgroup *A* can know what it is like from the outside is by examining itself in the mirror of its interactions with other entities. As with every mirror, one can look from a distance, picking up mere impressions of what self is like; one can choose to look when it is dark—keeping murky, distinctions that would be evident under the spotlight; or one can pull close, examining a troublesome part in microscopic detail. For subgroup *A* to decide, for example, whether it is strong, it needs to look in the mirror of its interactions with other subgroups. If *B* seems intimidated in *A*'s presence, *A* might deduce something about its own strength. If, however, *A* is intimidated in *C*'s presence, *A* might conclude that the reason that it felt so strong when with *B* was not because of its own strength but because of *B*'s weakness. In other words, *A*'s external "self-knowledge" is an internal synthesis of the external interactions with other entities that it is using as social mirrors.

   The implication of this is that the distinction between

self and other, in social reality, is somewhat arbitrary. Where and how the lines are drawn are due to social convention and are created via social negotiations. To claim that subgroup *A* and subgroup *B* are separate is both true and false. To say "this is *A*" is both true and false, and we are reminded of the territory inhabited by statements such as "I am lying" and "The following statement is false"/"The preceding statement is true," which of course contains the vicious cycle of self-referential renunciation. One difference in this situation, however, is that the paradox is often not evident, for only one-half of the statement gets made. It is as though instead of saying "the statement 'this is *A*' is both true and false," we acknowledge only one-half of it, the part that claims "the statement 'this is *A*' is true." Hence, the piece that would point us to the paradox is left out; accordingly, the paradox does not strike us: *the self-referential quality is hidden*, and the part that triggers the self-renunciation is left unsaid or unnoticed. We have *invisible paradox.*

We are now back to the important topic of framing. When *A* uses both *B* and its interaction with *B* (that is, the *A-B* relationship) to examine itself, it is doing so from the perspective of two frames that are in part self-referential. In addition, these two frames (that is, *B* and the *A-B* interaction) are logically different in kind. To illustrate, a woman's husband is a *person*. Their marital *relationship* is a configuration of interactive patterns. A person and a relationship are classifications of different logical kinds. One could never be substituted for the other in any logical proposition. Hence, *A*'s knowledge of external self emanates from at least two frames that are both of logically different kinds *and* partially self-referential.

To make matters even more complex, let us consider subgroup *A* to be made up of two individuals, *a* and *b*. Everything we have said thus far about subgroups *A* and *B* will be just as relevant to individuals *a* and *b*. Thus, subgroup *A*'s internal reality system will be a similarly swirling construction, manufactured from partially self-referential frames of logically different kinds. While this may sound overwhelming and ultimately beyond understanding, our overall point is to emphasize the notion that when dealing with a group caught in grooves that are

circular and self-reinforcing, it makes most sense to think *first*
and *foremost* about this in paradoxical terms. It will almost certainly be impossible to break down into component parts all that
is contributing to the group paralysis. However, starting with an
understanding of the paradoxical nature of collective experience
will suggest *very* different ways for how to act (be one a group
leader, a group member, or an interventionist) than if one did
not have a paradoxical perspective. To illustrate, if a group is
stuck, *how* the group is thinking about what it needs to do to
get unstuck is, in and of itself, an expression of the configuration of framings that are partially responsible for the stuckness.
Hence, one needs to look at these "potential solutions" to dis-
cern the frames that are being used. Only by adopting different
frames can one begin to understand the entrapping dynamics
within any one frame.

What we are suggesting is that it is possible to deal not
only with the content of experiences in groups but also the
frames within which that content has its existence. This is possible in a paradoxical conceptualization. Nonparadoxical theories
search for explanations and actions focused primarily on the experiential content. We are arguing that the paradoxical perspective opens up an array of choices about how to understand and
deal with group experiences that are not available within nonparadoxical theories. The paradoxical adds to the content theories the importance of the framework within which those con-
tents are embedded. It adds the notion that any experience can
be multiply framed and therefore can have multiple meanings,
each meaning being a consequence of the relationship between
the frame and the event. It adds the perspective that conflict
may emanate from a single source and that it is not always true
that a conflictful state is the result of two or more distinct,
separate, and conflicting sources. It adds the view that attempts
to resolve conflict can entrench that conflict further and that
often what is needed is a way to release it.

An example may illustrate these points. Consider the
reactions of dependency and counterdependency in groups.
These reactions can be conceptualized as opposite and their
management as a process of compromise, reconciliation, and

conflict resolution. When they are conceptualized through a paradoxical perspective, we see the very concept and experience of dependency as relying on the concept and experience of counterdependency and on the interaction of the two. One does not exist without the other; the expression of one is also the expression of both, since it is the contrast with dependency that gives counterdependency its meaning. In this sense, dependency and counterdependency are not opposites but more like Siamese twins who share vital organs. The twins are separate individuals, and yet they are not. Their lives depend on each other, since one lives or dies in direct relationship to the other, and the attitudes, moods, and health of one twin are intimately tied to the attitudes, moods, and health of the other, often in reciprocal or complementary ways. What we are suggesting is that if we were to adopt a paradoxical frame, the very conflicts that are so overwhelming because our frames tell us that they are bad or that they impair group functioning might become less important than the exploration of the "single source" represented in the two sides of the conflict.

Paradox in Small Groups

Groups, like all human relationships, evoke strong and often conflicting or ambivalent reactions. Perhaps because of the echoes that linger from our infancies, participation in a social unit is often both comforting and discomforting, satisfying and dissatisfying, supportive and alienating. The psychological experience of group membership involves the coexistence of these opposing emotions and reactions, and the group provides a setting for managing the tensions that arise from "holding" these conflicting and contradictory feelings. By managing these tensions, group life maintains the tenuous but surprisingly strong connection between individual and collective development. When groups stop "holding" the opposites and move instead toward extruding or subjugating one "side" of a conflictful issue, they often get "stuck," because the balance in the group so necessary for member involvement and participation is threatened. It is indeed a paradox that while the *existence* of conflict and opposition threatens a group's life, the *absence* of these same forces is also a serious threat. Emotionally, a group that does not provide room for the conflicting and ambivalent reactions evoked by group life is not a place where either the individuals or the group as a whole can thrive.

As we have discussed, groups often respond to the threat and anxiety aroused by the presence of opposition, conflict, and contradiction through the mechanisms of splitting and projective identification at the individual and interpersonal levels and ethnocentrism and social-comparison processes at the collective levels. Groups and their members seek ways to extrude, displace, or subjugate one side or the other of the conflict so as to reduce the tension and anxiety associated with it. Because this is usually an unconscious process, we lose sight of the inherently paradoxical nature of this conflict, of these coexisting opposites, and enter the conflict as if it were possible and desirable to move forward by eliminating or compromising one side of the individual or collective ambivalence. We lose sight of the common frame that gives meaning to the simultaneous coexistence of opposites, and it becomes hard to see the inherently paradoxical aspects of groups that express a complex and often anxiety-ridden "truth" about emotional life in groups. When we lose our ability to look through a paradoxical lens, we find it increasingly difficult to see the connections between the opposites, to explore and contain the contradictions, and to find a productive path in groups.

We turn now to an examination of some of the situations and conditions in groups that evoke contradictory and conflicting reactions. We present them in their paradoxical form, as if these opposing reactions were expressing a connection, a "truth," about the emotional life of groups.

※×※×※×※×※×※×※×※×※×※

Exploring Paradox

We commence Part Two with an examination of a dozen paradoxes of group life. These twelve are intended to illustrate, not exhaust, the paradoxical aspects of behavior in groups. Our purpose is to explore the implications of a paradoxical frame for our understanding of individual and collective behavior. We are going to examine a number of familiar themes in group life that are often experienced as contradictory or conflictual. By adopting a paradoxical frame, we will attempt to illuminate the self-referential, circular, and repetitive character of many of these dynamics. As we describe each paradox, we will be searching for the roots of the contradictions as they are found in both the individual and the group as a whole, in particular the common sources from which the contradictions spring and how these sources are made into contradictions through the experiences of groups and their members. We are interested in exploring the fundamental or essential elements of groups that are expressed in these contradictions, in the relationship between the "opposing" elements of the contradiction.

This last point is especially important. For paradox to occur, the contradictions must be *linked* to each other. It is the connection between two statements, emotions, or reactions that creates the condition of contradiction. The fact that collective activity evokes contradictory emotions, for example, testifies to the existence of a link between these emotions. We are inter-

ested in understanding what that link is and what it can tell us
about underlying group processes. Put still another way, since
paradox is necessarily self-referential, the contradictions of a
paradox must be expressing something about the "self." Paradoxes of group life should tell us something about groups.

The twelve paradoxes discussed in the following pages are
presented in three clusters, paradoxes of *belonging* (Chapter
Five), paradoxes of *engaging* (Chapter Six), and paradoxes of
speaking (Chapter Seven). In its most simple form, belonging is
about membership. In this cluster, we discuss the themes of
identity, involvement, individuality, and boundaries. The paradoxes of engagement deal with participation. In this section, we
explore the dynamics of disclosure, trust, intimacy, and regression. The third cluster, paradoxes of speaking, is about influence: the development of an individual voice potent enough to
have an impact within a group and the development of a collective voice strong enough to represent the group in exchanges
with others. In this third section, we explore the paradoxes of
authority, dependency, creativity, and courage. The twelve sub-
headings have been chosen because they are themes that have
been explored by researchers who have written about group dynamics. As we delve into each of these themes, it will be obvious that all of the paradoxes are interconnected. Issues that
surface as authority dynamics in a group may well be connected
to the paradoxes of dependency, individuality, regression, and
courage. In order to present and explore these paradoxes, we
will treat them as separate, mindful of the artificiality this presentation may convey.

It is probably not an accident that *three* clusters emerged
from our attempt to illustrate group paradoxes. "Threes" are
common in the theory and research on group processes (for example, three phases, three basic assumption states). Triads are
also unstable or dynamic forms; the number itself provides an
impetus toward shifting alliances and change. It is also probably
not an accident that each cluster includes *four* paradoxes. Four
is a number that expresses stability, partly through our associations with it and partly because of the balance inherent in its
easy symmetrical division. And, at heart, our discussion of para-

dox is an exploration of the ways in which *two* are often *one*. In addition to the content, the organization of the next three chapters also gives a message. There are both stable and unstable, static and dynamic, predictable and unpredictable aspects of processes in groups. The three clusters suggest instability and unpredictability at a time when the four, two, one analyses suggest stability, pattern, predictability, and control. Both suggestions are intended.

Having discussed these twelve internal group processes from a paradoxical perspective, we turn to the issue of the context in which groups are embedded. Many of the frames used by groups for understanding their internal experiences are imported by group members. Decisions concerning how these internal experiences are managed, avoided, confronted, understood, or distorted are in turn exported back out into the larger context by group members. As we explore the twin processes of importation and exportation, the close linkage between the internal and external life of groups becomes clearly evident.

With this as a base, we illustrate how the relations among groups can also be fruitfully understood using the same type of paradoxical thinking discussed for internal group dynamics. This is illustrated with a discussion of the intergroup paradoxes of scarcity, perception, and power that are in turn linked, for illustrative purposes, to the internal paradoxes of belonging, engaging, and speaking.

5

Paradoxes of Belonging:
Identity, Involvement,
Individuality, and Boundaries

There can be no group unless people belong to it. What does belonging to a group entail? The paradoxes in this chapter all involve the issue of membership. What are the conflicting and often contradictory emotions aroused by the fact of belonging? For individuals and for the group as a whole, the joining process is a continuous one. What must the individual give up in order to belong, and does this change as the group changes? How does a group come to determine what individuals can and cannot bring into the group except through the "in-puts" of its members? What does it mean to be "in"?

Each of the four paradoxes that follow illustrates an aspect of the paradoxical tensions surrounding belonging to groups. The *paradox of identity* examines the link between individual identity and group identity. Which one comes first? Which one determines the other? Which gives way before the other? Which must be settled and stable before the other can be known? These questions seek to break apart the confusing circularity of the paradox of identity. The *paradox of involvement* explores the relationship between involvement and detachment, observation and experience. Are these separate and distinct aspects of belonging to a group? Can there be involvement without withdrawal, or do the two spring from a common source of what it means to belong? This second paradox looks at both the contradictions and the connections in the coexistence of involvement and withdrawal. The *paradox of individuality* continues the theme of connection. The existence of a group requires connections among its members. There is nothing to belong to if no such connections exist. But if the connections are founded on similarities, if the *group* is founded on similarities, then what becomes of the *individual?* The group cannot come into existence as a psychologically meaningful unit unless individuals are able to express their individuality, their differences, so that connections can be found. Again, the circularity is both apparent and unsettling. And again we search for that which links the individual and the collective. The *paradox of boundaries* leaves us where we began. The fundamental question of belonging is the question of belonging to what. How do we know what the group is? A group must exist before the question of membership can be considered. Boundaries define what the group is, and yet they also define what it is not. They simultaneously give meaning to belonging and to not belonging. Paradoxically, the boundary around the group enables, even forces group members to confront the emotions around *both* belonging and not belonging. The boundary symbolizes the ever-present relationship between the two "opposite" conditions.

The Paradox of Identity

To be an individual, a person must integrate the variety of groups to which he or she belongs. In order to be a group, a collection of individuals must integrate the large array of individual differences that the members represent. These individual differences, however, are closely linked to the group memberships that the individuals carry around with them. The paradox of identity is expressed by the struggle of individuals and the group to establish a unique and meaningful identity where each is an integral part of the other.

When individuals approach a group, they invariably strug-

gle with what they are going to have to give up in order to belong. Likewise, a group as a whole often expresses concern over
whether its stipulated purposes can be achieved given the individuals of which it is constituted. These twin dilemmas can lead
members to look around for "good" groups, by which they
mean that individuality will be minimally compromised, and
groups to look around for "good" members—that is, people
willing to put the group ahead of themselves. The tendency for
individuals and groups to conceive of identity development in
such either/or terms can be seen in a variety of group dynamics.
For illustrative purposes, consider deviance and its relationship
to the often discussed topic of group norms.

Norms are informal ground rules that provide guidelines
concerning appropriate and inappropriate behavior in a group.
They are implicitly understood by members and are the sub-
strata beneath behavior in and of the group. In many ways, the
"character" of a group can be seen in its norms. If the norms
are very loose and easily adjusted from one situation to the
next, the group may have a somewhat "laissez-faire" identity. If
they are very strict, the group may be seen as "uptight."

When there is conflict between how an individual wishes
to act and how the norms prescribe that he or she "should" behave, the pressure is invariably on the individual to change and
adapt to the group. "If you want the benefits of belonging to
this group, you had better learn how to fit in." Group members
are rarely able to say to the deviating individual, "we are grate-
ful for your deviance, because it helps to loosen up our norms,
makes tolerable a wider array of behaviors, and in the long run
will make us a better group, because we will be much better
able to adapt to our world." The group's response to deviance is
usually to keep it in check, use it as an indicator of what is not
acceptable, or reject the individual(s) expressing the deviant side
of the group. Since the deviance seems counter to the group's
norms, the group is unable to see that its very norms created the
deviancy. The deviancy is informing the group about aspects of
its nature of which it would prefer to remain ignorant. If the
group sees the deviancy not as an expression of itself but instead as a characteristic of the individual who is expressing it,

then the group may elect to eliminate that individual or at least his or her troublesome behaviors. The group can then pretend that it has repaired itself without attending to the fact that it has just rejected a piece of self-knowledge. Such behavior by the group is implicitly based on "framing" its collective identity struggle as being in opposition to the identity struggles of individuals.

Individuals get into a similar posture with respect to groups. It is not unusual for an individual who does not like the norms in a group to develop a heroic stance toward changing the group into something that he or she would wish to be part of. This requires Herculean efforts to make the group into something that it is not. Such thinking on the part of an individual member is filled with a logic that views the group's character as different from and independent of the actions of its members. In this frame, the hero(ine) does not see the way that this "heroism" is itself an expression of an aspect of the group and accordingly "locates" the heroic powers in self. His or her "mission" in the group becomes framed in oppositional terms. When the group suddenly displays powerful resistance, equal to the hero(ine)'s own efforts, there seems no alternative to "upping the ante" and fighting even more vigorously. The cycle repeats itself until the individual conquers or feels conquered by the group or, more accurately, by the self that was put into the group.

Most often, however, the conflict between individual and group identity is not played out in such bold colors. It is more usual to see the tensions as requiring choices and compromises to be made by the individual and, occasionally, by the group. Consider a group in which the range of tolerable behavior is very limited, the stipulations about what everyone must do at different times are very precise, and the cost of noncompliance is quite explicit. This might conjure up an image of a tense group that would be hard to be a part of if one wanted room to express one's individuality. If this were a friendship group, most might conclude that it is not worth belonging to. However, for a group of surgeons in a hospital whose task is to conduct complex operations, these norms might be both tolerable and appropriate. In order for a surgeon to experience him- or herself individually as a good surgeon, these norms are necessary. The surgeon cannot be "good" unless the group is "good." In such an example, it is evident that individual competence is augmented when people both contribute their individual skills and subordinate their individualities to the collective norms. In a surgical team, the individuals are good when the group is made good, and the group is good when it provides a way for its individual members to be good.

A paradoxical approach to identity conceptualizes the processes through which both individual and group identity are formed as being one and the same. In this frame, individuals are seen as both creating and being created by the groups to which they belong. Even entertaining this possibility feels paradoxical, because the simultaneity of the two complementary processes creates a loop that is difficult to tolerate, both intellectually and emotionally. The paradox of identity conceives of the individual as deriving meaning from membership in the group while, at the same time, the group derives meaning from its individual members. Hence, any conception that separates group and individual identity is an oversimplification. The struggle so often observed *between* the individual and the group is predominantly a struggle occurring simultaneously *within* the individual and *within* the group over how to live with the tensions created by the mutual processes of adjustment of the individuals to the group and the group to its individual members.

A great deal of group life is involved with these identity struggles. This can be illustrated boldly by examining male-female dynamics within a group. All groups have to attend both to the fulfillment of their primary tasks and to the nurturance of their membership. To do only one or to do one at the expense of the other will quickly impoverish a group. At some level of awareness, all groups know this. Hence, they develop ways of attending to their mission and to their self-caretaking activities. It is not unusual for these tasks to be cast in gender terms, with nurturance associated with the feminine side of the group, while purpose and goal setting are labeled as masculine. Groups whose membership is predominantly male or female may find themselves using predominantly masculine or feminine terms. It is commonly noticed that much of the language structure of corporate America is laden with male sports terms, while social welfare groups often adopt female metaphors. These two "sides" may even be labeled as respectively hard and soft, especially in the larger culture. The key question is what happens when the necessary parts of group life are seen in gender terms and the group has both men and women in it? Will the females be free to be "masculine" and vice versa?

When men and women feel split into gender "camps" but compelled by the group to stay integrated, this is a clear expression that both parts are necessary for the group's wholeness and survival. However, once subgroups have formed, it is difficult for the group as a whole to conceive of integration in any terms other than some joining together of the subgroups. Given the nature of the splitting phenomenon, it may be hard for the group as a whole to conceive of a form of integration where individual members carry their own fair share of *both* caretaking and primary task activities. What then happens to the woman who wants to be other than nurturer, or the man who wants to be a caretaker? The natural response of the group is to resist this, especially if the initiatives or the resistances of an individual threaten the "balance" in the whole. This creates quite a bind. How does such a person use or develop the whole range of his or her personal and professional skills when the group has locked itself into this particular form of "integrated subgroups" as a way of staying whole? And how does the group learn about the ways it is impairing itself by ignoring or diminishing so many of the resources its members could potentially make available to the group?

The solution too often seems to be that the group, the individual concerned, or the subgroup feels pressured to abandon the drive for integration in response to the needs of the "other." Typically, this situation is seen in either/or and conflict terms, and the conflict is thought of as having emerged from different sources, in this case maleness and femaleness in the society as a whole. The alternative that views this split as being a manifestation of the group's internal life, displaced into the respective male and female parts, is not accessible to the group. As a result, the release that would be available if this dynamic were framed in this way is never realized. Instead, the "way out" involves one subgroup gaining dominance, restricting the potency of the other, or negotiating a compromise that both subgroups can live with. From a paradoxical perspective, the conflict is seen as having evolved from a common source, the collective needs of the group. Resolutions focused on bringing together those needs that were "artificially" split only end up reinforcing the conditions they are attempting to overcome.

The Paradox of Involvement

Becoming involved in and with a group requires some major commitments both to oneself and to the group. Membership means involving oneself in the search for ways to mesh individual needs and wishes with what the group has to offer and determining what one will give in the light of what the group needs and wants. As we discussed in the paradox of identity, these individual and group processes are mutual and co-occur. This generates a new dilemma, both for the group and for its individual members. If the parts and the whole are so mutually involved that individual identity cannot be preserved, then the group experience may lead only to a diminishing of the individual. On the other hand, if as a result of this mutual involvement the group becomes impaired by the loss of a part of itself, then it risks being unable to maintain a coherent sense of its identity as a whole in the face of inevitable turnover in membership.

There is an aspect of this dilemma that is central to our understanding of an individual's involvement in a group and a group's involvement in its individual members. If the processes of individual and group identity formation are so strongly linked, how does one avoid becoming lost in a group? And if one does get lost, how does one take actions to become more or less involved? Likewise, what happens to the group when it loses itself in one of its members or in some subgroup? How does the group take action to determine whether it is investing too much of itself, for little or no benefit, in some activity or concern of an individual part?

Consider the experience of a group of engineers in a large

organization that had become deeply involved in the alcoholism of one of its members. Walt had joined the group after several months in a rehabilitation program. His counselors had encouraged him to tell his potential employers about his "historical" problem with the bottle. Their view was that joining an understanding work group would facilitate his return to a normal life. Just before Walt was appointed to his new job, the other workers were advised about his situation and were asked to speak out if they had any concerns. All said, "Let's go ahead." Walt had impressed them with his professional skills, and the group he was joining took the attitude that they would be happy to help in his rehabilitation. Although not fully articulating it at this point, the work group took on Walt's "restoration" as a project of its own. For many months things were fine. At times of potential weakness, Walt found support from his colleagues and resisted the urge to return to drinking. The group became proud of him and in so doing was expressing pride in the parts of itself that had identified with his struggle. Walt's struggle became the group's struggle. His success became the group's success. The problem arose when the group and Walt began to lose a sense of what was his and what was the group's.

At a particularly busy time in the life of the group, members felt that they were going to be engulfed by more tasks than they could possibly handle. Having everyone work at high efficiency became important. For the first time, Walt felt significant stress in this job, and he turned to his peers for help. At the beginning of this pressure period, Walt's requests for help were "tolerated," but eventually people began to wish that he could contain his own problems. Walt felt abandoned, and, as he thought more and more of drinking as a solution, his need for group support increased. As members sensed that he was "losing it," their investment in keeping Walt dry rekindled. The prospect of Walt's failure began to look to the group like its own failure. At this point, the group was unable to separate itself from its investment in Walt's success and its fear of failure, both Walt's and its own. Rescuing Walt from the potential abyss became all-important, even at the risk of not completing essential projects. The group's sense of success and failure had become fused with Walt's. Walt stayed off the bottle as long as the group gave him enough attention precisely when he needed it. He had become, as it were, addicted to the group's support as a method of handling his addiction to alcohol.

With the group's loss of a sense of identity separate from Walt's, members began to feel emotionally blackmailed by him. Although this was never said out loud, individuals came to believe that if they did not give Walt his own way, he would go back to the bottle. Walt's needs seemed to say, "If I fail, you will have failed, so *you* had better make sure that *you* do everything necessary so that I don't fail." Predictably, the group came to see its imperfections as caused by Walt, and he continually felt responsible for the "group's garbage."

The special problem for this group and for Walt was that no one could get sufficiently outside of what was occurring to decide whether or how to get more or less involved. It was as though neither the group nor the members had any way of taking a larger perspective on themselves. The group lacked the capacity to see itself from an external vantage point analogous to the observing ego in the individual. The group seemed to have a sense of what Walt was doing to it, and Walt seemed to have a view of what the group was doing to him, but these two views were so enmeshed that neither the group nor the individual could see what each was doing to the other, or how the actions of each were contributing to a destructive pattern.

One's ability to take a perspective on oneself depends on one's ability to get outside of one's experience while at the same time remaining inside that experience. Although this is extremely difficult, it is essential for growth and is what is meant by the concept of an observing ego at the individual level. But what happens if one cannot do this? A classic "solution" is to try to place this observing function into someone else or some others and then use their reactions as the substitute for one's own. This is one possible perspective on what happened to Walt. Many group processes can be thought of as originating in the activities of many or all members to locate their observing egos in the group in hopes of having reflected back that which would be most gratifying.

How does a group get outside itself for the purpose of reflecting on itself? The dilemma is that the group does not have an observing function separate from the individual and collective actions of its members. Hence, the individual, as part of a group, is prone to use the group as a frame for understanding him- or herself; and the group is prone to use a part of itself (often its individual members) as a frame for understanding self. The dilemma is that the individual when using the group and the group when using its individual members for self-reflective purposes attempt to reject the part of self placed in others, setting in place the precondition for the vicious cycles of self-renunciation that lead so inevitably to paradox.

In the case of Walt and the group of engineers, the paradoxical dynamics become clearer if we continue the case. The group had to bring itself to the point where it did not care whether or not Walt returned to alcohol. When this happened, the emotional blackmailing and addiction became painfully obvious to both Walt and the others in the group. Then and only then could the group contemplate the ways that it could be and, in fact, was successful, independent of what was happening to Walt. Likewise, this separation, which had earlier seemed so threatening to Walt because it felt like abandonment, enabled him to confront the idea that substituting one addiction for another might be no solution. This gave him the chance to step back and take the next critical step in his personal journey out of substance addiction.

One might say that both Walt and the group would have been much better off if they had never come together in this mutual "project." On the other hand, because they both became so intensely *involved,* virtually losing key boundaries, they mutually created the conditions that enabled them to gain a perspective that might otherwise have been impossible. With some help, the group learned about the side of it that was invested in taking on projects that were destined for failure. Like many groups, it was struggling with how to distinguish between productive and wasted energy and to cut its losses on hopeless projects early enough that it was not continually driven by what was already invested. For the group, this was the learning that came from its involvement in self-observation, learning that would have been difficult, if not impossible, without involvement.

Although it may seem obvious that individuals' participation in a group and a group's participation in its membership require both experience *and* observation, action *and* reflection, these are most often conceptualized as separate and opposite and are therefore treated as being mutually exclusive. It is as if a group member is conceived of as either an actor or an observer; as if a group is not involved when a member is engaged in some action; as if a group in its observer state is not also acting; as if a member's noninvolvement is not also a group's noninvolvement in itself. This type of separation leads one to see group life as a clash between the active and the passive, between "doers" and "reflecters," between risk takers and risk avoiders.

In paradoxical terms, the ability to be involved is tied to the ability to be removed. The reflection informs the action, and the action forms the basis for reflection. In most cases, action and reflection occur simultaneously in groups, at the levels of both the individual members and the group as a whole. We observe while we experience. If we attempt to observe before we have experienced, there is nothing to observe. Likewise, observing is a form of experience that itself is a behavior that can be observed and reflected on. Through the playing out of the actions and the observations as in the Walt case, it becomes possible to talk about the simultaneous difference and similarity in the processes of action and reflection. This is the paradox of involvement. To develop the level of detachment necessary for self-reflection demands a kind of involvement that makes detachment appear impossible. Detachment through involvement *and* involvement through detachment are the essence of this paradox.

The Paradox of Individuality

The paradox of individuality is expressed by the statement that the only way for a group to become a group is for its members to express their individuality and to work on developing it as fully as possible and that the only way for individuals to become fully individuated is for them to accept and develop more fully their connections to the group.

We mentioned this paradox in our historical review of earlier writers on groups. Freud (1922) elaborated on the individual side of this paradox in his explanation of how individuality develops as one works on one's "groupness." Ironically, suggested Freud, it is the impairment of one's connections to the family that stirs the intense desire to be individuated in the first place. When one learns how to deal with one's groupness, the importance of individuation fades, and, through its fading, individuation is realized. Benne (1964) picked up on the group side of this paradox in his reflection on the way members divide over whether the group exists for its members or members exist for the group. He pointed out the importance of moving beyond this bipolar perspective to the stage where members learn to accept their groupness and the group learns to accept the importance of its members. The paradox is that the group gains its solidarity as individuality is legitimated, and individuality is established when the primacy of the group is affirmed.

This paradox of individuality often runs counter to the instincts that we have on approaching a group for the first time. To imagine throwing ourselves into it before we have developed a clear sense of the lay of the land sounds insane. Most of us have the tendency to be cautious, to hold back our energies, our individual wishes, our secrets, until we know what the group is like. Such reactions are a natural response to the fear of losing parts of ourselves to the norms, dictates, and imperatives of a group. The dilemma is that our very withholding is what contributes to making the group unsafe. The refusal of members to engage makes the group a hollow cocoon that no one wants to be part of. A group can become a group only when individuals put themselves into it, for it is the contributions of individuals that enable connections among people to form, connections that become woven into a fabric from which the foundation of the group is constructed. There is no group without these connections, and yet it is hard to discover connections without the support or foundation of a group.

One of the special ironies of this paradox is that members usually join a group because they feel some sense of inadequacy —to cope with aloneness (friendship groups), to develop competencies that cannot be acquired in isolation (educational groups), to earn income so that they can survive (employment groups), to meet intimacy and social needs (family groups or support groups). Hence, individuals come to a group looking for what they can get. Yet the overwhelming message is often "You can't get anything from here until you give!" So we look to see what others are getting and giving, as a way of determining whether it is worth putting in the required energy. What we see is ambiguous. "It seems like you have to join before it is even possible to work out whether joining is a good idea. But will they want me? I should put on a good face so they like me; otherwise, I'll get nothing. But it wasn't primarily the desire for confirmation that brought me to this group; it's my inadequate side that I want to have indulged. If I can't bring my inadequacies, what am I even doing here? I've got enough drains on my energy as it is, dealing with all this aloneness. . . ." If it turns out that others are in this group because they have similar inadequacies, what the individual expects to be demanded of him or her is a contribution from the very well that is already dry, making its emptiness seem even more troublesome. Mostly, individuals coming to a group with the hope that key needs will be met become less hopeful about this possibility as they actually join the group. Being fully an individual would seem to be problematic in groups.

When discussing the paradox of identity, we noted how easy it is for individuals in adopt a heroic stance toward the group. Out of the belief that the only way to become one's own person is by gaining mastery of the group comes the struggle between self and group, David and Goliath. In the paradox of individuality, we find a complementary dynamic to the heroic, expressed in archetypal form. On one side, we find expressions of the collective good, the call for a commitment to a common goal, the need for self-sacrifice, social conformity, and the compromises of the social contract. On the other side, we find the virtues of individuality, creativity, freedom of expression, and the stimulation and growth from which all human progress is sculpted. The tensions are symbolized in terms of the collective journey that humankind must take together until we reach the promised land, when it will be possible to bring forth to full life the many creations that come from the interaction of differences and the bountiful variation of the human species.

These heroic and archetypal forms often dominate our conceptions of the development of individuality in a group and contribute significantly to members' holding back until they have determined whether the group is to be supported or fought. This withholding, in turn, creates the very kind of group that leads members to take either a heroic or an antiheroic posture when confronted with the fear of a repressive collective or a dangerous renegade.

The paradoxical perspective emphasizes that the group exists, grows, and becomes strong and resourceful only if the individuality of its members can be expressed. At the same time that a group requires connections, conformity, and similarity for its existence, it also requires discontinuities and differences. Both the differences that come as expressions of individuality and the similarities, expressed as connectedness, simultaneously jeopardize and strengthen the group. In like manner, the similarities and the differences both support and threaten the individuality of group members. The expression of differences risks individual disconnection and collective disintegration while providing the possibility of connection based on personally meaningful commonalities. Similarly, the connections risk the stagnancy of conformity and the rebellious exit of individual members. The paradoxical struggle is again within the individual *and* within the group, to live with the tensions that emanate from the group's dependency on the individuality of its members and the individual's dependency on the commonality of the group.

The Paradox of Boundaries

One cannot talk about groups without implicitly invoking the concept of boundaries. There are boundaries in groups that explicitly indicate who belongs and who does not. There are boundaries drawn around subgroups that together form the group as a whole. There are boundaries that link the parts. There are boundaries around each of the individuals that make up the membership. There are boundaries less easily pointed to, though just as real, such as the psychological sense of belonging that group members feel and the attitudes that are acceptable or unacceptable to the group.

The concept of group boundary has been important in social science theories of collective behavior since the work of Lewin on field theory. He drew on the prevailing thought in military strategy, and so it seems reasonable to suspect that this concept has been around since humankind began to fight with itself. The places where boundary was most meaningfully elaborated as a pivotal concept were, at the collective level, in general systems theory and, at the individual level, in the object-relations work of the psychoanalytical school and the cognitive theories of Piaget. In each tradition, development is understood in boundary-drawing terms (for example, learning to distinguish between breast and self, me and not me, and so on). Once boundaries have been drawn, the possibility of relationship emerges. Without boundary, there can be no relationship. For example, only as the infant builds a sense of a self that is distinct from mother can it develop a relationship with mother. Without boundaries, there is fusion. In this regard, boundaries are at the base of everything in group life. For the group to have a sense of itself as an entity capable of acting as a whole, it must have clear external boundaries. For the group to develop an internal sense of itself, it must be able to see multiple possibilities for the arrangement of its internal parts. This requires the drawing of distinctions between the parts.

The paradox is that boundaries simultaneously make it possible for a group to take actions and limit those actions by what the boundaries define. For example, when a group's boundaries are drawn such that it is defined as management, the fulfilling of the management function becomes possible but the option of being labor is taken away. This paradox of simultaneous possibility and limitation is most evident in the boundary delineation associated with labeling. In human consciousness, the only way for us to think is via the symbols that we use to store our experiences of the world. These symbols make it possible to hold sufficiently constant images of experience for us to reflect upon those experiences. Our reflection, though, is not in terms of those actual experiences but in terms of the symbols that we use to store those experiences. If we have labeled an experience in a particular way, that is the frame within which we will think about it. To develop thinking beyond the limits defined by the symbol requires us to break frame, but even then the breaking out is shaped by that which is being broken out of. The deep paradox is that were it not for the symbols, experience could not be stored and would not be an ongoing part of our experience, yet, at the same time, those very symbols constrain the ways we are able to experience both the past and the future.

We must also point out that the same paradox is operative within our use of the symbol of boundary. As a metaphor, it tends to suggest, and even take on, physical manifestations like those of a fence or a ravine. If we fall into the trap of the paradox that we are attempting to delineate, we could easily start thinking of a relationship that connects what the boundary separates as being the actual *location* of the boundary. A relationship is not a place where patterns connect; rather, it is a concept at a level that hovers above, within, or beneath that which it refers to.

To illustrate this paradox further, consider belonging to a group engaged in hostile exchanges with a peer group. We may choose to label the other as "mistrusted enemy to be fought with." This label "enemy" gives us a frame for storing our experiences with this group. If the enemy does something kindly, we will code it as evidence of nonhostile behavior or of an attempt to get us off guard, to lull us into a nonvigilant condition, so that they can attack us. The key issue is that the initial symbol "enemy" provides a dominant template that then constrains how our future interactions are coded and experienced. Should our group someday conclude that the other group is not really an enemy, we are likely to break the old symbol of enemy and replace it with a similar one, such as "friend." "Friend" may be an equally inappropriate and constraining symbol, which we find meaningful because we no longer see "enemy." It may be that neither "enemy" nor "friend" is appropriate and that both groups may just be trying to coexist within a constrained environment, occasionally getting in each other's way and needing to make adjustments so as to avoid being pushed into behaving destructively toward each other.

The importance of boundaries is most visible in the experiences of those who have not been given adequate boundaries. Experiencing the constraints of boundaries gives one the chance to work out how one is going to deal with them. This is evident in the experiences of those who expect to be rejected or held accountable but are not. In a junior high youth club, every adult leader knows that kids expend a great deal of energy testing limits. Ganging up and behaving "counterproductively" are often so much fun for this age group, especially since they feel constrained in how much of this they can do at school or at home. In a way, the youth club is a forum where the steam can be let off. If, however, the leadership refuses to define and hold clear boundaries for the group, it takes away a lot of the fun for the kids; more important, it deprives them of the necessary lessons that can be learned only by encountering the limits and then dealing with them. For this reason, the testing of the authority figure does not necessarily mean that the kids want the authority to change his or her behavior; rather, it may mean that they want the experience of testing the authority figure. This cannot be done if the boundaries are inadequately drawn or if they "give" each time a kid bangs into them. Even boundaries that may seem cruel are more helpful developmentally than those not drawn.

One of the most critical functions that a group's boundaries provide is being a metaphoric container of the anxieties carried by individual members as a consequence of their group membership. If members are constantly put in the position of having to bear alone the anxiety of group membership, then the group will always be an overwhelming place. It is in the group's interest to provide a way for its members to deal wth the reactions that the group generates in them. The term *container* is a good one, because the most visible aspect of the container is its boundary system. In fact, it is the only property that the container has. The metaphor of group as container implies that "stuff" will not leak out and that if you lift the lid appropriately you can pour "stuff" into it. The group needs to be able to contain the "rage for order" that members bring to their experiences of the group, together with the rebelliousness emanating from the same individuals' "drunkenness with autonomy."

Jaques (1955) argued that much of the desire to structure experiences in groups comes out of both the individual and the collective wish to have a defense against these anxieties. But the paradoxical rub about "these boundaries that contain" is that they are the very processes experienced as structures that create the anxiety in the first place. Individuals do have their own individual anxieties that they import into the group, but collective anxieties are coalesced by that which binds the members together; that is, the group's boundaries. In recognizing this, it would be tempting to suggest that if the group's boundaries *create* such problems, then it would be best to draw the boundaries in a different way or to have none at all. But this provides no solution, at least in any absolute sense, for boundlessness has its own set of dynamics that have to be contained in some way or other, and each structural configuration will bring with it a shadowy coattail.

So, while boundaries constitute a containing process, they also contribute to creating that which they are designed to contain. Another illustration can be seen in the relationship between insiderness and outsiderness. When the boundary is drawn such that certain individuals are "in" and others "out," those who are outside the group adjust to this fairly quickly, either by deciding that they do not care about the group after all or by joining other groups. It is left to someone or some subset on the inside of the group to now carry the feelings of outsiderness on behalf of the group as a whole. The irony is that someone who is "in" begins to fear the possibility of being "out," and the group has to develop a way to contain the emotion associated with outsiderness, an emotion that it has created by its actions to include. But it must do this in a way that includes; otherwise, it will merely push out again this aspect of itself and undermine further the sense of inclusion that the boundary was designed to create.

A special consequence of effective boundary drawing in a group is that the container effect can make experiences very much more potent than would be the case if the boundary did not exist or if it were drawn more loosely. This is very evident in many experiential group-learning settings (such as group-relations conferences in the Tavistock tradition). In these groups, the boundaries are drawn so vigorously, both by the staff and by the design of the program, that the normal safety valves of letting unwanted or difficult emotions "flee" through the "walls" of the conference are effectively removed. This increases the potency of the emotions that members are confronted with. They get to experience the major consequences, constructive and destructive, of having boundaries tightly articulated. In most group situations, the external boundaries are drawn with sufficient permeability that unwanted parts of the group can be pushed outside. When this is experienced as not possible, the group finds itself face to face with elements of itself that it may not like and is confronted with the idea of dealing with them in ways that it would never encounter in ordinary circumstances. Likewise, the groups are not free to import things, such as distractions, from the outside. Resources from outside are not available, and the group has to solve its own "problems" when it might normally seek "help" from without. In such settings, it is possible to learn just how much of inside-group life is normally a playing through of outside issues that have been taken into the group and vice versa and how this blunts the capacity of the group to feel and know the full force of its own internal dynamics.

In its role as container, the boundary is both the life and the death of the group. It is the essential precondition for a collection of individuals to have a life together as a group; at the same time, poorly defined, it can be the vehicle for a group's demise. Too rigidly defined and the group feeds on its own anxieties until it explodes out of existence; too porous and the group dilutes its experiences, even to the point where the group's life is totally dominated by the outside, by that which it is not.

The paradox of boundary puts sharply before us that the complex processes of group life and death come from the same source. To handle them in a way that preserves life without separating it from death and vice versa requires a group's learning how to live "in" and "with" the tensions of the boundary.

Conclusion

In each of the four paradoxes in this chapter, tension is generated when links between the contradictory emotions and reactions evoked within individuals, within groups, and between individuals and groups are unrecognized. The anxieties evoked by the questions of belonging seem most debilitating for individuals and groups when the connections between the opposites go unnoticed and instead only their exclusiveness is attended to. The paradoxes of belonging suggest that it would be strange indeed to find a group where there was a group identity but no individual identities, or experience but no observation, or deviance but no conformity. One might wonder about the vitality of groups in which these polarities were not simultaneously in evidence. Their coexistence may be a sign not merely of conflict and disagreement but of the dynamic life of the group.

In this chapter, we followed a progression of thought that moved from identity through involvement and individuality to the theme of boundaries. Now that we have traveled along the contours of group belonging in this direction, it is obvious that the journey could equally have been taken another way. Boundary is at the root of any attempt to formulate the identity of individuals and/or the groups to which they belong, and the boundary drawing associated with identity development is essential for both individuals and groups as they struggle with how much to be involved and how to engage in the dynamics of self-reflection. In turn, self-reflection is a form of boundary drawing that helps to articulate individuality. The processes of individuation set boundaries both for individuals and for the setting being individuated from. In other words, each of these paradoxes, although discussed sequentially, both contains and is contained by each of the others.

6

Paradoxes of Engaging: Disclosure, Trust, Intimacy, and Regression

The paradoxes of belonging are evoked by the combination of individual joining and group-formation processes. These processes do not occur exclusively at any one point in a group's life, but they are more likely during its early phases. The paradoxes of engaging arise when members begin to ask how much of themselves they are willing and able to contribute to the group and how much is required of them for the group to be effective. In its most concrete form, a group works best when members know each other's strengths and weaknesses, abilities and disabilities, and when the group's tasks and ambitions are well matched to the limitations of its members. But under what conditions will members disclose their respective strengths and weaknesses? How much do the members engage each other and the issues that arise in the group as a whole, and how much of themselves will they allow to be engaged by the demands and concerns of the group?

The paradoxes described in this chapter seek to address some of these questions. They examine the apparently contradictory and often confusing dynamics within individuals, between individuals and the group, and within the group as a whole evoked by the issue of engagement in groups. Once again, in the analysis of each paradox, special attention is paid to the link between the "opposing" forces, between the hidden and the disclosed, the past and the present, acceptance and rejection, confirmation and disconfirmation. In the examination of the relationship between these opposites as they occur in groups, we learn more about the process of engagement. The themes being examined in the service of understanding engagement are disclosure, trust, intimacy, and regression.

The paradox of disclosure turns on the question of how and whether we allow ourselves to be known in groups. To disclose about ourselves, we often feel the need to know about others first, and yet, for us to know about others, someone must be willing to allow him- or herself to be known. The exploration of this paradoxical cycle takes us to the concerns about acceptance and rejection common among members of groups and to the paradoxical relationship between rejection and disclosure.

In the second section of the chapter, the development of trust in groups is viewed in paradoxical terms. How does trust ever develop if, in order for it to develop, there needs to be trust? The process of engagement is facilitated by a group in which members feel safe when they are vulnerable, when they have exposed a weakness or a hurt. Without this safety, the efforts of the group are hampered by the actions that individuals take to protect themselves and what they know, both about themselves and about the group. How safety is created out of fear is the question at the heart of the paradox of trust.

The paradox of intimacy explores the apparent contradiction that to know others we must know ourselves and that to know ourselves means knowing others. In groups of all kinds, it is often tacitly assumed that knowing others is an external task and that knowing oneself is an internal one. Much of the life of a group is based on the assumption that these two types of knowledge can be distinguished and separated. From a paradoxical perspective, we argue that self-awareness is a precondition for other awareness or vice versa. The paradox of intimacy suggests that there *is* a relationship between intrapersonal and collective intimacy.

The paradox of regression enters the past to unlock the present. Regression allows progression, and progression requires regression. The examination of this paradox reveals a very interesting link between individual regression and collective development. Only as it provides an environment that supports regression by its members can a group become an effective group, yet it is precisely this kind of environment that is resisted because it seems to retard the very progress that the group seeks to attain.

The Paradox of Disclosure

For a group to be capable of acting as a whole, members must know each other and know how each of them contributes to their collective action. While a group is not independent of its individual members, it does have a life beyond what any individual in the group is capable of understanding at any moment. For intermember knowledge to occur, members must be prepared to disclose who they are, yet it is not possible to know who one is in a particular group until such time as one knows something about that group. But little can be known until members have begun to disclose. This paradoxical circle is what we call the paradox of disclosure: for members to learn who they are going to be in and to the group, they must be willing to disclose; to self-disclose, members need to know about the group to which they belong.

This cycle is particularly prevalent in groups that are forming, when everyone is new to each other, but it also occurs when an established group goes through the process of bringing in new members. The disclosure paradox is clearly evident in the experiences of the new members, but it also can be seen in the behavior of the "old" members as well. For example, a group that is replacing two or three members may be quite reticent to show anything other than its good side to the new members until it is clear that they are committed and will not leave. The new members, in turn, may be reticent to disclose things about themselves until they learn more about the "problems" of their new group and the group's "true" identity.

The paradox of disclosure is tied to the process of social

comparison. To know oneself in a social context, one may reflect on one's inner experience, but one also needs to know how one is experienced by others. This external knowledge can be obtained only through the feedback of others. The reactions of others will not be very valuable unless they are in response to characteristics of ourselves that we care about, and these could be known to others only if we are willing to disclose. If one never takes any meaningful actions but remains at a level of trivial exchange, the quality of what is reflected back will be at the same level. In addition, feedback from others is self-disclosure on their part. If one is in a group where members will not disclose either their inner responses or their reactions to what others do, think, and feel, then personal and collective learning will be severely retarded.

Disclosure and feedback are the necessary conditions for the development of interpersonal relationships (Luft, 1970). The question that we each must face is what to disclose about ourselves when we are eager to gain acceptance and what we keep hidden. The most natural thing to do is to reveal only those things that we are sure will be accepted and keep private what we anticipate others will reject. Yet this sets in place the inner sense that, when others do accept us, it is all a sham—they are not in a position to reject the "real me" because I have kept it hidden. If others were to know "what I am really like," if I let them see the ugly parts of me that are unacceptable even to me (which is, after all, why I keep them locked away inside), then they would reject me. Thus, the acceptance I gain is unacceptable to me, because it is not based on the parts of me that I "know" are unacceptable. I set myself up to construe those who are accepting me as being unacceptable, paradoxically rejecting the very source from which I crave acceptance when I am given the acceptance I seek. Of course, were I able to accept myself, with all my flaws, acceptance by others would be less important to me, and hence I would be less prone to reject the acceptance that I am offered.

In this cycle, it can be seen that acceptance and rejection are integrally linked. For our discussion here, the key issue is what happens when the place from which acceptance is being sought is a group made up of individuals all engaging in processes such as the above. The answer is that all find themselves rejecting the group that accepts them, creating a feeling about the group as a whole that it is like quicksand. It is only when the group breaks out of this conundrum by itself rejecting the members who are treating it this way that individuals begin to feel that the acceptance is at all authentic. The expression of the group's rejecting side paradoxically enables individuals to feel more secure about letting their rejectable sides be known, which in turn sets up the possibility that the rejectable can be tolerated by the group, making the acceptance that is offered feel more real.

Luft (1970) contended that disclosure and feedback are the necessary conditions for the development of interpersonal relations. Of particular interest to us are those things known to self that one might wish to keep hidden. The desire to hide is often stirred by the fear of being rejected by others. The fear that others will be rejecting may emerge from the parts of self that are rejecting. Fearing our own rejecting sides, we suspect that this is a potent feature of others, and so we work hard to gain assurances that others will not reject as a precondition for our own disclosure. No matter what assurances are given, the proof remains uncertain until the disclosure is attempted.

This kind of paradox was evident in a team of surgeons with a homosexual member who felt it necessary to keep his sexual preference hidden in order to remain in good standing in the group. He discussed his dilemma at length with friends in the gay community. His desire for others to know grew out of his sense that his acceptance at work was predicated on a lie. "We spend a great deal of time together dealing with life-and-death issues. I feel like a fraud living behind this facade." When his friends encouraged him to tell his co-workers about his homosexuality, he would reply that it was too risky. "You're talking about my career! Someday, maybe, when I am well established and don't need to rely on others' opinions to hold down a good job! But not now." Though he craved the acceptance now, he was acting to perpetuate the conditions where authentic acceptance was not possible. Perhaps because of his own sensitivity to the issue of "authenticity," this man was acutely attuned to the inauthentic behavior of the rest of the surgical team and used this as his justification for the following guideline: "I can risk disclosure only when others have become authentic." When he eventually did tell his colleagues about his homosexuality, the response was "That's OK by us." The reaction was relieving but ultimately unsatisfying, because it left him unable to engage the rejecting feelings that he "knew" existed in the group. As he remarked to a friend, "Their reaction implied that they didn't care. I know they do, but I would have felt so much more accepted if someone had said he was troubled by it; then we might have talked, maybe even fought a bit, but I would have had a chance to tell a little of my own struggles. As it is, they now know I'm gay, but they don't know *me* any better, and I don't feel any more acceptance than I did before."

This man now faced another choice point. His impulse was to let it pass and accept that *this* surgical team was not going to be close. Yet a voice inside said, "You cannot be a good surgical team if you are indifferent toward each other." The question now was whether he was prepared to reject the superficiality of the other group members' response to him. Paradoxically, in order to gain others' acceptance, he was finding that it was necessary to embrace his own rejecting side. He was painfully discovering the link between acceptance and rejection. He decided that it was worth a try. When he raised the issue again, someone said "What do you want, acceptance or rejection?" There it was. He wanted both. He admitted this, triggering the somewhat disdainful response of "When you've worked it out, let us know, and we'll oblige either way!" The response hurt, but at that moment he felt this person's rejection and preferred it to the earlier indifference. He said as much. A long conversation ensued, which initially focused on homosexuality but eventually moved to a discussion of feelings about the life-and-death dimensions of their daily work. After a while, the fact that he was gay receded in importance, to him and to the others, as they talked about their shared anxieties.

In this surgeon's experience, his fears of being rejected

for disclosing his homosexuality gave way before his willingness
to *be* rejecting. In expressing his own rejection of others, he
allowed them to know more about him, which in turn led them
to disclose more about themselves; that is, more about the rejecting feelings that they had suppressed. Ultimately, the disclosure of feelings of rejection created the foundation for some
degree of mutual acceptance.

The key point in this, as it concerns the paradox of disclosure in groups, is that only when one gets reactions from
those who are different can one's self-knowledge develop, but
those very differences make it probable that one will feel rejected when the reactions are given. Defending oneself against
possible rejection by closing down or refusing to risk being experienced as rejecting blunts the group members' capacity for
individual and collective self-knowledge. The group will not
alter in the desired ways independent of members' actions. Paradoxically, only as individual members in the group risk self-disclosure, with all the uncertainty about how the group will deal
with it, does it become safe to self-disclose in the group.

The Paradox of Trust

Once group members start to engage in the dynamics
found in the paradox of disclosure, they encounter those of trust.
Group life is filled with dilemmas in which one needs to trust
others but where the development of trust depends on trust already existing. Before we are willing to trust others, we want to
know how they will respond to us, not just at the level of acceptance or rejection but with respect to our weak parts as well as
our strong ones, our fears as well as our hopes, our ugliness as
well as our beauty. In order to discover how others will respond, someone in a group must be willing to expose his or her
weak, fearful, and ugly sides. The willingness to do this depends
on the trust in the group.

The paradox of trust may be symbolized by the conundrum of a cycle that depends upon itself to get started. The
problem of developing trust has often been represented by the
prisoner's dilemma "game." In this "game," the sentences of

two isolated prisoners depend on their respective stories about a crime that they allegedly committed. Most versions of the game have the following flavor: If neither prisoner implicates the other, both are set free. If both prisoners blame each other, they both receive long prison terms. If both accept some responsibility for the crime, they receive moderate sentences. If one prisoner accepts some responsibility for the crime and the other blames the first, the first receives a long prison term and the second goes free! The "game" is created because neither prisoner knows the rules at the outset but each gets repeated opportunities to "tell a story" and is told the consequences after each story; that is, the length of the prison term. The paradoxical nature of this game lies in how it begins. The prisoners begin with a two-pronged struggle over trust—trust in the jailor, who is inherently untrustworthy from the prisoners' perspective, and trust in the fellow prisoner. The concern over the other prisoner is whether she or he will opt for self-interest over their joint interests. This is an issue for each inmate, because the structure of the situation requires each to consider the option of looking after self at the expense of the other. The concern about the jailor is focused on whether she or he will (1) abide by the rules of the game, (2) not alter the rules in response to prisoners' choices, and (3) accurately and reliably transmit information about the choices of the other prisoner. Trusting that this will occur, the prisoner acts and in turn finds out whether that trust was founded. Of course, the smart prisoner makes an initial test of the waters, not risking too much until there is confirmation that the trust being expressed will be honored. One can imagine an exchange between a prisoner and a jailor that goes as follows: "I want you to do such and such!" "Why should I?" "Because it will be good for you." "You mean good for you, don't you?" "Well, of course, it will be good for me, that goes without saying. But it will be good for you, too!" "How can I be sure of that?" "You can't! The only way to find out will be by doing it!" The power of the prisoner-jailor example is that, in a state of distrust, the way to gain the necessary knowledge to make trust possible is by trusting.

Some of our understanding of group experience can be

enriched by using the jailor as a metaphor. He is a despised figure, yet he is also valued as a provider of security as well as a
constrainer. The jailor, while supposedly protecting the outside
world from the prisoner, is also keeping out the lynching tendencies of that world, assuring due process, no matter how bad
the crime. Most critically, however, prisoners count on the jailor
to protect them from each other, to regulate interactions so
that the explosions arising from the intense and impacted emotions of living in close quarters are contained.

The group plays a similar role for its members. It would
not be unreasonable for the members to ask the group, if there
were some clear entity to talk to, whether they can count on
the group to give the security that members feel they need. We
could imagine a conversation between the members and the
group that paralleled the one between the prisoner and the
jailor: "How can we be sure that belonging to this group will be
good for me?" "Well, there are no guarantees, but the group has
the best interests of its members at heart." "Well, I thought that
was the case in the last group I belonged to, yet we ended up in
a real mess." "That was probably because that group was poorly managed." "Well, I want some assurances that this group will
be different." "It will be different, because everyone has the investment in making it good." "How can I be sure? It sounds like
you're asking me to trust you, and I don't know that groups can
ever be trusted!" "The only way for you to find out is to trust,
for the trustworthiness of the group is made up from the trusting behaviors of the members." "But if I trust and others don't,
then I will be out on a limb. . . ." "Look, the only way to find
out is to trust and see what happens. That's how it is. Take it or
leave it!"

Many of the key dynamics of members' trust in the group
and the group's sense of its own trustworthiness can be understood by exploring the operations and implications of positive-
and negative-feedback systems. Positive feedback simply encourages a system to continue doing what it is doing; it provides
no self-corrective information. A system receiving only positive
signals has no way of discovering when it is doing poorly or
why. In addition, such a system cannot reflect on how what it

is doing leads to what it defines as positive outcomes. It may have the experience of success (in part because it does not know how to pick up the signals of failure), but it could not describe the actions that make success possible. In this regard, such a system is deprived of learning. It may "get things right," but it does not know why, and it cannot self-correct.

Negative feedback, on the other hand, tells the system that what it is doing is not working and that it needs to stop, reflect, contemplate other alternatives, adopt an experimental approach, and discover anew what works. In this context, positive feedback can help learning to occur. This is possible because the negative feedback provides a contrast. It is out of the "in-formation" created from the distinctions between the positive and negative that a system's self-reflective capacities are molded. The special dilemma represented in the positive- and negative-feedback processes is that the very thing that is necessary for a group to survive, negative feedback, is also the thing that assaults it, telling it, as it were, that it is "not OK." If the group heard only the "not OK" message, it would find itself forever attempting to adjust to externally induced pain to a point where its ability to function would be seriously undermined.

A further complication is that individuals, like groups, both want and do not want negative feedback. We want to know whether the concerns we have generated from our own attempts at self-understanding are valid, but we also hope that they are not. In the extreme, we hope that our process of self-understanding is flawed, since this would mean that our "self" is not. And, though we know that we are imperfect, we hope, however irrationally, that the feedback we attend to will prove us wrong.

In group settings, the intertwining of individual and collective feedback processes is complex. A group may need to be able to receive negative feedback about its processes in order to learn and grow. Yet the source of this information may be a member of the group who is not valued because of his or her tendency to give negative feedback to the group. If the group does not listen to this side of itself or elects to act as if this information is merely "inside" the one person who is speaking,

then it may be disconfirming (rejecting) that which is disconfirming. In order to confirm its collective identity, the group
may have rejected the negative feedback it needs to survive.
Negative feedback to an individual aimed at disconfirming the
individual but confirming the group may have precisely the opposite effect. This leaves us in a very confusing circumstance.
How can a group that is struggling to know itself do this while
its members are struggling to know themselves in the group?

It is very common for groups to give negative feedback to
members who give the group the negative feedback that it needs
to both survive and grow. In the process, the group masks the
parts of itself that do not want to change. Rather than acknowledge openly the resistance to change, the group continues to remain the same while affirming its interest in changing, but it
accuses those giving negative feedback of pushing their own self-
interests instead of the group's. On this basis, the group justifies
its rejection of those advocating change. This negative feedback
by the group to the members who offer negative feedback to
the group can be used as a smokescreen, enabling hidden agen-
das to remain hidden. This is especially relevant if those giving
negative feedback to the group are driven away, in which case
the individuals never get "wise" to what the group is up to.

On the other side of this coin, a group often needs to buy
time to adjust to the changes proposed by those it rejects. As in
other dynamics that we have discussed, often the group will say
"no" to the changes being suggested in order to set in place the
possibility of eventually saying "yes." It comes to recognize
that the very thing that it is rejecting is what it wants. Then it
says "OK." The variation being suggested via the negative feedback is rejected by the group because the group lacks the capacity to deal with that variety. It is only as it struggles with the
repetitive rejection that the group comes to the point where it
is able to accept what it is rejecting.

A paradoxical approach calls upon us to change the frame
in which we struggle with the issue of trust. It suggests that
staying within the self-referential dynamics of trust and mistrust, confirmation and disconfirmation, leaves one hopelessly
confused. The more we attempt to sort it out, the more confus-

ing it all becomes. However, if a group and its individual members trust that the individual and collective feedback processes, operating in tandem, provide the possibility for self-correction and growth, then the confusion is less of a problem and may turn out to be the very condition necessary for learning to occur.

The issue becomes learning how to trust what logically makes little sense until the kind of assurance and growth associated with trusting has been created. When that point is reached, not understanding the logic ceases to be a reason for not trusting. The issue of trust has been changed to one of trusting that which seems untrustable and discovering that engaging in the *process of trusting,* rather than the content of the trust, creates a group in which people feel increasingly safe disclosing the weak and the ugly.

The Paradox of Intimacy

In this chapter, we have been weaving our way through a complex set of dynamics at both the individual and group levels. It is evident that a person's willingness to disclose thoughts and feelings in a group requires an acceptance of these, both by the person and by others. However, the development of that acceptance comes only when one has disclosed and discovered through others' disclosure the commonality of those thoughts and feelings that seemed initially so risky. This leads us to the paradox of intimacy: acceptance of self depends on acceptance of others, and acceptance of others depends on acceptance of self. It can be expressed in the form of the person who needs to listen to be understood.

The difficulty of this issue can be seen in the example of the expert review panel convened by politicians after a troubling accident at a nuclear plant. Panel members had been invited from various parts of the country. One criterion for the composition of the panel was that the members not know each other. Several disciplines were represented, ranging from physics to administration to law enforcement (since there was a suspicion of sabotage). The panel was asked to do its investigative work as quickly as possible, because the community was deeply distressed. The longer the anger raged, the greater the possibility of protracted lawsuits that could be economically devastating.

To speed up the process of getting acquainted, a necessary first step given the selection process, the chairperson of the panel decided that it would be best to bypass the trivia of introductions and get quickly into a substantive discussion. He suggested that each person say something about the special expertise that he or she brought to the panel's work, and the members agreed that this was a good idea. The difficulty was, however, that this group was rather prestigious, and most were feeling rather awed by each other. In addition, each was feeling some anxiety about the limits of their collective capacity to be rational about a subject so charged with emotion.

So this group in formation began a process that each member felt was a little risky. After a moment's quiet reflection, the first person spoke. It so happened that no one listened to what was said. Each was so totally preoccupied with what to reveal that listening to someone else was impossible. As each spoke, the pressure mounted to be more revealing than the previous individual. At the end, those who had gone first felt that they had not been sufficiently self-disclosing. At the conclusion of the activity, very little of the content shared could be remembered by those in the group; it was as though each had been so invested in listening to his or her inner anxiety that others' revelations seemed unimportant in comparison. As a consequence of not listening, very little understanding was advanced, and the tension characteristic of any first meeting was still present.

Someone suggested talking about what they had done and whether it had given them the kind of start the group needed. Everyone agreed that it had not, especially as it became clear that everyone had been listening to him- or herself and not to anyone else. As they talked further, the recognition emerged that each of them had been so concerned about acceptance and what seemed like the impossible mandate that they had been given that the attendant anxiety had blunted their collective capacity to listen. As the members spoke to each other about their individual difficulty in listening, everyone listened, leading to an increasing sense that people had indeed felt similar things during the introductions. By the end of this review session, the listening had enabled each to recognize the collective nature of the individually experienced anxiety. Through the individual speaking and not listening, the group was saying something at the collective level that could be heard only through the not-listening behavior occurring at the individual level. When this group-level statement was heard, it became possible for individuals to listen to each other in the way that they had presumed they would do in the beginning.

Consider a second example, the experiences of Dr. Malakoff in his role of professor of marketing in a prestigious business school on the East Coast. Classrooms are groups, too, and display similar dynamics to those observed in the expert panel. Let us listen to this example through the words of the professor involved:

> In this school, our students arrive for their first semester having left influential jobs where they were receiving indications that investing an arm and a leg and two years of their lives in professional education would return valuable dividends. For many of them, it is done with considerable sacrifice, uprooting spouses and tearing themselves away from locations where they were beginning to develop meaningful connections. It is undertaken with the hope that at the end there will be a high-paying, worthwhile job to justify all the investments.
>
> The first day at school is filled with excitement. All the waiting is over. By the second day, it has become terribly confusing. It is the middle of orientation, fellow students seem intolerably aggressive, and the administration of the school is turning out to be remarkably inflexible. As one student expressed it, "I wanted to be able to organize Wednesday afternoon off so that, along with

the whole of Friday, I will be able to work to put food on the table for my family. But I have my introductory accounting class on Wednesday afternoon, and I am told that all other sections are closed. The only way to get in is by permission of the instructor, but all of them say they can't add anyone until someone else drops. And three of them aren't even back yet from their European travels." This type of experience, or some variation on the theme, is prototypical for virtually all students. Everyone seems to think that his or her concerns are more important than others'; the level of collective anxiety is high but denied and derided.

Walking into the opening class of first-semester M.B.A. students is something amazing. The shared angst and the obvious hope that the professor will not turn out to be a disaster are very intense. It would be really easy, if I didn't know anything about the larger environmental dynamics, to see this class's potential chemistry as explosive and therefore feel that I must contain it in the service of the education. The first things I say seem to be dissatisfying to the students. If I begin by laying out the syllabus and the structure of the work for the course, the majority of what I say is not listened to; and then one person will speak up about some nitpicking element of the structure that is unsatisfactory. It is not until we start talking about grades and the evaluation system that people begin to pay attention.

This is how I now do it. And it is amazing what a difference it makes to the beginning of the semester for all of us. I open by saying that it will be possible for every one of them to get credit for the class. I indicate that they have already been chosen as someone who will succeed and that it is my responsibility, as a faculty member, to make that happen. I proceed to tell them what the class

evaluative anxiety

requires for success and that if they follow these
procedures they will be given the appropriate cred-
its. I say that if anyone's work turns out to be unsatisfactory along the way, they will have a chance
to redo it, under guidance, until it is satisfactory.
The first time I did this, I assumed that this would
be sufficient to take the evaluative anxiety away.
Quite to the contrary. It made things worse.

I then ask them to think about whether they
believe what I said. At that moment, every eye is
riveted on me. The expression on their faces communicates immediately that I have hit a raw nerve.
I proceed as follows: "The problem as I see it is
that we've admitted you to this school because we
believe you are qualified and deserving of the training you will get here. We believe it, as did all the
people who recommended you and the various financial institutions who have lent you money; no
one is acting out of altruism, the problem is that
the most important person to believe this doesn't.
Isn't it true that many of you simply don't believe
you belong here? Some other prestigious school
turned you down, and your belief is that we made
a mistake in admitting *you,* not everyone else, just
you. You are the one person who scrambled in under the gate or through the back door, and although what I've said about everyone being able to
pass might be true in general, there is going to be
one exception this semester, and *you* are it."

At this point, the tension in the classroom is
great. I then suggest that they look around the
room and see how many other people seem to be as
disturbed as they themselves feel. I ask for a show
of hands as to who felt while I was speaking that I
was describing just them. Gingerly at first, but then
in the context of emerging laughter, about 75 percent of the hands go up. We then talk for fifteen
minutes or so about what arriving at school was

humble acceptance

like and what the anxiety means to them. And as
we do this, the tension fades away as the bonding
among the students begins to develop. Suddenly
the big ex-football players and those who are into
preening look as human as everyone else.

The special value of this illustration for our discussion is
that the paradox of intimacy suggests the necessity of bringing
to the surface the collective dimensions of shared experience in
order for the members (the parts) to be able to develop meaningful relationships with each other. However, there is no way
for that collective phenomenon to crystallize unless members
work directly at connecting first with each other. If they try to
connect with the group first, they will be creating a vacuum
that is then very elusive to engage. If they work to understand
their own emotions and to engage others in an exploration of
those emotions, they create an opportunity for the connection
to occur out of which the group fabric becomes constructed.

There are facets of this that are rather distressing, unless
we can learn how to exist with a paradoxical view of the world.
To connect at an individual level as members of a group, we
have to be willing to engage each other and apparently experience the failure of connecting. The paradox of intimacy suggests that meaningful connections with others are limited by
one's willingness to "connect with" or learn about oneself, and
vice versa. In this sense, "listening" is simultaneously a means of
understanding oneself and of understanding others, while
"speaking" is simultaneously a means of connecting with oneself and connecting with others.

The Paradox of Regression

When individuals join a group that is either formed or
forming, they are approaching experiences that are unfamiliar.
They attempt to create some structure for thinking and acting
that will enable them to manage the joining process. The available structures that an individual can draw upon come from his
or her personal history. Each person will bring into this new

joining process an approach (or set of approaches) from past encounters with groups and will use this as a guide for managing the unfamiliarity of the new setting. At a surface level, the ease with which this joining takes place will depend in large part on how similar the present situation is to past experiences and how accurately the individual delineates what overlaps with the past and what is unique. If the overlap is small but the individual fails to recognize this, then a great deal is being transferred into this encounter from elsewhere. If the overlap is large, the transference is less evident.

Consider, for example, a person going to a country that he or she has never been to before. He or she takes along the map that previous explorers created and refined across numerous visits. Most of the terrain encountered appears on the map, and this is a comfort. Only when the traveler runs into things that do not fit is it suddenly clear how much he or she depends on what has been carried from the past to manage the uncertainties of the present. In addition, the discovery that the map is not perfect serves as an impetus for the traveler to pay more attention to what is in front of him or her at the moment. Had the map been a very poor one and this recognition come earlier, he or she might have noticed more about the terrain because of the necessary increase in vigilance.

A similar process is at work in group experiences. Whatever the case, be the overlap small or large, a transference is occurring that can be characterized as treating the present as though it were the past, so that members can move quickly through the uncertainty of the present toward a more certain future. This transferential process involves an individual's return to an earlier mode of operating in order to deal with the present, a dynamic called regression. Paradoxically, individuals eager to be very present in a new situation need to be able to engage in this regression in order to learn what of their experience is merely an importation from previous history and what is meaningfully rooted in the here and now. Those most invested in resisting the regression process are least able to separate out the past from the present and deal with the present on its own terms. The paradox of regression is that in order not to *be* in a regressed state, one has to be willing to regress.

This process of regression is both complex and important to understand. The complexity starts with the fact that much of what is transferred into the present is the unfinished business from the past. Perhaps the use of previously established approaches would be less problematic if these approaches had been fully explored, but that is rarely the case. More often, earlier experiences have parts of them that are incomplete, and each "present" situation provides the individual with an opportunity to obtain closure on that which had been unfinished in previous settings. A largely unconscious dynamic at play in the new setting is the tendency to use the present as a way of making over the past. In this regard, the regression associated with the unfamiliar is a transformation of the present into past in order to make the new easier to deal with and the past more manageable as well.

Certain theoreticians, Bion (1961) among them, have observed that individuals often become intellectually regressed when they are in a group. There could be numerous explanations for this observation. If the group situation evokes feelings of anxiety, for example, the loss of "IQ points" associated with any anxiety attack may be adequate explanation. Or, if group members split off their own sense of competence and deposit it, through projective identification, in the leader, then those individuals are likely to function at a lower intellectual level than they would alone.

Bion, however, went further, and argued that the regression in groups is massive and is associated with the earliest phases of mental life. He suggested that this regression has two main features: (1) the belief that the group exists as an entity over and beyond its individual members, which leads individuals to believe that it has the particular characteristics the individuals impute to it, and (2) the change that occurs within group members as they feel their individuality overwhelmed in the light of the attributions they make about the mammothness and power of the group (Sutherland, 1985). The utopian fantasies that

individuals often create about what groups or communes can do
for them in the face of the sense of fragmentation, isolation,
and impotence experienced when living and working alone testi-
fy to the power of these beliefs. Such fantasies, while often
understandable, make a group so powerful that the individual's
sense of potency is necessarily diminished. Whereas Freud believed that the intellectual ability of the *group* was impaired as
a result of this regression by its members, Bion saw it differently. He argued that the appearance of impairment hides the very
sophisticated creation and assimilation of interpretations that
are going on in a segregated and nonvisible part of the group's
information-processing system, and that this is work that must
take place at a collective level for the group as a whole to develop a functional understanding of itself and its world. Hence,
the apparent cumulative intellectual regression of the members
may be a necessary (though not a sufficient) condition for
group growth.

In other words, individuals who walk into the group as
whole and separate entities are in the process of becoming parts
of something larger than themselves. In order to prepare for
their "partness," which is necessary for a whole (the group) to
come together as an integrated entity constructed out of the
parts, the individuals have to allow themselves to experience
some fragmentation. Such fragmentation, of course, means a
loss of wholeness, which is invariably threatening and counter
to many of the developmental struggles that they have been
going through as individuals. To resist this process of inner partitioning, while perhaps making it easier for the members,
makes it very hard for the group as a whole to do what it must
in order to come together. The propensity for these tensions to
be set up in either/or terms (either the group gets to be whole
or the members remain whole) sets up a conflict that is additionally fragmenting. Members feel split from the group, which
heightens even further the artificial sense that they are separate
and independent entities.

When individual members do allow the necessary regression to take place, they are thrown back to those locations in
their own individual histories when fragmentation was so prob-

lematic, to their earliest experiences. The regression of the group members is regularly to those experiences in the family of origin when one's sense of self, as an individual unit, was developed. While such individual regression is taking place, the group as a whole, in order to function with these members constituting its parts, has to work out a collective way to contain the anxieties, splittings, and projections stirred in its members as they regress in the service of the group's development. When members are willing to regress, they give the group both the time and the chance to become an adequate container of their anxieties, making the group into a potentially safe place to be present as a part. This also gives the group the opportunity to build into its foundation a method for drawing together elements (the individuals) that are no longer demanding that their original versions of wholeness be maintained. If and when such a foundation can be created, the members are able to experience their partness (as elements of the whole group) and their wholeness (as a part of that group).

It is the playing through of dynamics such as the above that makes real the proposition that for a group to grow into a condition where it is not severely limited in its ability to function as a unit, the members must be willing to become regressed, and that through the individuals' regression, the group is given an opportunity to develop into a form where those individuals are no longer regressed when existing as parts of a whole.

In this discussion, we have been exploring the most primitive form of regression, namely, to infancy and to the early experiences in the family of origin. There is no reason why the regression need always be so severe, especially if individuals have learned in the past how to become effective parts of groups. One of the fundamental tenets of group psychotherapy is that individuals who have so much difficulty containing their anxiety in collective settings and in interaction with others get a chance to have their anxiety contained by the group so that they can do the necessary individual regression to enable early group experiences, such as family-of-origin experiences, to be reworked. It is clear that groups that learn how to deal with the regressive tendencies of their members can create the conditions where those individuals will not require such extensive regression in the future. Hence, paradoxically, the group and the individuals who are able to embrace their regressive sides can learn about how to interact such that they do not end up remaining regressed.

Conclusion

The dynamics involved with the themes of disclosure, trust, intimacy, and regression deal with a side of group life that is hidden. These four interconnected paradoxes are activated as individual members vacillate over how much and in what forms to engage with others and with the group as a whole. Simultaneously, the group is sorting out for itself how to manage the various ways members engage with it or remain detached from it. To engage others in a group, members must explore what they hide from others and maybe even themselves, as well as what is kept hidden from them. This means that the process of engagement is operating on multiple strata that lie beneath the surface behaviors of groups and their members in their mutual attempts to connect.

These paradoxes suggest that when certain aspects of shared life are actively engaged in, other domains of engagement are displaced into a hidden arena, where the process of engagement continues in a manner not readily accessible to those involved. The polarities of acceptance and rejection, trust and mistrust, and progression and regression are not as separate and unconnected as they are often experienced. By allowing these polarities to coexist, members and groups paradoxically can progress while regressing, create acceptance out of rejection, and develop trustworthiness in the midst of mistrust.

7

Paradoxes of Speaking: Authority, Dependency, Creativity, and Courage

The paradoxes we discuss in this chapter all involve the dynamics of influence. The major theme that runs through this cluster is action: What do members and the group as a whole do that makes some kind of difference? Were it not for the inevitable association with the theater and the dramaturgical distractions this would produce, we would have labeled this constellation of group processes the *Paradoxes of Acting*. We have chosen instead to refer to them as the *Paradoxes of Speaking*, with the term *speaking* intended to evoke associations such as speaking up or speaking out. The key issue is how members and the group as a whole find a voice to give expression to what is going on. By focusing on explicit behaviors, patterns that develop iconic meaning for group members, and what is left unsaid along with what is expressed, the many ways voices develop in a group can be examined. Acting while remaining silent and being visible while remaining hidden are both ways of speaking in a group, and each mode may be giving expression to important facets of group life.

Participation in groups presents us with many questions of influence. How much do we want to influence the direction of the group? How much are we willing to be influenced? If our influence changes the group, how much change do we want, how much can we tolerate, and how much do we want to feel responsible for? Ultimately, one of the ways influence is attempted and realized in groups is through members speaking or not speaking to each other. Speaking or not speaking, being or not being, and acting or not acting are all forms of influence in a group and may become sources of conflicting and often contradictory reactions for individuals and the group as a whole, depending on how the associated messages are framed.

The following pages explore some of the paradoxical dilemmas that arise as group members struggle with influencing and being influenced. As in the previous two chapters, the temptation to frame influence processes in either/or terms often leads us to construct a view of group life as inherently competitive, with mutually exclusive positions vying for control. When the direction of the group is at stake, the relationship between opposing forces gets lost in the process of choosing between them. Sometimes it is the group that seems to stand in opposition to one or more of its members. At other times, two internal subgroups—for example, the powerful and the powerless—seem to stand in opposition to each other. In either case, the meaning contained in the relationship between the opposites is obscured, and the "whole," the group, is crippled by its inability to attend to the connections as well as the distinctions. The four paradoxes of speaking explore the connection between the apparent contradictions evoked by the influence process in groups.

The section on the paradox of authority starts with the link between authorizing others and authorizing oneself and explores the paradoxical nature of resistance to authority, one's own and that of other group members. It is through a mutual authorization process that groups have the potential to be greater than the sum of their parts, and the management of resistance is a key to this process. This section describes the way in which resistance is also acceptance and acceptance involves resistance. The link between these two "opposite" phenomena is the heart of the paradox of authority.

In our discussion of the paradox of dependency, we explore the proposition that to be independent in a group, one must fully accept one's dependence. How are independence and dependence linked? What role does independence play in a group that, by definition, is founded upon mutual dependency? When an individual "speaks out," does that contradict or threaten the stable dependencies that enable the group to function? The essence of the paradox of dependency is that, upon examining dependency, one repeatedly finds independence, and upon examining independence, one repeatedly finds essential dependencies.

The paradox of creativity is born of the link between creation and destruction. Many of the struggles in groups around creation are "shadowed" by fears and concerns about destruction. In order to create new patterns, patterns must exist and must be changed or destroyed. The relationship between these opposites is a difficult and painful one for group members and gives rise to some very disturbing conflicts. It is precisely because the link is so difficult to accept, understand, and live with that groups find it easier to "split" the paradox and live with the battle between apparently opposing processes.

Finally, the paradox of courage is that courageous action, the willingness to speak one's mind and to act in accordance with it, is courageous only when it is undertaken in the presence of doubt and uncertainty. Without doubt, there is no courage. Without ambiguity, imperfection, and anxiety, the acts of speaking, influencing, and giving direction cannot be courageous, because one is free of the uncertainty that gives courage its meaning. It is a fitting end to this chapter, since paradox can, at one level, only create uncertainty and ambiguity no matter how hard we search its contradictions for a simple and straightforward answer. Living with paradox demands courage.

The Paradox of Authority

One of the most critical developmental processes in a group is the creation of an authority system. Usually authority is thought of as something that flows down from above: a boss derives authority from those higher up, and subordinates accept this as a direct consequence of the employment contract; professors derive authority from the university, and students accept this as part of obtaining a degree; the judge in a courtroom derives authority from the relevant branch of government, and those who participate in the judicial process accept this because of the societally sanctioned powers of the court.

The authority invested in a person can be understood to be a derivative of an authorizing process. If we focus on the *dynamics of authorizing* rather than on the authority itself, it is clear that authority is something that is built or created. It flows from many places to many people. For example, in a group, members can authorize an individual to enact certain things on their behalf. The members' willingness to accept the activities undertaken by the authorized individual as an expression of the parts of themselves that they have given over actively creates authority in the group. The acceptance makes it possible for those with authority to be effective in representing group members' collective interests.

The process of authorizing creates the conditions in which individual contributions can have an influence on the work of the group and the group can be influential in the larger system to which it belongs. In this regard, authority is closely linked to empowerment. One develops power as one empowers others. Taking the power that is available and using it often creates a vacuum, because it is experienced as depriving others of a scarce commodity. As a result, power taking is resisted. Individuals often refuse to accept or exercise the power that is available to them in a group simply to avoid the accusation of having stolen it from someone else or having gained it at others' expense. Yet the very avoidance of taking and using the available power makes individuals in a group, and ultimately the group as a whole, feel powerless. The feelings of powerlessness create an even greater wish for power, making it even harder for anyone to seize it, because the feeling of deprivation is correspondingly larger, and the resistance grows. On the other hand, if one takes the available power and uses it to empower others, the total amount of group and individual power increases. Taking power when it is dangerous to do so and then acting to empower others defuses the terror and breaks the cycle. Of course, the empowering of others is a very tricky endeavor, since ultimately no one can empower someone else. So the work of those who have or create power is to create the conditions in which others can move toward their own empowerment.

Authority can be defined as sanctioned power. The sanctioning can come from numerous places, but it must always come from those most influenced by it. The special bind, however, is that in sanctioning another's authority, one might be deauthorizing oneself. If one deauthorizes oneself while authorizing another, then one may be placing oneself in the position of having so little personal authority that, should the authorized person act inappropriately or consistently work against the group's interests, one may feel unable to take the authority back. This fear may make group members reluctant to authorize, creating the conditions where authorizing would again seem dangerous. The converse also presents a dilemma. As group members learn to authorize themselves so that they can be effective authorizers, are they in fact deauthorizing others? This fear, too, makes group members reluctant to authorize both themselves and others.

One of the essential developmental tasks of a group is to learn how to do both facets of this authorizing simultaneously. One without the other is not sufficient. A paradoxical perspective on authority in groups looks at the relationship between authorizing oneself and authorizing others without assuming that, if one person has authority in a group, others cannot have it also. The implications of this perspective for anyone occupying an authority position in a group are numerous. The most potent is how one understands resistance. When a group member resists another's authority, it is as much an affirmation of that authority as it is a denial. In resisting, a member is making a metacommunicative statement of the form "your authority is so strong that I have to engage everything I have to keep it from overwhelming me." If a person with authority can see resistance in affirmative terms and not exclusively or primarily as a denial or a threat, he or she can use it to empower both self and other. If, however, the resistance is resisted, then the relationship will focus on the battle, with each person trying to escape the paralysis that comes from being preoccupied with the prospect of losing.

Accepting resistance means that the authority figure must learn to manage the splitting process that is represented in the resistance. If splitting is treated as pathological or infantile, it is unlikely that any of the participants will be able to work with each other. If it is seen as part of the process of authorizing, then the first wave of splitting and projection onto the authority figure can be treated as growthful. Consider the contrast between the initial responses of two different group members to someone with authority: "Yes, I'll do whatever you want" and "Wait a minute, I'm not at all sure that is a good idea." In the first case, the authority figure may feel quite happy because the individual has acquiesced. What has also been communicated, though perhaps not recognized, is that the subordinate is bringing only part of him- or herself to this encounter. The part that is reacting, thinking, challenging, wondering aloud is being left out. In a way, this individual is bringing first and foremost the dependent, compliant aspects of him- or herself in groups into the encounter. If the authority reinforces this too vigorously, he or she may set up a pattern that retards the individual's ultimate value to the group. The second individual is more clearly engaged in splitting, because the "negative," suspicious affect in the encounter is being expressed toward the authority. The first individual is just as vigorously engaged in splitting, but the "positive" affect is not understood in these terms. Although splitting is occurring in both cases, in the "positive" case, the authority is unlikely to recognize it as splitting, since the affect toward the *authority* is benign. The danger is that the negative affect, too, is being split off and projected somewhere. The question is how and when it will surface. Here we can see once again that the "negative" is potentially more useful than the "positive," so much so that at times it feels like we have come to label these responses in ways that are opposite to their meaning.

How does someone with authority deal with the resistance and resentment that often come with being subordinate, and how can this resistance be managed and used in a way that authorizes and empowers both the subordinate and the person in authority? The following case fragment illustrates the connection between authority and the process of authorization.

> The warden was on the cellblock talking to the inmates, many of whom were deeply distressed over the death of a fellow inmate. It was mid 1985, and this inmate was the prison's first-ever AIDS victim. No one knew much about the disease. It was not that the victim was particularly loved, but over the last few hours, several of the inmates had come forward asking to be tested for AIDS because they had been in sexual contact with the victim. As more and more individuals came forward, the collective anxiety on the cellblock was increasing exponentially as it became evident that the network of sexual contact in this closed environment meant that virtually everyone was at risk, especially if one included inmate fights and spitting as potential ways for the disease to be transmitted.
>
> Suddenly, one young inmate who was very bitter and upset approached the warden with what seemed like a trivial complaint about the inadequate medical treatment he had been receiving during recent weeks. His approach was filled with anger, and it would have been understandable had the warden viewed it as a nuisance complaint and summarily ignored him, especially in light of the serious medical problem the warden now had on his hands. But the warden reacted differently. He let the inmate express his anger, incoherent though it seemed, with the assumption that there was a valid basis to this young man's concern and that it might take a little ventilation of unfocused feelings before it became clear what the issue was. The inmate was struggling to control the full force of his anger, but it was obvious that he held the warden person-

ally responsible for the actions of the medical staff that were the basis of his complaint. After taking a lot of abuse, the warden asked the inmate what he could do for him. Suddenly the young man ripped his hat off, revealing an exposed wound on his scalp, and, pointing to the air above him, exclaimed with deep despair in his voice, "Warden, AIDS germs could be flying into my head right now and killing me."

The warden was struck by two things: (1) how hard it must have been for this young inmate to be that vulnerable with him, given that symbolically the warden's authority to restrict inmates' freedoms was despised, and (2) the paucity of information these incarcerated individuals had about existential issues that related to life and death, hope and despair. He was able to assure the inmate that his fears about "flying AIDS germs" were unfounded. More important, the warden had become instantaneously educated, through this one individual's outburst, about the massive need for an immediate educational program to keep the inmates informed about social and medical issues such as AIDS.

If we examine the process of authorizing that was going on here, it is possible to see the warden using his authority to authorize this young inmate, through validating the feelings that were a massive displacement of concerns that the inmate was keeping hidden. This validation, in turn, provided information for the warden that authorized him to do the type of caretaking that the inmates wanted and needed but had been unable to express because of their rage at authority. Paradoxically, this inmate enabled the warden to be a more effective warden by taking the authority offered when the warden asked what help the inmate felt he needed. All this was occurring in the context of the expression of feelings that, on the surface, also threatened the warden's authority.

There are times, however, when authorities must be willing to say "no," to set limits and to abide by them. There is always a judgment to be made about the projected emotions of a subordinate in an authority relationship. How does one accept these emotions as information to be dealt with and understood without accepting the responsibility for them that resides with the subordinate? For example, this same warden's next encounter with an inmate was over another young man's complaint that his appearance before the parole and probation board had been postponed. When the warden asked why, the inmate revealed that his recent drug test had shown illicit substances in his system. He thought that it was unfair that he was being incarcerated any longer "just because of a little weed," and he wanted the warden to take action to "be sure I'm treated justly." The warden smiled and said, "The easiest way to deal with this is to keep away from drugs. Then there will be no issue at the parole board hearings." In this case, refusing to accept the projection, saying "no," was the much more empowering and authorizing act.

The Paradox of Dependency

In the human life cycle, growth involves the development of a good measure of independence. However, in most ways, our strivings for independence are closely linked to the development of new dependencies. We vigorously attempt to break away from our families of origin, so that we can create families of our own. In the severing and transformation of one set of dependencies, we become free to create new dependencies, upon spouses, upon our own children, upon networks created or chosen by us. Paradoxically, the work of becoming independent actually involves giving expression to many of our dependencies.

In groups, we observe behavior that, on the surface, can be described as dependent, counterdependent, or independent. Although these concepts are usually defined as nonoverlapping, there are strong experiential and epistemological connections among them. If, for example, we are dealing with dependency, the other two forms (counterdependence and independence) may well be active at the same time. While a group member's refusal to accept guidance from a leader may express some degree of independence, it may at the same time be a counterdependent denial of the leader's authority, a denial that unwittingly gives that authority more power than would be the case if some degree of dependency were acknowledged. In many ways, the counterdependent individual is as much imprisoned by the dynamics of dependency as someone who accepts the leader's guidance without question.

It is clear that a group can function only if members are able to depend on each other. It is ultimately the mutual dependency that makes the group a group. To deny this dependency or to try to make it into something other than what it is retards the group's capacity to come together as a whole. The metaphor for the paradox of dependency is ecological. For any part of a system to be able to act independently, it must accept its dependency on the other parts with which it together makes up a whole.

If we examine group behavior, it is very noticeable that the times when a member seems most troubled by feelings of dependency are when those who are being depended on are asked to be something that they are not or when they are perceived as untrustworthy. In both cases, the desire of the individual member to be independent is very strong. If one is independent, it is much less important to trust others, or so it seems. The dilemma is that the condition of extreme independence creates its own vulnerability. What happens when the "independent" person needs something that can be obtained only from a collective setting? Then the independence sought after and created to compensate for the "untrustworthiness" of the world of others makes the individual's need for trust even greater than it would have been had independence not been so strongly pursued in the first place.

This is especially evident when a group views being cohesive, or speaking with a single voice, as all-important. Unions and tenant groups, for example, are forever caught in this bind. As classic powerless groups, they adopt the posture that they must remain united, no matter what differences may be felt internally. In the public arena, they act as if they are of one mind and ask those who do not agree with the dominant position to suppress their dissent in the service of unity. What happens to the individual who does not want to go along, who would prefer to be independent of the group position? If he or she accepts a dependent position when this feels wrong, he or she may experience the group as undependable in times of conflict and distress. It is precisely at these times, when individuals struggle with their own independence, that the group's dependability will be most in question, making the desire for independence even stronger and the attendant binds accordingly more acute.

An example of the dependence-independence paradox can be seen in the behavior of the Supreme Court of the United States in its controversial ruling on abortion. During the court's initial hearing, the majority of the justices were opposed to legalizing abortion. The reasons behind this decision were complicated, but it was necessary to construct both a majority and a minority position in order to untangle the legal issues, as well as the political one, latent in this case. Harry Blackmun, a recent appointee to the court and a long-time friend and colleague of Chief Justice Burger, was assigned the task of writing a position for the majority, the group opposed to legalizing abortion.

Under these circumstances, the court as a whole depends on the justices to behave consistently. What would happen if, partway through the case, the person writing for the majority switched sides and two minority positions were drafted? Would this then make the original minority position the majority? And what would happen to the conventions about the assignment of the opinions? (Tradition has it that the senior justice on each side allocates the relevant writing tasks.) These questions were raised when, while preparing the argument, Blackmun changed his mind. Had Blackmun voted initially with the minority, it is most unlikely that William Douglas, the senior member on that side, would have chosen him to write the opinion. Yet new circumstances had arisen, throwing the procedures on which they all depended into a state of flux. The sudden burst of independence by Blackmun, against the background of his previous dependability, had made the court's inner dynamics undependable. New procedures had to be created in the context of the particulars of this case. At one level, this was most undesirable, since there were court conventions to ensure coherent practices across cases. The court would seem like a very strange beast if on some occasions its decision rules were majority vote, while other times consensus was deemed critical, while at yet other times the individual preference of the chief justice was accepted as all-determining. When Blackmun behaved independently, after having expressed his link to a particular subgroup that had formed around a specific legal position, the court's capacity "to rely on him" in this case was brought into question. That is, the independence at one level called into question the patterns of dependency at another.

In this particular case, it is important to realize that Blackmun was not simply being irrational and inconsistent, nor had he suddenly become an undependable person. His independence in this group was a reflection of his dependency on other groups. As he involved himself deeply in the legal issues, he found himself engaged by both medical and feminist issues that had not seemed salient when examined exclusively through the lens of the law. On the medical side, he brought into focus his ten years of personal experience as general counsel with the Mayo Clinic. On the feminist issues, he listened to his own family, his wife and three young adult daughters. When he allowed himself to depend on these two important personal referent groups for additional information and perspective and to let them sit as copartners with his identity as a lawyer, the case became much more complicated. In a way, it was his attempt to develop meaningful interdependencies among the divergent groups he identified with that brought him to a position that ultimately translated into what appeared to be an independent stance in the Supreme Court.

The special nature of the paradox of dependency is that to experience independence in collective life, one has to be constantly giving expression to one's dependent side. For only as reliable dependencies are established does *inter*dependence emerge. It is the creation of collective interdependence that provides the notion of independence with meaning. To be independent but not connected is nothing more than isolation. To be dependent with no sense of autonomy is symbiotic enslavement. These are processes that need each other to be fully what they are. At a group level, there is no way for a group to develop a fabric of reliable interdependencies unless its individual members give expression to their dependency, even when this may mean depending on (trusting) that which has yet to be proved to be dependable. Only as individuals depend upon others in the group does the group as a whole become a dependable entity. A network of interdependencies is created that frees individuals from the kind of "independence" that is based upon a fear that the group is an unreliable place in which to be dependent.

The Paradox of Creativity

The paradox of creativity is that the making of something new brings with it the destruction of something old. All change is predicated on destruction. At the very least, the status quo is destroyed. This paradox is founded on the idea that no matter how invested one is in the creative act, there is also some destruction occurring at the same time—just as there can be no light without the dark.

Destruction is usually considered bad and creativity good. Rarely do we take pride in destroying something. Nor does a creative artist receive accolades for his or her destructive sophistication. In peacetime, we laud the creative and loathe the destructive. In war, we do the opposite. There are no medals for military heroes who were very creative during battle, unless it was for developing a new and more effective way to destroy—and that would be metacreativity; that is, being creative about destruction, an activity of a different kind. It is hard to conjure up the parallel image of being destructive about creativity. We do not praise artists for their capacity to destroy the creative process.

We can see intense splitting occurring in the ways we think about creativity and destructiveness. For example, when a community struggles to decide whether an old building should be torn down "to make way for progress," those invested in change are accused of being callous toward historical preservation, while the other side is given a derogatory label that implies that their wish to preserve is misguided. It is rare that the tension between creation and destruction is "held" and contained. It is so unacceptable to actively engage our destructive sides that we feel obliged to use euphemisms to make our destructiveness appear to be something else. Glidewell (1970) describes a refreshing exchange with a woman student when he tried to blunt the pain of professorial "constructive criticism" by suggesting that it was meant as an attack not on her but rather on her idea. She responded that "the most important thing about me right now is my idea." Glidewell found this to be a sobering realization, and he was paralyzed. The student continued, putting an entirely different frame on the exchange: "I should be most disappointed if you did not make your criticism of my idea, but you mustn't think it won't hurt. It will, and I shall need your help and your patience if I am clearly to understand what you have to say" (Glidewell, 1970, p. 24). What she was saying was that in order for her to grow, she needed to be around a teacher who was willing to destroy. That way, she could learn how to be creative. However, this would not be possible if the destruction was being denied. The destructive side of our creativity is hard to own, as is the creative side of our destructiveness.

From the very beginning of a group's life, there are activities focused on establishing patterns that have some order to them, that are consistent across time, and that provide a basis for the interactions among members. The creation of these patterns does two things. It precludes the establishment of other patterns that might have been formed if these had not been put in place, and it sets the developmental paths for the future. To make changes, it will be necessary to modify these patterns or to destroy them so that new constructions can be built. While these two implications may make the creation of initial patterns seem undesirable, to attempt to avoid this would, in effect, be avoiding the creation of the group. To become formed means, in essence, to give up certain options. It also creates options that would not have been available had a form not been established.

Of particular importance is the issue of group growth. Were it not for the development of patterns (traditions, rules, conventions) that give coherence and wholeness, there would be no form to set the stage for the transformation that is the heart of growth. The very shaping that restricts is the shaping that makes change possible. Before change can occur, the patterns to be changed must be established. We discussed elements of this in our exploration of the paradox of boundaries. A group also needs new ideas, new possibilities to go along with its stabilizing forces. If it is unable to incorporate the new, the group will quickly die. While it builds in mechanisms to provide stability, the group must also create the possibility for incorporating novelty. That is, it must have a way of destabilizing itself, even in the midst of its investment in remaining stable.

To put this into concrete terms, consider the example of the Wellsborne Community Agency, a nonprofit charitable group deeply committed to providing services that traditional agencies overlook. After months of effective functioning, buoyed greatly by the start-up energy that came with its counterculture mentality, the group was having difficulty keeping its records straight and was unable to plan effectively in the absence of any method for accurately estimating the resources available for the rest of the year. They concluded that they needed help and decided to employ a business manager. The most skilled person was a woman with a business background. Not surprisingly, when she came to work with them, the group proceeded to reject her, both personally and professionally. When she pointed out that she was just attempting to do the job for which she had been hired, the group acted as though it did not need the assistance it had seemed so desperate for during the recruiting process. Soon the business manager was being asked to help in the relief work of the agency, an understandable request given how overworked everyone was. She refused and continued to leave the office at five o'clock instead of the implicit norm of eight or nine. When she made it clear that she would do only the tasks for which she was employed because these were the aspects of the agency that had to be brought into line for it to survive, she was almost fired. It was as though the group members could not stand coming to grips with the new patterns they knew they were going to have to incorporate in order to remain viable. They seemed to fear that the changes would ultimately undermine the delivery of the human services that were most important to them. They had all come from government agencies where they felt that the bureaucratic record keeping overwhelmed their capacity to work. The debates raged for days. Individuals had formed this work group to avoid the problems that came from what seemed like destructive systems in their former workplaces. They tried to create something that did not have the destructive elements of the past, but in so doing, they had neglected to create some of what was necessary for their survival. When they recognized this, they took action to self-correct (hiring the business manager), only to proceed to undo their self-corrective actions (almost firing her). In so doing, they again began to risk their ongoing viability.

A critical element in the paradox of creativity is turbulence that comes from a group's struggle to be innovative, creative, and responsive to the demands for change. As the group as a whole establishes its own sense of collective orderliness, its search for novelty often takes the form of bringing in a new individual. That individual then becomes not only the source of the group's creativity but the repository for the emotions that the group's orderliness is designed to overcome. More generally, groups often locate the chaos associated with novelty in one or two individuals. The tensions in the creative process often stem from the split that exists between the group as a whole and one or more of its members. Groups deal with their destructive sides in a similar way. Since destruction is as destabilizing as creativity, the group is prone to locate this in individual members as well. If there are negative consequences to the collective destructiveness, the group can deposit it at the feet of an individual who can then be scapegoated. As with all paradoxes in group life, the link between creativity and destructiveness is difficult to acknowledge and difficult to live with as it occurs in groups. Often, the tension created by the coexistence of these apparently contradictory processes is managed by separating them, locating one in the group and the other in a group member. The conflict that results from this artificial split can immobilize the group and harm its individual members. This is the danger of splitting the paradox.

The Paradox of Courage

It takes a great deal of courage to live in the midst of the many paradoxes that fill collective life. It demands courage to fully *belong* to a group, to struggle with forming an identity through involvement with others, especially when this means giving up one's individuality in order to gain it. There is a precariousness to self-discovery that is like living on the edge, swinging between the tensions of what is and what might be. The boundaries, the thin lines between security and stagnation, between hope and despair, between creativity and chaos, are often such that a miscalculation can mean the difference between success and failure.

Becoming *engaged* with a group also demands courage. To trust enough to self-disclose, when the available signs suggest the instability of the social contexts in which we find ourselves, requires courage. For it often means that we have to regress to levels we long since have outgrown, to grow out of the restrictions those earlier patterns have placed upon us. To become intimate with others means dropping barriers that protect and letting light fall on what we privately cradle in the dark. And this, too, takes courage.

It requires courage to find one's *own voice* in a group, to speak with personal authority in the presence of institutional authority. To accept one's dependency when the inner desire is to reject those upon whom one must depend requires courage, as does accepting the dependencies of those we wish would grow independent—to say nothing of the burdens of being creative, especially the risks inherent in destroying that which is, in the service of bringing to life that which might be.

Courage itself is paradoxical in that only when one is floundering with all the uncertainties of not knowing what to

do, feeling totally without courage, can one's actions be courageous. It is much like faith. One cannot believe unless one
doubts. For faith was never built on the "castle of certitude"
(as Tillich, 1952, expressed it) but on the foundation of simply
not knowing. It is often when in despair that we feel the need
for courage. While it is easy to view courage as the opposite of
despair, it is not. Courage is the capacity to move ahead *in spite
of* despair, as Kierkegaard, Camus, Sartre, and other existentialists have suggested.

Many of our contemporary views of courage come from
mythology, where the heroic act springs from the capacity to
affirm death and, in so doing, affirm life. The special paradoxical nature of courage becomes visible when we examine how the
existential philosophers link it to self-affirmation. In most ways,
courage, especially the kind evident in the heroic act, appears as
"a giving up of self." By making Other or God above self, the
hero achieves divinity. But on closer examination, the opposite
is true. Rather than giving up oneself, total self-affirmation
turns out to be an act of participation in the universal and, as
such, is an affirmation of the divine over the human—or, perhaps more appropriately, the divine through the human. The
critical element is the word *total*. The dilemma with human self-
affirmation is invariably the partialness of it. It is the fact that
much of our humanness is so terrifying that we need to deny it.
And it is that denial that leads first to splitting, then to projection and disowning. This leaves us needing to master ourselves,
the very beings that we have so severely truncated. Our striving
for self-mastery is undertaken as though it were a part of the
universal mastery, which is how we so often think about the divine. "God has control of everything. If only I had the powers
of God, or could be assured that he was on my side, then I too
would have total control and be able to master myself and have
mastery of my life." The existentialists contend that it is our refusal to *be* fully human that leads us to diminish our divinity,
because it seduces us into believing that our partial selves are
our whole selves and that, through making these selves larger
than life, our shadowy sides can be overshadowed. Paradoxically, then, he or she who seeks to be heroic is making a mockery

of heroism, for under these circumstances, the acts undertaken for other are for self and as such disconfirm both other and self. On the other hand, those acts undertaken out of a sense of personal confusion but grounded in the fullness of one's total humanity may end up being heroic in that they tap the universal that is present in the particular. The paradox of courage, in the existentialist's language, is that to *be* courageous, one must act in the fullness of doubt and uncertainty, affirming that which seems unaffirmable. But it is the unaffirmable that spawns doubt. Therefore, to affirm makes doubt larger.

In his treatise on courage, Tillich (1952) suggests that "self-preservation and self-affirmation logically imply the overcoming of something which, at least potentially, threatens or denies itself" (pp. 25–26). The actual psychological experiences of either protecting or asserting oneself leave a great deal of uncertainty about whether this is the best thing to do, what the consequences will be, what unknowns will be discovered as a result, what activities will be necessary if things go wrong or someone unexpectedly gets hurt, and so on. No matter what one does, there is ambiguity. Suggests Tillich (1952), drawing on the writings of Nietzsche ([1911] 1961), "courage is the power of life to affirm itself *in spite* of this ambiguity, while the negation of life, because of its negativity, is an expression of cowardice" (p. 27).

This tension between affirmation and negation is important to understand. There are so many forces in groups that seem to resist or undermine our efforts to *be* the best we can. This can be demoralizing, especially when we find ourselves with problems that seem like they must be solved. We experience that which blocks or thwarts us as being a negation, at least of our efforts, if not of ourselves. To carry on, or to do "better" next time, we often conclude that we must work to diminish that which undermines, blocks, or destroys. The logic, when developed to the extreme, goes as follows: If we do not conquer those negative forces, then we might be conquered by them. This position involves us in attempts to negate negation. No matter how justified this may be, the process being engaged *is* the same kind as that which it is designed to overcome.

Hence, even if it were successful in eliminating the external negation, it would be unsuccessful, because it would have become like the very process it sought to destroy. When confronted by negation, the question is whether we can affirm that negation as being a part, or some embodiment, of the actual affirmation. To do the alternative of negating negation would only create negativism. In this frame, courage is the act of affirming that which negates even though that very affirmation threatens.

The paradox of courage in groups can be seen when members go toward those very things that are most troublesome. Justice Harry Blackmun, in changing his mind in the Supreme Court decision on abortion, displayed courage. Whether one agrees with that overall decision or with the particular position he took is irrelevant. He was attempting to integrate a much larger array of his group memberships and to let the many voices within him, introjected through his identification with more than just the legal system, speak in a single and combined voice. He had the courage to act in concert with his attempts to integrate, even though he had little idea what the consequences would be or the way the other justices would relate to him after he had changed his mind. Blackmun's courage is further illustrated by the fact that there is no way for him to *know* whether the position he took in this specific case is "right." So, having courageously expressed himself with the voice he found fit him, he has also to continue to live with the self-doubt he experienced prior to his judicial decision.

As we contemplate the paradox of courage, we are drawn back to the other paradoxes that have been discussed. In each case, there is an underlying theme: the actions taken to avoid or overcome create the experience of needing to overcome. What is the substance or content of the avoidance, on the one hand, and the overcoming, on the other? As it relates to groups and individual members, it is associated with the dynamics of emptiness and nothingness. The group attempting to form is struggling to give shape to the formless, to create that which did not exist prior to the group's coming to life. The group attempting to develop or to change itself so that it can function better is trying to create something that currently is not. And the individuals who make up the group are searching to create or transform something larger than themselves that would not exist unless that collective entity were formed or changed. They are also struggling to avoid being less than they are as individuals in their efforts to be more than they are as parts of the group. At some level, all social structures are organizations of emptiness. If the structure did not exist, in its place there would be nothing. Paradoxically, the structure that was developed in the service of containing emptiness (in the sense of controlling or transforming it) also contains the emptiness that it constantly struggles to evict.

It takes enormous courage to understand this and not to pretend that meaninglessness and emptiness can be structured away or overcome but realize that they can only be drawn out of one's visual field, to return into sight in their own time and their own way. Those who find such courage do not need the courage to live with this reality. It is those without the courage who need it but who search for it by wanting to get more control over the structures that they believe will rescue them from the angst of both structuredness and unstructuredness.

Conclusion

Circles. One cannot escape the feeling that an exploration of paradox is like walking in circles. It is hard to know where you have come from and where you are going. But the more one lives with a paradoxical perspective, the more one develops a tolerance for circles and for the places where two apparently contradictory paths join. In groups, the search is for the single source of tension that prompts the split between individuals or subgroups and the group as a whole. Most often, the split becomes the focus of emotion and activity while the source of the split, the confusing and self-referential connection between the opposing forces, remains unexamined, hidden from view by the power of contradiction to define reality. The paradoxical quest is the search for the link that one cannot see. When we are in groups, it is because we cannot always see this link that we learn to develop the courage to believe that it exists.

❦❦❦❦❦❦❦❦❦❦❦❦❦❦❦

8

Contextual Influences:
The Process of Importing
and Exporting
Frames of Reference

Up to this point, we have been discussing group paradoxes as though the only relevant dynamics are those that emerge from the inner life of a group, from the interactions among individual members and between the membership and the group as a whole. In many ways, we have been acting as though groups exist in a vacuum, free of any outside influences. This, of course, is not true. Groups are always located in a context, and that context has a profound effect on the groups that exist within it. We now want to pause and add the additional perspective and complexity to these internal group paradoxes that come from the relationship of a group to its context.

There are three critical ways the context is important. (1) As we have been discussing, many internal group processes are embroiled in paradox because of the frames that are used to understand them. Often these frames are indigenously developed within each group. However, many are also brought in from the outside, from an environment that "advises" any group about the frames that are appropriate for its use. (2) Individual members of a group are usually members of other groups as well. As they move from one group to another, they carry with them frames for understanding. This means that ways of dealing with group paradoxes can be imported into and exported from any group via the membership. This is particularly relevant since groups treat many of their members not as individuals but as members of the other groups to which they belong. (3) There are numerous direct ways a group is influenced by its context, simply because it must fit into a larger environment in order to survive. In many cases, the price is subordinating certain internal processes to the demands of the external.

In this chapter, we will explore the first two of these issues. In the next chapter, we will address the direct influences of the context, drawing special attention to the fact that, although there is minimal discussion of conflict in the literature on internal group processes, *in the literature on relations among groups, there is little discussion of anything other than conflict.*

To set the stage, we return to our earlier discussion about framing. A group's frames come from many places. They are latent in the multiple facets of internal group life, in the activities and interpretations of individual members, in the configurations of relationships among members, in the realities of the subgroups, and in the interactions among subgroups. Frames for interpretation of group experiences are also readily accessible in the environment, carried around in the experiences of individuals who can bring them along when they come to belong to any new group. To illustrate the radically different understandings about group experiences available through use of different interpretative frames, we turn to two examples.

The Strange Memo

Five young managers who carpooled to work sometimes stopped off at a local bar. One evening, after a couple of hours of drinking, they had a car accident on the way home. It was not serious, but the car required extensive repairs. The following morning, the five of them met to draft a memo to their vice-president telling how they *as a group* had been responsible for causing the accident.

They described how they had been telling jokes, giggling, and providing a constant barrage of unwarranted distractions for the driver. A few minutes before the accident, the car had swerved onto the shoulder of the road. Rather than encouraging the driver to slow down, the group had dared him on to cut the next curve even more closely. They acknowledged that one of them had drunk very little that evening and that, had they been more responsible, they would have asked him to drive. But the group had not been thinking in terms of responsibility. They talked about how over recent weeks the driver had become their informal leader and about the fact that they drank longer when he was the driver. They suspected that this was related to his assuming a leadership position, because the group was less responsible when he was driving. One thing was sure, the group had never before encouraged the driver to take a corner dangerously. In its memo, the group also acknowledged that these informal drinking sessions released work-based tensions from the day that would otherwise be taken home to their families. The final statement in the memo was a strong affirmation that the accident had been caused by the group as a whole.

When this account is read from the vantage point of Western culture, it sounds very strange. But this was in a plant in Japan, a culture that thinks about and understands experience primarily in collective terms. Imagine how a typical American executive would handle such a memo. It would be assumed that what happens to employees after hours is of no concern to the company unless it affects their ability to work or gives the company a bad name. The executive would probably destroy the memo or ask those who wrote it what they wanted done with it. He or she might assume that it was written for the inevitable insurance company investigation and accordingly send it to personnel for appropriate filing. Or perhaps it was a company-owned car and the group was trying to cover up for the driver, so that he would not be singled out when company cars were next being considered as part of compensation packages. The executive might put a copy in the personal file of the driver but would probably not put copies in the files of the others in the group. It is virtually certain that a file would not even exist for coding this accident as a piece of data about the functioning of this group as a whole. The chances are that a car-pool group would not even be seen as a part of the company.

It is also certain that this accident would not be considered as furnishing possible data about the company itself. There would not even exist an organizational thinking pattern of the form "what does it tell us about us, that our managers have to anesthetize themselves with alcohol so as to avoid taking work-based tensions home to their families?" If an employee constantly brought the leftover tensions from his or her family to the workplace, this might provoke questions about whether the manager could adequately contain the pressures of personal life and, if not, whether leaving the job or getting a divorce would be the best solution. But the other way around? Not likely! Most organizations expect workers to use their families or their personal support networks to recover from the work-based problems of the day. It is as though the workplace is viewed as having the right to draw upon the families of the nation to sustain it, and not to have to attend to the fact that work organizations may be undermining those families by exporting many of their tensions through their members at the end of the day.

Most important, however, the responsibility for what can be seen as individual behavior is clearly placed on the individual. If the group had a role in influencing the driver to behave irresponsibly, it was still the *driver* who acted irresponsibly, not the group. The driver might be asked why he was so weak that he would let the group affect him in this way. The law and the insurance company would place all the blame at his feet. Imagine the situation, when the time came for assessing premiums for the next year, in which each of the five argued that any increase due to the accident should be divided into five equal parts and applied to each of their premiums. Perhaps even more outrageous is the idea that the company might be expected to pick up a portion of the extra premium because it was partly responsible for the tensions that the group was getting rid of by drinking on the way home. Causal attributions in Western thought tend to be made to the actions of the parts of a group and not to the group as a whole or the relations among the parts.

The Shuttle Disaster

On January 28, 1986, the United States experienced the worst space "accident" in history. The booster rockets of the space shuttle *Challenger* exploded shortly after takeoff, killing all seven astronauts and, in the view of many, substantially setting back the space program. The mourning of this tragedy was made especially painful by the fact that one of the astronauts was a woman schoolteacher who had captured the hearts of the nation. A presidential commission was appointed to investigate the cause of the accident.

For the next few weeks, the press published many reports focused on the question of whether knowledge existed that might have enabled this accident to be avoided. The concern centered on what were referred to as the O-rings. It appeared that they had failed. Had people known that they could fail? Were the manufacturers responsible? Did NASA rush the launch? Were decision makers pressured by all the press attention and a nation waiting impatiently? Were the astronauts informed of the specific risks being taken? The questions were endless.

What was most striking about these investigations, especially in the early days as the press speculated on the findings, was the tendency to focus on what, *in particular,* had caused the problem. It had the flavor of trying to find an appropriate scapegoat, so that certain parts of the system could be free of blame. There was very little public thinking that sought explanation in the system as a whole. Unlike the example of the Japanese group of managers, attributions were made to the parts as opposed to the whole. It would have been difficult to think through who would have to be included as actors in the accident if a system-as-a-whole perspective were to be adopted: the White House, with its vigorous suggestion to send a teacher, a proposal that generated the publicity that engaged the press and the nation; decision makers on both sides of the argument who publicly debated the use of tax dollars for space exploration; the subcontractors milking the nation through NASA by charging $159,000 for fans that cost $5,000; the Defense Department's investment in the militarization of space; the press, who were and are relentless in keeping certain events in front of the public, especially if doing so translates into high ratings and more revenue; the history of Soviet and American competition over the domination of space—the list is enormous.

In each of these examples, our understanding of the critical events is as much a consequence of how they are framed as it is a result of the events themselves. Frames that pull one's interpretive attention toward the parts create very different "realities" from those focused on the system as a whole. In our technological, commercial, and political world, we rarely understand any occurrence as being a statement about the system as a whole. Instead, we focus attention on the parts. Frame the car accident in individual terms, and the issue is a driver who cannot hold his liquor and who cannot handle group pressure. Frame the shuttle disaster in terms of the demand for a scapegoat, and very different explanations emerge than when the whole pattern of relationships is used as a frame.

The question is, what produces one choice of frames over another? And how do the self-referential dynamics that may exist in the situation get created, camouflaged, or avoided via a particular framing? Is it possible, for example, that an internally based group paradox can be displaced onto an external location by choosing one frame over another? Could a group be "seduced" into using a particular frame by an environment that is "attempting to deal" with its own difficult dynamics by getting one of the groups that belongs within it to play a role on the environment's behalf? Members carry around inside themselves frames for understanding group experiences. These frames are often encoded into our and others' very beings, and in ways many of us do not recognize. For example, consider the groupness latent in our identities as individuals. While most of us think of ourselves first and foremost in terms of our own individuality, it is usually articulated to others in terms of our group representativeness.

Group Representativeness

What we mean by representativeness is that every member brings to each group his or her memberships in a variety of other groups. In one way, no one can act just as an individual and have these actions seen by others in purely individual terms. For example, a black female physician always carries her identity-group memberships (black and female) into group activities. If the group is racially and sexually mixed, *her blackness* will be very salient both in how others see and respond to her and in how she interacts. If the group consists of only black women, her blackness is not likely to be the dominant group identity to which she or others respond, but if she is the only physician in this group of black women, her professional identification may be treated as an important group membership.

Just as no person is merely an individual, neither can an exchange between two people in a group be thought of completely in interpersonal terms. For example, two white males in a work team arguing over the best way to proceed on a project may be thought of as expressing the different experiences that they bring from other groups to which they separately belong. Even events that we characterize in group terms can be seen in representative terms. A clash between a follower and a leader may well be a microcosm of larger authority conflicts existing in an organization or a society. In each of these cases, the individual can be seen to be acting as a representative of identity groups such as race, age, or gender or of organizational groups such as profession, function, or level of authority. Any group dynamic is a function, in part, of the reactions of group members to the representative aspects of each other.

To highlight the special dimension the group representativeness issue brings to our understanding, consider how individuals introduce themselves on first encounters. The most common practice is to list one's group memberships. While this may not be self-evident, each introduction depends a great deal on what can be communicated by identifying one's salient groups. "Hi, I'm Joseph Levinson!" One's name alone can reveal membership in an ethnic group, evoking different reactions from others than if the name had been Roderick Fitzpatrick, especially if it is being said to a group of Irish Catholics.

If Joseph continues, "I'm a nuclear physicist, working at the power plant at Three Mile Island, having just moved to Pennsylvania from Berkeley, where I was an associate professor," a whole host of other group memberships are introduced. Joseph has said things about (1) his professional identification, which may be responded to favorably or with hostility, depending on how one feels about the nuclear power industry, (2) his Californian roots, which may or may not play well in the East, (3) his identification with a prestigious academic institution, which may fuel others' identification, competitiveness, or indifference, depending on their own education, (4) his "new boy" status, which may trigger different responses than if he had been around at the time of the Three Mile Island accident, and so forth. Further, Joseph's introduction contains other unspoken group memberships (age, race, gender), and his thick European accent announces his foreignness.

Joseph also communicates a lot about himself by the group memberships he has elected not to identify. For example, in not wearing a wedding band, he leaves ambiguous his marital status, and by merely stating his group identifications, he leaves out how he is emotionally linked to those groups, an ambiguity that might disappear if he had included belonging to the KKK, or the Committee to Restrict Free Speech at Berkeley, or Scientists Against Militarizing Space, or the Political Lobby to Free Soviet Jewry.

It may well be that Joseph, along with everyone else meeting on this first occasion, feels concerned about acceptance and hence is reluctant to say more about himself until he knows things about the others. Yet everyone is playing it safe, looking for acceptance prior to risking self-disclosure, thereby creating the vicious cycles of the paradoxes already discussed. By staying with simple group identifications, Joseph could attribute any nonacceptance both to others' not knowing him and to their attitudes about the groups he belongs to. In announcing themselves in terms of group identities, Joseph and the others may paradoxically be seeking a way to manage the uncomfortable feelings created by their methods of introduction. The group members have provided each other with information that brings with it, from each person's experiences in society, an entire set of associations and reactions. Some may have strong positive reactions to certain groups mentioned in the introductions, while others may have negative ones. And, in a way, each person will have deflected any specific reactions, replaced them with stereotypical responses normally triggered by group memberships. In so doing, individuals end up sharing with each other the attitudes and prejudices that they carry toward various groups.

Another way to explain this is that an individual anxious about potential acceptance within the group imports how he or she normally gains acceptance in the society at large. Joseph may have received a lot of kudos for being part of the Berkeley community and therefore expect similar acceptance in this new setting. However, acceptance depends on how others view Joseph's group memberships. A professional think tank will respond differently to the Berkeley link than the nuclear-cleanup crew who may still be angry about being exposed to dangers that might have been avoided if the scientists had not been so sure that they could build safe power plants. In this regard, individuals may not intend to be representative of anything specific but can be made so simply by how others respond to them.

Interpersonal interactions between two individuals in a group can be understood as an enactment of the representativeness each brings from other groups, via their respective identifications. For example, a white male manager and a black female worker, no matter how personal they are with each other, have the environmental intergroup forces of management-labor, male-female, and black-white folded into their interactions. It is inevitable that they will carry into the group some variation on the classic tensions that society has located in black-white, male-female, and management-labor exchanges. Even if they, as individuals and as a pair, attempt to mute the forces tied to their group representativeness, it is likely that others will put these traditional tensions into them and that they will be expected to carry them or sort them out on the group's behalf. In addition, these individuals will import into the group societally developed methods for handling these tensions. Likewise, how these two individuals manage their interactions will lead to an exportation process. If they manage their relations poorly, then the internal group tensions that were present in their exchanges will be carried back out into the environment, making labor-management, white-black, female-male relations even more entrenched than they were before these two "representatives" met. On the other hand, the splits in the environment could be diminished a little if what was exported was less polarized than what was imported. In this regard, much of the internal life of a group can be thought of as containing within it many of the dynamics of the interactions among groups in its environment. And, in turn, many of the dynamics in the environment may be viewed as a playing out of internal group relations that have been exported into the context via the group representatives.

Illustrative Cases

To illustrate how external group tensions are imported into a group via the membership and then exported back out into the environment whence they came, we will discuss appropriate examples from four cases. This discussion will create the foundation for the examination of another dimension to our paradoxical theory of group life.

Situation 1. By the third week of this newly formed work group of eleven people, individuals began to feel that they were getting to know each other well. Their assigned project had started successfully, and everyone was feeling self-congratulatory. They decided to have a special lunch together to celebrate. During idle chatter, one person commented, "I'm very happy being in this group, but I must say I often feel intimidated. I feel vulnerable around you all!" This caught everyone's attention, and all other conversation ceased. After a brief pause, another member exclaimed, "What is there to feel vulnerable about? We're all very supportive." "That's true, but it doesn't stop me from feeling vulnerable." "But no one is going to hurt you. There just aren't grounds for having such feelings!" For several minutes this conversation proceeded, with all others in the group being intense but silent spectators.

From an observer's vantage point, this circular exchange expressed in interpersonal terms could be looked at from a group-as-a-whole perspective. The person expressing fear might be understood as "giving voice to" feelings of vulnerability that all members of the group shared, although certainly not in their conscious awareness. If a group-based paradoxical interpretation were adopted, it might be argued that the very expression of vulnerability triggered its counterside, such as the existence of frightening forces that needed to be denied to maintain a sense of safety, on the one hand, and the fact that some significant level of trust was being enacted in the mere voicing of these concerns, on the other. Then the expression of defensive reassurance, such as "What is there to be afraid of here? No one is going to hurt you," and "This is a really trusting group when people can talk about such things so openly," are the complementary expressions of the unspoken aspects of the statement about vulnerability.

In this example, as the interpersonal exchange continued, some of the group found themselves increasingly identified with the feelings being expressed about vulnerability while others were drawn to the position that the group was a solid and trustworthy place for members. In no time, what started interpersonally appeared to have taken on a different character as those not originally involved became invested in one side or the other of this interpersonal tussle. In this way, the interpersonal could be seen to have both created and become the arena for expressing the internal struggle between two subgroups.

Now in this particular case, the person expressing the vulnerability was a woman, and it was a man who countered with the comment "What is there to be afraid of?" While the other women in the group initially remained silent, they mostly identified with the voice expressing the vulnerability, while the men generally felt that the group was a secure place to be. As the interpersonal exchange between the woman and the man continued and others began to talk, it seemed that the tension between vulnerability and trust as companion feelings existing in every group member went through an evolution. Eventually, the following transformations appeared to have happened: the tensions emanating from the multiple sides of being vulnerable became experienced by everyone as a tension between vulnerability and trust in the group; it then moved to being tension between a "vulnerable subgroup" and a "secure subgroup"; finally, it became an issue between the women, who felt vulnerable, and the men, who felt secure, leading to the position that the women felt vulnerable *because they were women,* and the men felt secure *because they were men.*

In looking at this dynamic as it unfolded, the following was evident. The group's attempts to manage the tensions between vulnerability and trust triggered a set of roles that enabled the paradoxical tension within each person to be expressed through the medium of subgroup conflict. The gravitation to a male-female split drew on the familiar patterns for expressing this tension that are present in the society at large. In this way the group, in its attempt to deal with certain internal dynamics, could be understood to have imported from the environment a "solution" that freed it from having to struggle with the tensions that were a central element of its own group life, responding instead as though these tensions were a result of the different characteristics of the male and female members of the group.

For the group, this "external" way of dealing with the conflict brought some advantages and some disadvantages. The benefit was that the group did not have to keep struggling with its own unique way of dealing with these tensions. It borrowed, as it were, a script from the larger society that everyone knew how to enact, whether they liked it or not. It also enabled the group as a whole to experience itself as actually being without the conflict. "Sure, there was conflict, but that was not because of some problem in the group but because of the fact that there were men and women in the group. That's a societal problem, and, after all, the group was able to be a safe enough place for these normally suppressed feelings to be expressed." This set of "thoughts" or "rationalizations," of course, let the group move on to other things. The disadvantages were that the group might never come to develop alternative ways of dealing with these splits, thereby locking both men and women in the group into positions that limited the group's collective capacity to undertake its tasks, to say nothing about how the men and women might be diminished by the roles to which they were restricted.

In addition, having dealt with its internal struggle by borrowing an external approach, the group reinforced a particular view of male-female conflict and exported that perspective, via its members back into the environment, increasing its availability for future importation.

Situation 2. In a large engineering firm, a new work group, consisting of several white and a small minority of black men, was assembled to undertake a particular assignment. During the first few weeks, the black men remained relatively silent, doing their work and going along with the wishes of the white men. As the group got more deeply into its assigned task, there were numerous struggles as members sought to gain influence in the group, engendering anger and resentment that went unexpressed. At one point, one of the black members made an observation about how competitive everyone had become. He was immediately cut off and asked where he was coming from. He responded angrily with explicit aggressiveness that matched the implicit and angry aggression that had been directed at him. His action made public the angry feelings that had been alive in the group for some time but that had been suppressed and dealt with through intense interpersonal competitiveness among the white group members.

Had the group as a whole understood then what was going on, they might have been angry at this black group member for stepping out of the framework of denial that they had been using for some time. Instead, one white male made the attribution that the black man had become angry not because of what was occurring in the group but because he was black and had a chip on his shoulder about white people. In no time, the other black members joined in, arguing that this attribution was racist. The white members seemed unable to recognize this, and the blacks were put in the position of either "cooling" the event, backing down and remaining angry, thereby fueling the racist attributions of the white members, or taking on the task of attempting to reveal to the whites why their actions were seen as racist. The problem was that no matter which option the black members chose, the original difficulty that revolved

around the struggles for control and the attendant competitiveness would be obscured. Once this white-black dynamic had begun, all members of this group were in exactly the same positions that whites and blacks had historically occupied in the
country as a whole. In this sense, the dynamics being played
through in the group between blacks and whites looked like a
microcosm of the racial dynamics in the larger social system.

By diverting them into a racial exchange, the group as a
whole avoided confronting the angry feelings that came with
the intense commitment to the difficult project at hand, together with the attendant intermember competitiveness. This
anger, cloaked in rhetoric about the best way to do the job, had
been transparent to those, in this case the black members, who
had kept themselves out of the struggle. When they spoke from
a more observing than acting perspective, those deeply involved
denied what was happening and instead expressed their anger at
those bold enough to point out the presence of anger in the
group. The eventual intensity of the anger expressed between
the whites and blacks about racist attributions could be seen as
an importation of an external way of understanding and "dealing with" conflict that left the group as a whole deflected from
the anger that was endemic to its internal experience. The racial
explosion ended up giving expression to the anger of the entire
group, but about a different issue, and, once again, it was as if
the black members were being required to carry the anger on
behalf of the group. The black members were being made the
repository of the collective anger, exporting back out into the
environment and ongoing social history the very thing that had
been so historically debilitating for both blacks and whites.

Situation 3. A top management group for a medium-
sized public utility called in a consultant to advise on how to increase the competency of middle managers, who seemed reluctant to take initiatives or to exert control over the workers. The
group consisted of a number of vice-presidents of the functional
areas and a number of senior staff directors. Six of the nine
members were male, and all were white. The consultant's arrival
caused a bit of a stir. He was a tall, well-built black man in his

late thirties who, the group had been informed, was a recently hired associate of a local management consulting firm.

After the two-hour meeting, the top management group discussed the session. Most members felt that the consultant had been extremely formal, to the point of condescension, continually speaking to the group rather than to individuals and lacking warmth. A number of participants felt unfavorably evaluated by the consultant's comments and assumed that he was angry at the group, although they had no idea why this might be. Although all group members had been eager to hear what the consultant had to say to them, most had been unimpressed with his presentation and thought that his ideas had little relevance for their organization.

The consultant described his experience as follows. Upon his entering the room, two of the white males had introduced themselves to him and begun talking about the previous night's college basketball game. When the consultant mentioned that he was neither a basketball player nor a fan, the other two men seemed surprised and at a loss for a conversational topic. It was as though the way of developing rapport with an athletically built black man that they had in the society at large was not being successfully imported into this group setting as a way of diffusing their specific concerns about relating to this particular black consultant. During the first half of the meeting, the consultant felt as if each question put to him was a test—of his expertise, his willingness to work with a group of all white people, and his appreciation of the complexity of the managerial problems that they were struggling with. Try as he might to address their concerns, his impression was that the participants rarely listened to what he said.

As the meeting progressed, he became more and more frustrated and finally decided to take the type of risk he had been discussing in his description of alternative ways that the management group could operate. He suggested to the group that the tension he suspected that everyone in the room was feeling might be released if they could all talk about his being black. The reaction to this comment was unanimous. No one in the room thought that race was affecting the dynamics in the meeting. Nor was anyone interested in discussing this subject. To the consultant, it seemed that everyone was upset that he had brought up the issue. The remainder of the meeting was tense and unproductive.

For the top management group in particular, the disturbing effects of the meeting did not dissipate quickly. Participants slowly began to explore with each other the thoughts and reactions that existed below the surface. Mostly in two- or three-person conversations and briefly at their weekly staff meetings, they began to piece together a somewhat different explanation for the dynamics of the meeting. In fact, all of the members had *noticed* the consultant's blackness. Some thought it odd that the consulting firm would send a black man to work with an all-white group. Others secretly wondered whether the consultant's position in his firm had been a result of affirmative action policies. The two men who had spoken with the consultant about the basketball game were at first surprised that an athletic-looking black man was not interested in basketball and then embarrassed at their own stereotypes. Most of the group admitted that their impressions of the consultant as aggressive, hostile, condescending, and aloof were consistent with their stereotypes about black people in general. And some of the members could not remember much of what the consultant had said during the meeting, having made a judgment about his competence early in the encounter. Finally, two of the participants remembered that during the session they had kept thinking about slavery in America, which in turn raised the question for them of white society's guilt for past racial injustice. Neither man felt responsible for past treatment of black Americans and remembered feeling angry during the meeting over the guilt that they thought they were supposed to feel.

Clearly, the consultant's racial identity group had a strong influence on the meeting. Upon reflection and analysis, the top management group discovered that many of its reactions to the consultant were responses by representatives of one identity group (whites) to a representative of another identity group (black). These reactions (1) dominated their impressions of the consultant as an individual (which people were hard pressed to recall); (2) made it difficult for the entire group, consultant included, to accomplish the purpose of the meeting; and (3) even made it difficult to examine and intervene in the process dynamics of the meeting.

For the consultant, too, identity-group memberships had a powerful influence on his behavior. As he sought to understand the "failure of the meeting," he realized that, under the pressure of being an outsider and the only black person in the group, he too had invoked his stereotypes of white people. He found himself worrying about the insensitivity of the white members of the group, was angry about how everything he did or said seemed to be turned into a test of his competency, and felt that his historical experience of white people led him to mistrust what they said, which in turn he suspected might have limited his capacity to hear what they were saying.

In this case, the individuals imported into these exchanges between group members and the outside consultant a set of ways of dealing with complex internal emotions. Any group entering a consultation has to deal with the part of itself that feels inept, that feels unable to manage without help. The dynamic issue that must then be struggled with is how the group is to maintain its integrity and identity while moving to a dependent position that may feel somewhat regressive. These feelings might lead to some resistance to the consultation, even though the group had actively sought the project in the first place. In this case, having to manage these difficult internal conflicts, the group resorted to a "solution" that the members brought into the group via their whiteness and what they had learned about dealing with white and black issues in their larger social world. The all-white group resorted to the familiar practice of denigrating the black consultant in a way that left them not having to confront the insights he was offering to them or their own feelings about their inept and dependent sides.

The black consultant, too, on being placed in this conflictual position in the light of the defenses being used by the group, fell into the posture of seeing the group's behavior as rooted in the members' whiteness, not in their struggles to manage their own ineptness. The group explicitly sought the assis-

tance of a consultant because they did not know how to get
their subordinates to behave more competently and because
they thought it had something to do with the way authority
was being managed. The relationship with the consultant, whom
the group immediately pushed into a subordinate position due
to his blackness, as opposed to a superior or equal position that
would have been appropriate given his credentials and his job,
could be seen as a mirroring of what the members of this managerial group was doing to their subordinates—namely, seeing in
them the side of themselves that they experienced as incompetent.

 Situation 4. Professor Ruth Glass walked to class recall-
ing the last time that she had met with the eighteen students in
her course on social behavior in organizations. The session had
been devoted to an exploration of racial and ethnic relations in
organizations, but by the end of the class period, it seemed to
Dr. Glass that the energy in the discussion stemmed from the
unfolding ethnic relations among the students. The ethnic minorities represented in the class (Jews and Hispanics) were identifying strongly with the experience of minorities in the literature assigned for class discussion. Similarly, the white Protestant
men and women in the class seemed to find themselves forced
into explaining the perspective of the majority cultures. What
Dr. Glass was coming to recognize was how she, too, was involved in the ethnic dynamics in the class. Immediately after
the previous week's session, two of the Jewish students had
"cornered her" to ask her what it was like to be a Jewish woman professor in the university. Dr. Glass's initial impression was
that the two students were seeking support in the face of an
emotionally difficult and potentially threatening class discussion. Her judgment told her to avoid getting too engaged with
these students outside of class so that she could more effectively facilitate learning for all the students, but she also felt a desire to provide the Jewish students with both support and
understanding. All this went through her mind as she stepped
into the classroom to implement the design the students had
agreed upon the previous week.

After some discussion, the students divided themselves into three ethnic groups, Jews, Hispanics, and whites, and for the next half hour the groups talked among themselves about how their ethnic identity affected their relationships with the rest of the world. The whole class reconvened so that each group could "report" on its discussions. For the Jews, the conversation had touched on a number of points. In the first few minutes, people shared their experiences as victims of discrimination or as observers of anti-Semitism in the larger society. One of the Jewish students reported how difficult it was to discuss anti-Semitism with WASPs for fear that the WASPs would think that the Jew was paranoid, thereby fueling the stereotype of the Jew as overly sensitive to any form of criticism. The Jewish group found itself discussing the topic of intermarriage and the reactions of parents and grandparents to intimate relationships with non-Jews. Finally, the group remarked on how good it felt to spend some time with the other Jews in the class.

The Hispanic group was the smallest numerically and consisted of students from a variety of national origins. Their discussion had centered on how few of them there were in the class and at the school and how this made it difficult for them to participate in classes. They experienced the pressure of being treated as a representative of all people of Hispanic origin whenever they spoke. Not only did this make them feel that their individuality was unrecognized and unappreciated, it was even more disturbing in that all of them had different national origins. In a direct comment to the Jewish group, the Hispanics noted that they, too, had had a discussion about intermarriage, with the role of parents and grandparents occupying a central place in the conversation.

The WASPs were the last to report. They seemed uncharacteristically reticent. They reported their discussion with a series of adjectives, capturing the following sentiments: envy because they did not have a strong ethnic identity; pride because of their achievements; guilt because they had no experience of strong ties with each other. The WASPs had also discussed intermarriage and remarked that they felt excluded by the Jews, both socially and in work situations. One of the Jewish students responded to this statement with surprise and an admonition about the pervasiveness of exclusionary practices *toward* Jews. In one of the more tense moments in the class, one of the WASPs suggested that perhaps the Jews brought this on themselves by their own ethnocentrism.

A white woman said that during the WASP discussion she had begun to empathize with how white males must feel in a discussion of male-female relations arising out of the women's liberation movement. Another white woman had been very upset by the class and said that she had previously viewed them all as one group that had been developing cohesion but that the preceding two hours had seemed to fragment them. She found herself very distressed by this current situation. In contrast, a Hispanic woman expressed surprise at this comment and said that she was now feeling much better. Before this class, she had felt alone in bringing to this group an ethnic group membership that influenced her perceptions of others and their perceptions of her. Now it was clear that everyone brought to the class their own group identities and the attendant experiences and perceptual filters. In a tangible way, this made her feel more like everyone else and therefore closer to the others in the class and more comfortable with her own ethnic identity in the setting.

Professor Glass pointed out how the different ethnic groups in the class had imported from the society at large the prevalent models for feeling cohesive. The dominant elements in society seem to experience more cohesion when differences are unnoticed or suppressed. However, minorities come to sense more cohesion when those differences are acknowledged by all parties so that the shared experiences have a more common base.

Summary. In each of these cases, the issue we want to understand is what has happened to the internal group tensions associated with the contradictions inherent in group life. We observe that the contradictions are first split and then avoided by a process of shifting the attendant paradoxical dynamics out of the internal struggles of the group and into the patterns that have been imported into the group from the external environment. We know, for example, that in history, culture, and mythology, women and men have carried the emotionally expressive and the forthrightly assured positions, respectively. If

the group plays out its expressive and assured sides in intergroup terms, aligned along male-female lines, then the original
group-based dilemmas will have been transformed into gender
struggles that have less to do with the internal life of the group
and more to do with the external modes of managing gender-
based relations.

What is the link between the paradoxes internal to a
group and those that exist in the relationship between groups?
If we return to our discussion of the problems of self-reference
in Chapter Four, we can see that the same issues associated with
splitting inside a group—the partitioning of a whole into parts—
also apply to groups' attempts to understand their relationships
with each other. When two interacting groups use each other
and their relationship as a looking glass through which to discover characteristics of themselves that are being mirrored back
to them, the conditions for self-reference are created. If, in
addition, they use each other as repositories into which they
put parts of themselves that are disowned, then each reflection
back from "other" is a reflection from a "self that has been displaced into other" via projection. The self-referential framing
will have again been created without those involved in the circularity being aware of it.

If we consider, for example, the social evolution of the
relationship between males and females in the society, and the
attendant definitions of what it means to be male or female, it
is evident that both male and female depend on each other to
be defined. It is through the distinguishing of differences and
similarities that the very concepts *male* and *female* derive their
respective meanings. Placing maleness beside femaleness, and
vice versa, enables us to give these concepts meaning. They are
concepts whose similarities provide the foundation for their differentiation from each other. This means that maleness and its
relationship to femaleness are used as a frame for understanding
femaleness, and femaleness and its relationship to maleness are
used as a frame for understanding maleness. When "maleness" is
indicated by what is "not female" and "female" is delineated
by pointing to "not maleness," the self-referential circularity of
self-renunciation is in place, and we have paradox. In other
words, the apparent contradictions in the concepts of maleness

and femaleness derive from a common source but are split and placed respectively into males and females, who then "take on" the differences. When conflicts emerge in the areas of the male-female differences, they are experienced as conflict between male and female groups, as opposed to paradoxical dynamics associated with the phenomenon of gender.

This means that when a group imports, through its representatives, the external patterns of managing gender conflict, what is being brought in is an intergroup paradox that is not recognizable to the group or to the male and female representatives through which the importation has occurred. When internal group contradictions have been managed by using the classic external methods of dealing with gender relations, the paradoxical binds for the group may be experienced as having been avoided. It is more likely, however, that ways of managing the external intergroup paradox involving male-female relations will have been enacted instead, complete with the processes of splitting and projection discussed earlier. This lets the group "off the hook" in terms of the particular paradoxical dynamics being located in its male and female members. In addition, it reinforces the ways in which the external intergender paradox is being managed when the members move on to their new group experiences. On the other hand, when a group consisting of males and females struggles to deal with its internal paradoxical tensions without *using the patterns of gender relations* in the external world as a basis, what gets exported back to the environment may be a new approach to the paradoxical intensity of intergender relations.

A similar pattern is involved in the examples dealing with black and white members in groups. Blacks and whites in society have a long history of adversarial relationships rooted in the dynamics of dominance, servitude, and disenfranchisement. The legacy of this history is a contemporary situation filled with both expressed and repressed anger. If a group splits along the lines of noticing and expressing anger, on the one hand, and ignoring and avoiding it, on the other, and these are seen exclusively in racial terms in the group, then, as with the gender case, dynamics that are group specific are being deflected into the cultural and historical ways of dealing with them. This can lead members to believe that if only there were no blacks in the group, there would be no anger, or if there were no whites in the group, there would be no domination, both of which are devastatingly inaccurate.

In the last case, we can see the dynamics of inclusion and exclusion that are a central feature of any group as they take root in an interethnic setting. The minorities in this class move to understand their struggles with inclusion and exclusion as yet another enactment of historically established patterns. This may be true. But it may also be the case that when the interactions become disputes over who is more excluded by whom, the group is deflecting the tensions associated with its own group-based contradictions involving inclusion and exclusion. The process of disentangling the historical intergroup tensions from the internal group issues is made more complex by the tendency of group members to *use* historical patterns to explain and manage the anxieties that arise from the inherent paradoxical tensions of group life.

In each of the above cases, external and historical "solutions" were brought into the group via its membership and used as a means of "managing" or "containing" specific group tensions. The benefit was that energy did not then have to be invested in creating new ways of dealing with these tensions. The price, however, was that revitalized ways of understanding and working with these tensions were not developed. Further, these particular external intergroup "solutions" became reinforced, making it increasingly likely that the environment from which the importation comes would remain the same. That is, the external was imported into the group, reinforced, and then exported out of the group and back into the environment, making those conflicts in the environment more rigid.

The Dilemma of Part-Partness and Whole-Wholeness

In all of these discussions so far about importation and exportation, we have deliberately left ambiguous a distinction that is now important for us to make. We will refer to this as *importation dealing with the part-part versus the whole-whole.*

By this we mean that there are times when the partitioning that exists within a group clearly represents a set of parts that together make up a whole, whereas there are other times where the internal partitioning is much more the attempted accommodation of two wholes trying to work out how to be parts of each other. In these two variations on a theme, there are certain importation-exportation dynamics that are substantially different.

To illustrate the difference between part-part and whole-whole processes, consider first an organization that assigned a group of architects and a group of engineers to the same project team. Each group came to the project with its respective autonomy intact, in that its own internal ways of viewing the world, professional practices, values, and relative standings in the organization and the society at large were accepted. Although these autonomous groups had to work out how to interact in a complementary manner, they could each look to the organization of which they were a part to find relevant frames within which to embed their differences and formulate integrative and complementary systems.

This stands in stark contrast to a group of medical practitioners from the United States joining with Swiss financiers in an attempt to work together on a project providing relief in famine-stricken Africa. In this case, the American doctors wanted to enact their two key group identities, the standards of their medical profession and their commitment to American political values of liberty and freedom of choice for all. Likewise, the Swiss group, with their long commitment to principles of financial management and humanitarianism, brought their dual identities of political neutrality and maximum social impact for dollars spent.

In the hard choices around resource allocation, the Swiss and American groups entered a very difficult struggle over how much money should be spent directly on medical assistance for the desperately ill for whom immediate survival meant only a brief postponement of death, swapping disease for starvation. The Swiss group argued that the imminent loss of life of those who were very ill could be only minimally influenced by medical aid, no matter how much money was spent. However, if dollars were given to agricultural assistance in areas where life-threatening diseases could be contained, the benefit to the next generation could be substantial. While not saying it directly, they also implied that the current staggering death rate, while overwhelming to watch, was reducing the population to a level where economic development could make a significant contribution. The American doctors took the position that their charge was to help the needy and to heal the sick, no matter what the cost, and that the importance of life while it lasted could not be traded off for a brighter future for others, that life and liberty were the rights of the living and should not be abandoned with the express purpose of rekindling them in a subsequent generation.

In these debates, the Swiss financiers and the American doctors were searching for a way to create a unity within which their separate wholenesses could be maintained. There was no larger organization in place to which they could appeal for guidelines or for help in mediating the tensions that they were having to live with. The metaframes within which they had to have their conversations did not exist but had to be created, and it was only out of their interactions that such metaframes could emerge. This was different from the architect and engineering groups in the project team. While each of them came to the work at hand as complete and autonomous groups, it was evident to each of them as to how they could preserve their respective autonomies *and* orchestrate a system of interdependencies that would lead to a united product created out of the contributions of their separate groups.

A major difference between these two processes, which we are labelling part-part (the architects and the engineers) and whole-whole (the American doctors and the Swiss financiers), is in what gets imported into the exchanges from the worlds that each group has come from. In the part-part case, each group brings from the environment a model through which the respective autonomies can be preserved as each moves into its partness. In the whole-whole case, no such model exists for the two groups to import into their interactions. These two groups have to create, out of their whole-whole interactions with each other, a metaframe larger than both of them that enables them to enter into their partness so that a new sense of whole can be created. The importation, in other words, brings in the conditions of conflict but no structure for dealing with potential difficulties. In the former case, the overall frame was imported, worked with, maybe refined, and then exported out again into the environment whence it came. In the latter case, the metaframe had to be created out of painful struggles and interactions, and then, when the project was terminated and the struggles between the two groups ended, the metaframe vanished. It no longer existed to be exported back to the environment.

Another major difference in these two examples is how the members of the part-part group (architects and engineers) might go about recognizing or understanding paradoxical tensions when they emerged, in contrast to the whole-whole group (the American doctors and the Swiss financiers). In the part-part situation, members can look to two clearly established frames of reference. They can refer to their architectural or engineering parameters and work out what those frames respectively tell them about appropriate actions to take, or they can go to the organizational perspective within which they are located and use this organizational metaframe as a vantage point from which to determine their actions. That is, it is possible for these members of the work team to get relatively clear about when they are operating within a microframe and when they are in a metaframe; and if there is conflict between what is appropriate as a consequence of one framing as opposed to another, then choices or negotiations can be enacted to sort out which will be used, in the light of anticipated consequences for both the groups and the organization of which they are a part. In this regard, members can simultaneously learn how to *create and maintain a part perspective and a whole perspective.* And, most important, what looks contradictory from a micro vantage point may be seen as complementary from the larger frame, especially if that metaframe makes the connections among the parts focal.

This is radically different from the whole-whole situation. Here each group must be able to put itself into a meta-frame that does not exist except as it, at the same time, is fully within its own internal microframe. In other words, there is no place to locate, let alone store, this metaframe, even as it begins to develop shape. The metaframe is always in the position of residing in the space, in the cracks, in the midst of the interactions, between the groups struggling to maintain their respective wholenesses as they attempt to become a part of a larger whole that does not exist until they can work out how to be "parts." The tension is obvious. It has the quality of attempting to have the perspectives of an eagle and a worm at the same time.

When whole groups come together in a context where there is a method in place for them to enter their partness, as opposed to the situation where this is not the case, there are immediate implications for how the internal life of the newly formed group will be played out. Consider, for example, our earlier discussion about the paradox of authority. In the part-part situation, the group as a whole has a frame for struggling with its own issues of authority, with how to deal with the authority of its parts and how to link to the authority of the setting in which it is located. The process of authorization can include the relationships among the parts (that is, how they will authorize each other) as well as the relationship between the parts and the group as a whole (that is, how the parts combine to authorize the group in its relations with the outside world). In other words, the part-part situation includes elements necessary for it to engage the simultaneous authorization process.

In contrast, imagine the whole-whole situation of the doctors trying to explain to their peers in the American Medical Association the conditions under which they were willing to bend their commitment to the Hippocratic oath or to explain to the State Department their willingness to band together with Communist insurgents because, in their judgment, the future medical well-being of these famine-stricken areas would be better sustained under ideological systems antithetical to American values! The authority dilemma would be most visible if, when they returned to the United States, the American Medical Association contemplated decertifying the doctors for their "abandonment of their responsibilities as medical practitioners," with the price being withdrawal of the right to continue in the practice of medicine. The doctors might argue that while in Africa they had subordinated their medical authority to a larger system, so that the collective endeavor they had joined could be fully authorized. The next question would be, "What larger system?" The doctors could not point to the metastructure that they and the Swiss financiers had created, for it vanished the moment their project ended, since there was no institution available to take on what they had created or to embody it in retrievable form. To those listening to the explanations, the doctors would sound very strange, and it would be hard for them to explain how or why they were willing to subordinate their high medical and democratic principles to something that was so amorphous and that existed only vaguely, as if in their imaginations.

What we are addressing here is the idea that if a group imports into its midst, through its representatives, competitive authority systems that the members do not feel free to subordinate to the whole of which they are becoming a part, then an intergroup version of paradox has been created that has all the hallmarks of the internal paradoxes discussed earlier. The group merely becomes an arena in which the struggles among the larger groups who have representatives in this setting get played out.

What happens is that external intergroup relations, locked into symmetrical, either/or battles, are once again imported into the group via the representatives. As a result, the internal life of the group is driven by the symmetrical attempts of each to remain whole. But this can be possible, so it seems to the protagonists, only if each can get the group as a whole subordinated to its interests, that is, interests that are but a part of the whole group. This is an inversion that cannot possibly be accomplished. For if the group were to allow itself to be dominated by a part of itself, the very concept of the group, the idea that it is embodying something larger than its mere parts, will have been destroyed. As a result, the group as a whole will resist such attempts to dominate it, setting in place a struggle between the group as a whole and the factions that it contains. If there is any doubt about the importance of not letting a part of the group gain control, the protagonists that see themselves losing if others gain domination will vigorously remind the group of its existential responsibility not to allow this to happen. Either way, the group will be put in a position of fighting with itself. The outcome is usually the group's destruction through fragmentation, or paralysis. In either case, all that is available to be exported back out into the environment via the representatives is the "unresolvable" conflict, which simply makes the environment an increasingly conflictual place. This conflict is subsequently taken back into other groups, which proceed to interact with each other in even more polarized ways than before.

Conclusion

If we think back to the paradoxes described in previous chapters, it becomes clear that individuals, subgroups, and groups involved in a part-part relationship that is embedded in an organization are more *able* to explore links between the contradictions that emerge as they work together because the fact of the embeddedness asserts the existence of these links. The interdependence of the parts is actually and symbolically revealed in their mutual embeddedness. The dynamics of the part-part relationship import *both* the contextual ways of handling the paradoxical tensions (for example, negotiation, compromise, attributions to gender or racial dynamics) *and* the possibility of framing these apparent conflicts in paradoxical terms. This possibility exists in the part-part relationship because the link between the opposing parts is in place, even if it goes unnoticed, at the level of the "whole," be it a group or an organization.

In contrast, the whole-whole relationship can influence only the contextual ways of handling contradiction through the membership of its parts in other groups and organizations. It is very difficult for the whole-whole relationship to import the possibility of a paradoxical view of the tensions in the relationship, because there is no larger system in which the "wholes" are "parts." In the whole-whole case, the paradoxical tensions reside in the *relationship* between the wholes. In order for the metaframe to be retained so that the paradoxical can be contained, each whole must tenaciously hang onto its portion of the relationship. If it does not, then the relationship collapses and the metaframe that connects the wholes vanishes. The contradictions embedded in the relationship become split into parts that get carried by the separate units that go their separate ways without the relationship to guide or sustain their actions. Each unit that has been split off from its complement is the poorer for the split; it feels this, and tries to be more whole again by influencing the other, its split-off complement, to change in some major way.

The real rub for those of us caught in these group and intergroup paradoxes is the judgment call as to whether and when to subordinate the interests of the groups that we primarily identify with to some larger frame and when to hang onto our part of the struggle. In the part-part case, looking to the larger frame opens the window to the paradoxes in which we are embroiled. In the whole-whole case, it is only as we keep asserting our experience that the relationship remains, a necessary condition for the paradox to remain whole.

As we move increasingly into a world of professional and organizational specialization, it becomes more and more difficult for groups and the individuals in them to see the "larger system" or the "critical configuration of relationships" to which they belong. This makes it harder for interdependent parts to see the connections between the contradictions that are an inevitable aspect of their relations.

9

Intergroup Influences:
The Paradoxes of Scarcity,
Perception, and Power

While discussing the literature on internal group processes, we commented on how rarely researchers included conflict as an important topic for consideration. The exact opposite is the case with the literature on relations among groups. Here, frames that highlight conflict dominate the published record. Books are filled with propositions about intergroup conflict: cohesion is strongest when there is an adversarial or hostile group around (Simmel, 1955); ethnocentric dynamics enable groups to feel good about themselves because an "other" can be construed as bad (Levine and Campbell, 1972; Alderfer, 1977); management of intergroup relations is basically the management of conflicting interests (Rice, 1969). In a way, developing conflict-based explanations about intergroup relations seems to have been as easy as understanding the interior of groups in conflict terms has been difficult.

Our exploration of the part-part and whole-whole dynamics in the last chapter suggests a possible reason for the predominance of the conflict theme in relations among groups. In their attempts to deal with each other, groups need a larger framework in which to place an understanding of their relationship. If a framework exists, each group must evaluate the extent to which the framework produces a conception of the interaction that is compatible with its view of itself. If it does not produce such a conception, one or both groups may be in conflict with the framework and accordingly feel the need to change it before attending to the relationship issues that prompted a scrutiny of this framework in the first place. Thus, the architects and/or the engineers in the example we discussed may find themselves concerned with how the organization they are working for deals with integrating their respective contributions. If no larger framework exists, then both of the parties must be willing to hold up their ends of the struggle, because only then does the relationship continue. Since such group interactions are not embedded in an entity that provides a "framework" for the groups, the framework gets carried by the relationship and would cease if both or either party were to let go of its side of the interaction. We illustrated this with the experiences of the Swiss financiers and the American doctors in the African famine project.

In addition, an examination of the context in which a group exists leads us to make several observations about factors that heighten the likelihood that conflict will prevail in intergroup interactions: (1) since groups belong to a world populated by other groups, they tend to be forever banging into each other, each struggling to find its own place and identity; (2) each group, to maintain that identity, makes attributions about other groups and encourages them to act in ways that support this particular self-definition; (3) the very notion of multiple groups in the same context means that there are multiple interests that may not overlap, creating the potential for conflict among groups; (4) how groups regulate their interactions creates a system of interdependence that each comes to depend on for its ongoing vitality; and (5) the context of a group is not automatically given, for how a group elects to act can create a context that is hospitable and sustaining or hostile and adversarial.

Given the predominance of conflict in the contexts groups find themselves in, it is not surprising that the frames for understanding imported from the environment are conflictual in nature. In turn, since it is internal conflict that members are attempting to manage or avoid by importing external frames, it is understandable that what is exported back into the environment is also conflictual in nature. This sets up a cycle in which the environment becomes increasingly conflictual and, therefore, filled with frames for importation that are conflict based.

There is another side to all of this, which we began to acknowledge in the last chapter: relations among groups, just like relations within groups, contain paradoxical dynamics in their core. Groups with their internal paradoxes are located in an environment that also contains paradox. This means that the internal group frames that trigger self-referential, circular self-renunciation are themselves located in metaframes that have self-reference, circularity, and self-renunciation operating at the intergroup level.

In this chapter, we will discuss three intergroup paradoxes common in the relationships among groups: *the paradox of scarcity, the paradox of perception,* and *the paradox of power.* We will then look at how these influence the internal group paradoxes of belonging, engaging, and speaking, respectively. While we believe that all of these paradoxical dynamics influence each other in multifaceted ways, we will trace the specific links between these intergroup and intragroup paradoxes to *illustrate* how intergroup dynamics can be enacted in the internal life of a group, and vice versa, and to show how thinking from a paradoxical perspective can illuminate certain facets of group life that are often obscure in other theories of group dynamics.

The Paradox of Scarcity

Scarcity as an Intergroup Paradox. The intergroup paradox of scarcity can be observed in the corporate project that brought together the teams of architects and engineers in our part-part example from the preceding chapter. Before the project began, corporate headquarters allocated resources for the project. Initially, these were only rough estimates, but they provided a basis upon which the two professional teams began their relationship. The architects felt that they had not been given enough resources in light of the magnitude of the engineering task being proposed. The corporation's first response was to ask the architects to simply sort it out with the engineers; if it was not possible to shift resources to cover the problem, the architects should submit a revised budget for reconsideration.

When the two groups first met to discuss this, the architects indicated that, with the budget that they had been given, the plans that they could draw up would not come close to matching the designs the engineers believed they needed. On the other hand, if they simply did the best design possible within the limits of that budget, the engineers would not require as much money as they had been allocated, because the construction would have to be substantially more modest than originally conceived. Realizing this, the engineers began negotiating a reallocation of the available monies to provide an appropriate fit between design and construction. The architects asked the engineers how they wished to conceive of the project so that they could work out what resources they would require for the design process. But the engineers responded that, before they could give the architects the guidance being asked for, they needed to know the possible options that architecture could offer. They pointed out that all of their plans so far had been based on the guidelines of the original budget, which had led them to develop unrealistic expectations in light of what the architects could design, given *their* limited budget. Each group began its interaction with the posture that only as the other took an action would it know what to do. This created an obvious stalemate, based on a circularity that both groups helped to establish.

Unable to find an easy solution, the groups simply asked the organization for more money. But they did not acknowledge that the problem involved their inability to work out a reasonable reallocation process. The organization was in no better position to determine how to do this now than when the original proposal was made, so they responded by simply increasing the overall budget by 10 percent—10 percent more for architecture and 10 percent more for engineering. This produced no solution, for the two groups were in the same comparative dilemma as before the increase. The simple reality was that the groups were going to have to work on this together; they could not maintain their independent postures. The more they struggled, the less engineering found itself interested in surrendering a portion of its resources to architecture, and the more architecture adopted the position that it had to be funded at the same comparative level as engineering. In no time, the groups were again turning to the organization to ask for more funds, framing the inability to distribute funds adequately as a problem of scarcity. Each group was finding it impossible to work out what it needed because the only way it chose to frame its experience was in terms of its relationship with the other group. The result was an intergroup version of self-referential circularity, such that the actions that might solve one problem created another one.

The theme of scarcity is evoked whenever a new group is developed. As Sarason (1972) indicates, the creation of a new group *implies an indictment* of the context in which that group is being formed. By implication, the new group is saying, "What you currently offer is inadequate, and we are going to do it *better*." This idea clearly states that the very birthing of a group contains within it the seeds of conflictual relations with other groups in its context. New groups often emerge to do that which the present groups refuse or are unable to do. However, they invariably have to go to the same pot as the established groups for resources, setting in place a struggle that is defined in comparative terms. The new argues for its position in terms of the established; since the established is the basis out of which the new has its birth, the relationship is in part self-referential from the beginning.

Consider the example of environmental groups that were developed in the United States when it became evident that more attention needed to be paid to the long-term well-being of the ecology. These new groups were taking on the task of containing what "spilled over" from the existing groups and thus were born into a potentially complementary relationship with them. If the new groups had merely picked up the obviously necessary task of cleaning up the environment, then the established groups would have been able to proceed with their familiar patterns; thus, they would have supported the new groups, and their relationship would have remained complementary. But the new, responding to what the old had been doing, tried to get them to change their behavior. For, after all, if those groups would change, it would be unnecessary to have separate environmental groups cleaning up after them.

Thus, the new groups set out to convince the old groups to adopt something new, thereby triggering an adversarial relationship. The new was saying to the old that the old must become new if it were to have longevity. If the old refused, the new might have to destroy it or trim its wings, so that the agenda of the new could be advanced. Such an adversarial position inevitably leads to a struggle about resources. Can the society support the technological advancement "necessary for ongoing economic viability" *and* have "a clean environment"? If not, which faction should win, that "for progress" or that "for environmental conservation"? The two groups can easily become locked in struggles over resources, each feeling that the context provides inadequate resources, in large part because of their inability to see their connection amidst the adversarial relationship.

The intergroup paradox of scarcity addresses the way groups use each other and their relationship as a frame for understanding themselves, taking the contradictions associated with their commonness and splitting them in a way that pits the groups against each other. Whatever resources are available are seen as inadequate, because what one gains is seen as being taken away from the other, as opposed to being given to the part of self the other is carrying on behalf of the system as a whole.

There is an old fable that illustrates the way that the paradox of scarcity is produced by how groups in conflict frame their experience and in turn how their frames generate the experience of scarcity. After the revolution, two groups of starving peasants in postfeudal Russia laid claim to the lord's storehouse of grain. There was only enough grain to support one group comfortably through the year. Conflict seemed inevitable, and several skirmishes broke out as the two groups battled over who had the right to the grain. Within a few weeks, the fighting had killed almost half the population of each peasant group. It was at this time that a stranger happened upon the scene. He requested food, but the peasants told him that there was not enough to feed even those who believed that they had a right to the grain, let alone anyone from outside. The stranger was saddened by their myopia. He argued that since the fighting had reduced the total population of the two groups to the size each separate group had been originally, there was now enough for all. But the two groups were so entrenched in their struggle that they refused to see it this way. He suggested that they could ration the grain for the next few months and plant the remainder so that at the end of the year there would be plenty for everyone, strangers included. The peasants listened, then drove the still hungry stranger away, accusing him of attempting to create a fight between the two groups.

The Link with the Paradoxes of Belonging. In this section, we examine how the intergroup paradox of scarcity intersects with the cluster of internal group paradoxes that we called *belonging,* the paradoxes of identity, involvement, individuality, and boundaries. Belonging deals with the mutual processes that individual members and the group as a whole go through in an attempt to develop a meaningful identity. It is concerned with the struggles of individuals to sort out what parts of themselves they will invest in the group. It focuses on the need of the group for its members to express their individuality in order for groupness to develop and on how individuality grows when members give themselves over to the group. Finally, it is undergirded by the notion that boundaries create processes that then have to be contained.

When a group is in an environment of scarcity, it frames its experience in terms of survival. This raises the question of whether it must fight with groups that it also may have to depend on. Such a fight may disable the group, especially if a great deal of energy has to be poured into dealing with external conflicts, draining the resources needed for working on its own internal identity struggles. But there may also be some advantages to engaging in these external battles. If the group is having difficulty getting organized because its members insist on retaining their individuality, the external conflict may make certain internal structures seem "necessary," thereby helping the individuals to let go of their personal investments "for the sake of the group." While this may mean that the internal structures are at odds with what the group as a whole needs for the development of an adequate identity, it at least saves the group from the disastrous possibility of never being able to form any identity at all because of its internal diversity. Groups struggling with their own identity issues often look for situations of scarcity and feed off them once they are found. If they are not available, they can be created, for by not cooperating with external groups, the conflict that is really a facet of the groups' internal life can be pushed to a higher level of social structure, and, in turn, this structure can be blamed for creating the conflicts through its lack of adequate resources.

In the meantime, the group is able to say to its members, "Look, be patient. If we can get this external stuff worked out, we may get enough space to make the internal adjustments necessary for the maintenance of your own individual identities, but you will not be able to have everything all at once." Meanwhile, it says to groups that it interacts with, "We have to pay attention to our internal group life, and we cannot just do and be whatever you want of us." In other words, the identity development for the group depends on its working out how it is going to *be* in light of the differences that it has with others in its external world and those that it carries around inside itself. The special paradoxical dimension of this is that the group has a tendency to use its internal differences as a frame for understanding its external identity issues and to use its external differences when managing its internal identity struggles. This means that the frames for understanding group identity are, in large part, self-referential and that they set up the possibility of a group renunciating its parts while attempting to affirm its place in its larger contextual whole, or of renunciating its part in the context while affirming the parts of which it is made into a whole.

The intergroup paradox of scarcity can easily become entangled in the internal paradox of involvement. Since a group needs to keep a part of itself "out of the firing line" so that it can provide perspective on what it is involved in, external conflict places another face on this issue. Groups in conflict usually call for "all hands" to help in the external battles. The part that is staying distant on behalf of the group as a whole to facilitate reflection on what is going on can be silenced by being told that it obviously does not care enough about the group to even join the fight for the group's interests. The part intensely involved can ignore the importance of examining how its actions reinforce the very conditions it is dedicated to overcoming. These two parts of the group, each of which needs the other to maintain the identity of the group as a whole, often take opposite sides in the debate over whether and how to deal with the external conflict. In so doing, they bring to the surface an internal struggle that must be managed before the external one can be considered. As a result, the group is in a position where the precipitating external tensions *appear* to have created internal tensions that were not a problem until the arrival of the external conflict. Actually, these internal differences were always present, though they may well have been latent. What often happens next is an internal fight over how and whether to engage the external fight, making the actual external fight somewhat irrelevant. In a very real way, the external conditions of conflict will have been internalized and enacted within the group.

Another option is for the discordant internal parts to put aside their differences and act in a cohesive manner. In this case, the group will have compressed its internal tensions into an explosive ball and placed them into the external conflict, making that conflict more excessive than it otherwise would have been. The part of the group that did not want to get into the battle will have been seduced into abandoning its "observing" posture, reinforcing the group's nonreflective actions while in battle. If the external battle goes well for the group, then afterward the part of it invested in being involved will be prone to remind the reflective subgroup how it had been wrong to argue for staying out. On the other hand, if the external conflict goes poorly, the reflective side is likely to say "told you so." Either way, the internal parts representing involvement and reflection will struggle with each other again, leaving the internal landscape of the group looking like it did before the external struggle occurred.

In paradoxical terms, the internal conflict between the acting and reflecting parts of the group is framed by the conflict between the group and its external adversaries and is treated as a conflict separate from the divisions within the group itself, setting up a self-referential system that has self-renunciation and self-affirmation occurring simultaneously. Conversely and simultaneously, the external conflict is caught in a similar displacement and is framed by these internal conflicts. One major contribution of the intergroup paradox of scarcity is that the associated external conflict often encourages individual group members to believe that heroically taking on battles with others will enable them to sort out their place in their own group. The pattern of this thinking is "if I can win one for the group, then the group might accept me, maybe even the parts of me that presently seem so unacceptable to it." This thinking leads individuals to try to be more than they actually are, so that they can master the group. In the process, they make the group into more than it actually is by treating it as something gigantic in the light of their own sense of smallness. This also puts the individual in the position of giving up, or temporarily putting on hold, the individuated parts of him- or herself, taking on only the part of self fused with the group's identity. Once members have made their individuality subservient to the interests of the whole, the group will be able to deal with its external conflicts. But the very act of group unification will have created for its members the experiences of deindividuation that motivated the heroic striving for mastery in the first place. The result is a cycle that intensifies, making the level of deindividuation worse than before the drive for individuation began. In turn, the internal conflicts that seek relief by engaging in external fights also intensify.

The Paradox of Perception

Perception as an Intergroup Paradox. One reason for the existence of different groups is the existence of different goals and values. One reason that there are different goals and values is that the world is divided into various groups. The existence of diversity among humans leads to the clustering of individuals of like mind and purpose to pursue their shared interests. The very differences among groups enable them to take on separate tasks and fulfill different functions. Were all groups the same in every regard, differentiation around interests and values would not be possible, and it would be much more difficult to divide up those tasks required for the survival of a system as a whole. While these differences are important, they have meaning only because of the similarities that also exist and provide a basis for collective endeavor.

Goal differences may emerge from the internal interests of each group or because the system in which the groups exist allocates specific functions to the various groups. The different goals of interdependent groups may be complementary when examined from the perspective of the larger system, while being experienced as competitive or contradictory by the groups actually involved (Landsberger, 1961; Lawrence and Lorsch, 1967; Walton and Dutton, 1969). It is important to note that it is not the interdependence that creates the conflict but rather the group differences that are needed for the division of labor necessary to undertake the task. The intergroup paradox of perception is that the very differences that help to create the basis upon which individuals can meaningfully form a group and that enable the system as a whole to allocate the differentiated tasks necessary for overall well-being also reinforce ways of perceiving that threaten the fabric of the whole and make the necessary integration of the differentiated parts very difficult, and often impossible, to achieve.

Consider our example of the African famine project. The fact that there was a group of medical specialists willing to come together with the financial specialists made possible actions that otherwise would never have occurred. Their different backgrounds, professional values, and skills created both new possibilities and the potential for debilitating conflicts associated with difference. The conflict, however, was embedded in the simultaneous existence of their differences *and* similarities. The differences were framed by the similarities, which depended

on the differences for their meaning, and the similarities were
framed by the differences, which depended on the similarities
for their meaning. The conditions for circularity, self-reference,
and self-contradiction could be found in the very processes
upon which their different and similar perceptions of the world
were based.

One of the prerequisites for task differentiation to contribute value to a system is that the groups that embody separate goals have to be willing to pursue them wholeheartedly,
even when they appear to be clashing with the goals of others.
If they do not do so, the value of having different goals and interests carried by separate groups would be undermined. For
example, organizations usually divide their labor in a way that
creates functional groups, such as marketing, finance, production, and so forth, each expected to respond to different pressures. The primary task of marketing, to deal with the interests
of customers, may not match production's interest in manufacturing quickly, efficiently, and in sufficiently large batches to
limit unit costs. Such goal differences are differences only because they are complementary elements of a larger goal, the
economic viability of the organization of which they are a part.
When these goals are pushed with all the energies of the separate
groups, the task of integration by the system as a whole is made
more difficult, often leading those who speak on the collective's
part to ask that the groups tone down their investments in specific interests. But such a message becomes double binding, for
it runs counter to the other dominant message: "The system as
a whole depends on each group to pursue its group goals fully."
So the world of groups in interaction is filled with messages that
seem contradictory. In view of the different world views that
each group brings to its interaction with other groups, the possibility of conflict among groups is vast. But it is conflict that
grows out of contradictions emanating from the same source, in
this case the very differences and similarities that give separate
groups their meaning in the context of the whole.

A critical dynamic associated with the differences and
similarities of groups and the paradox of perception is the view
that "if we are to be *pure* in our pursuit of our goals, we must

be sure we do not let any of the goals of other groups influence us; otherwise, we will be achieving their interests rather than our own." This is easily translated into a secondary membership dynamic—"we must keep others out; otherwise, they will contaminate us, and then *we* will no longer be *us!*" Under extreme circumstances, this can be transformed into "we must keep their perspective out of our group; otherwise, our thinking will become contaminated." As this type of thinking grows, groups begin to deprive themselves of the capacity to understand others and thus diminish their capacity to understand self, for the meanings of self and other derive from the same source. This cycle also blinds each group to how its actions contribute to the relationship as a whole and diminishes the group's ability to understand, and cast in an affirmative light, the adaptations it must make to live meaningfully in a world populated by other groups.

The Link with the Paradoxes of Engaging. The paradoxes of engaging (disclosure, trust, intimacy, and regression) are concerned primarily with making the group a safe place to interact, where the experiences of giving up some things to and for the group do not simply leave one depleted and therefore "less" as a result of attempting to be "more." For a group to become "whole," individual members must be willing to enter a condition of "partness," so that the group can work out how to integrate its elements in a way that enables its members, in turn, to feel whole when they are parts of the group. This requires members and the group to trust in a process that seems untrustworthy and to engage in self-disclosure when all the clues suggest that being cautious makes most sense. In this section, we explore how the intergroup paradox of perception is linked to these internal paradoxes of engaging.

Every group has to work on two forms of integration. It must learn how to bring its members together so that it can act as a unified whole, and it must develop ways of integrating itself with other groups. This means that members are being required to make two types of adjustments, so that the group to which they belong can cohere and so that the group can fit in with the demands of other groups. A problem emerges when the external relationships become conflictual. Members who have already become less than what they perceive they could fully be so that the group can become more fully what it wants to be are required to change yet again for the sake of the group. This stirs a wide range of attributions. Members feel that they had to trust the group to be willing to regress, yet, no sooner did they do this than the group, which has benefited from their willingness to subordinate individual interests to the collective interests, asks this "sacrifice" of them again. There are always some members who feel that the group has abandoned them and therefore do not want to go along with this request, "only to be ripped off again," feeling that the group as a whole is being more accommodating to other groups than to its own members. The emergence of this internal perception leads some members of the group to argue that the group has no alternative because of the external pressures it is subjected to. This can set off a conflict among group members over whether or not to capitulate to the group's requests of them.

Meanwhile, the other groups expect some adjustments so that mutual interdependencies can be created, and the group's only possible defense of its slowness in responding is that it will take time for all members to come along in the desired ways. This leaves each group seeing the problem as the inflexibility or uncooperativeness of the members of the other groups, and it leaves members perceiving that their own group cares less about them than about the group's position in the external context. Given the perception that the others are cooperating so minimally, this seems unjustifiable. Such attributions end up transporting the internal struggles between members and the group into the relationship between the group and other groups with which it interacts. It simultaneously takes the external tensions and places them into the relationship between the group as a whole and its members.

When this conundrum is alive, problems with disclosure increase. Individuals may no longer know what to say and do but feel that it would be very risky to express their confusion. This caution is used as justification for remaining or becoming disengaged, which lessens the sense of intimacy among members that might, under other circumstances, keep them sufficiently bonded together to be willing "to carry on with the struggle." The disengagement, in turn, lessens individuals' willingness to offer the kind of feedback that is necessary for the group's self-knowledge and capacity to self-correct when on a nonproductive path. Withdrawal or withholding of reactions often traps the group into believing that silence is consent. However, although silence may mean that members' commitment is still firm, that they are still invested in the group as a whole, it may actually be a sign of apathy that will galvanize into revolt or abandonment the moment an opportunity presents itself. So, while individuals are making attributions about the group, the group as a whole is also making attributions about its members. Yet it is so hard to sort out whether any of these are accurate. The traps of self-reference are in place again, for the internal system of attributions is used as a frame for understanding the external, and vice versa, bringing the circularity of self-renunciation as each reflection of other unwittingly becomes a self-reflection.

The Paradox of Power

Power as an Intergroup Paradox. When differences in values and ideologies lead to conflict over whose values are to be subordinated to whose, and under what conditions, the conflict can easily transform intergroup exchanges into a power struggle. Value differences, in and of themselves, do not always lead to conflict among groups. Differences in values can coexist in mutually enriching ways, as in the case of melding music and drama in the production of musical theater. This does not mean that the tension created by the differences in values disappears; rather, it is out of these tensions that the overall fabric of the production is created, generating an outcome not possible within the medium of either music or drama alone. When these tensions are not managed, however, conflicts between the musicians and actors can take on a warlike quality, making the whole performance less than what music or drama alone could have offered. It is not immediately self-evident what conditions precipitate the switch from potentially complementary value differences to contradictory ones. Clearly one major ingredient, however, is the difference in power that accompanies these groups in their respective settings.

In every organization, groups differ in the amount of power that they have. This may result from their differential access to resources, or from having control over critical information, or from being in a position to influence significantly the destiny of others. Power can also emerge from the perceptions that groups have of each other. A group may achieve power because others are convinced that it will exercise that power in a way that does not undermine the interests of those without power. In some cases, groups will even reject possibilities that would be in their interest, simply because they do not want those who suggested them to have the power resulting from coming up with something that was universally accepted. Power may also result from a group's sense of its impotence. Feeling powerless, a group may relate to another group as though this other group were powerful and in so doing give the other group power over it, not because it *was* powerful but because the powerless group imbued it with power. In this sense, power is an attribute of the relationship between groups, rather than of any group itself. It may also happen that some groups always end up on the powerful or powerless side of exchanges and hence experience the power or powerlessness as an attribute of themselves. Despite this, however, their actual power in the larger social system is an element of their relationships with other groups.

In organizational structures, groups are invariably arranged in some type of hierarchy where power is the underlying dimension. Some groups seem to be in a position, either legitimately or illegitimately, to define how interactions among groups are to be conducted. Such groups behave in a proactive way, setting goals, placing demands on others, and energetically pursuing whatever it is they want to achieve. There are other groups forever in the position of reacting to the initiatives of others, not setting their own goals directly but borrowing from what others want of them or deciding their priorities on the basis of rejecting others' demands. These differences can be thought of in terms of proactivity versus reactivity. We also find groups caught in the middle between these two, seemingly without their own reasons for existing but needed as a buffer or mediator between proactive and reactive groups. Those groups define themselves not so much in terms of the others as in terms of how the others *interact* (Smith, 1982a). Power differences set the stage for *both* a large number of potential conflicts *and* creative possibilities that would not emerge if the conflicts were taken away. The conflicts may be played through directly as power struggles, or they may be fused with value or goal differences or struggles over who has access to what resources, and for what purposes.

The intergroup paradox of power is that when one group has more power than another, the less powerful invariably redefines its condition as *absolute powerlessness*. This creates the belief that only if the more powerful give up some of their power can the less powerful ever have a chance to improve their situation. In the process, the relatively less powerful group turns a blind eye to the power that it does have and defines its condition only in its comparisons with the powerful. The social comparison processes of groups that get to this position trigger the circular, self-referential self-renunciation that we are all now familiar with.

The attempt of the powerless to define its condition exclusively in terms of the powerful is experienced by the powerful as an attempt to seduce it into giving away or letting go of its well-deserved, hard-earned position. This is experienced as an "assault that must be resisted," setting up the inevitable reactive conflict between those who are conceived of as the "haves" and the others who are the "have-nots." In the extreme form of this, the "have-nots" become blind to all that they have, and the "haves" overlook all that they do not have. The attendant polarization leads both to make attributions that intensify the polarization, setting the relations in a permanently conflictual form. The conflict serves well many of the ways each group prefers to relate to those who are different. In particular, conflict with an external group is often used as a way to maintain cohesion (Coser, 1956). When external conflict exists or can be created, it is easy for a group to generate a convincing rationale for members to put aside the differences that might otherwise fragment it. Then the group can ignore its deviant or convince its warring subgroups to stop their fighting in the service of the group as a whole.

The Link with the Paradoxes of Speaking. Our third cluster of internal paradoxes (authority, dependency, creativity, and courage) is concerned primarily with the issue of speaking out. In particular, these paradoxes deal with how and when to speak, in what voice, and with what levels of certainty and ambiguity. Actions that initiate, structure, and regulate have to be authorized both by those who perceive themselves as having the power to do so and by those influenced by it. The authorizing is a multidirectional process, in that if those who would lead are not followed, there is no leadership. Leaders depend on their followers to make their leadership effective. To become independent, group members must have the courage to affirm their dependency, the very thing they are trying to overcome and that they fear will eventually destroy them. The intergroup paradox of power is closely linked to these paradoxes of speaking, especially the issues that tie together the management of internal and external conflict and how leadership is exerted both within the group and in the interactions among groups.

In the paradox of authority, we observed that those who are dependent shape the character of that upon which they depend. Such character does not come into being, however, without initial actions by the leadership. For followers, in their dependency, are not in any condition to articulate what they will follow. They may indicate what they will *not* follow, but defining that does not suggest what they *will* follow. It is only as the leadership takes an initiative, usually against a backdrop of uncertainty, that the followers come to sort out what they will follow, thereby making leadership possible. This means that potential leadership must have the courage to create that which may be ignored or destroyed, for "leadership" is undertaken in a context of not knowing. Then the followers are given what they need to work out what they will follow and the conditions under which they are willing to be dependent.

There are special internal group dynamics associated with leadership and followership when the group is embedded in relationships with other groups that have differential power. For a start, the leadership is expected to keep the external boundaries tightly regulated so that any divisive forces from outside can be warded off. In addition, the followership's interests shift from a leader who provides internal guidance, such as goal clarification, division of labor, participation, integration, and so forth, to someone who can handle the external functions, such as negotiating, leading the battle, coalescing the group energy, and so on. When a group is in an external power struggle, it is important that the leader present a clear embodiment of the group's image of itself and the power of its emotions. The importance of this symbolic element of the leader can be seen in the ancient practice of settling disputes through the combat of each nation's champion, in which it was crucial that the champion represent the entire army's or nation's view of its skills, strengths, and passions, since victory or defeat determined the fate of the entire group. Vestiges of this ancient practice can be seen in the feelings that groups and organizations have about their leaders. The leader must not only *be* a leader but must *look* like a leader, whatever that means, for even though the fate of a group may not rest exclusively with the leader, external power struggles do increase the symbolic importance of the leader's qualities and characteristics.

When groups with differential power are in conflict, the authorization process is very complex. The leader not only must deal with the tensions inherent in the group but must devise or create an authorization process at the level of the intergroup struggle as well. If, for example, a leader has great internal credibility but those outside refuse to deal with him or her, then the capacity of that leader to represent the interests of the group in the larger conflictual context is effectively nonexistent. This means that the leadership must be able to create a frame for the authorization process that has internal and external concerns as copartners, experienced in complementary forms. If the internal authorization is pitted against the external authorization, then internal processes can end up being subordinated to the process of external conflict, or vice versa.

This pattern is evident from time to time in Yasir Arafat's leadership of the Palestine Liberation Organization. The times when he receives the most powerful authorization from the Palestinians are when he takes recalcitrant positions with those that the Palestinians must relate to. This leaves others unwilling to negotiate with him, because it always leads to pointless deadlocks, ultimately undermining the Palestinian concerns and Arafat's capacity to keep these issues before the world forum. When Arafat becomes externally more conciliatory, he almost always must then confront internal schisms that threaten his leadership, sometimes even his life. This swinging into either/or authorizing guarantees stuckness and the constant oscillation that creates a lot of motion but little movement.

The cycles associated with dependence, independence, and interdependence in groups take on a particular flavor in situations of conflict with groups with differential power. A group in isolation may be able to develop a relatively stable and reliable network of internal interdependencies, but these will quickly be thrown into disequilibrium on encountering external conflict. The issue then becomes how to mobilize for combat or how to reorganize to adapt to external demands, and these issues call into question the internal arrangements set up to manage the interdependencies created to enable the group to act as an independent unit. In the intergroup conflict setting, the patterns that stabilize internal struggles around dependence and interdependence throw external dependence and interdependence out of alignment, and vice versa. This produces a cycle in which any solution creates the conditions demanding its destruction. Awareness of this calls for a particular type of courage in the leadership. The leader in this situation must know that the world of action is uncertain and that only by taking action will clarity emerge but that even this clarity will turn back in on itself and make things opaque again, demanding more courage to act yet again.

It is hard for any group to manage the dynamics embroiled in the paradoxes of speaking. They produce remarkable tensions, for the group has to struggle with the awareness that each new arena it enters, each new developmental stage it approaches, each new artifact it creates, also involves a destruction of some kind. It is difficult to keep the destructive side by side with the creative and to see it as a central part of the group's internal life. If, however, there is an external group that can be used as a repository for the uncomfortable feelings associated with the destructive, the group can disown its destructiveness and remain attuned only to its own creativity, goodness, and beauty. Then, if the other group, not wishing to have this "muck" dumped upon it, strikes back, the original group can feel justified in unleashing its pent-up aggression, the destructiveness within that it did not want to own. It will experience this not as a displacement of something within it but as a force actually created by the action of the other group. In this way, the group can feel well served by the power differences that it experiences with groups in its environment and, in fact, prefer them. If equality existed, a group might feel obliged to behave collaboratively, and it has already worn out that side of itself trying to deal with its internal issues. As a result, external adversaries are courted, for they enable the groups involved to gain respite from the internal tensions associated with the paradoxes of speaking.

Conclusion

In this chapter, we have argued that the external context of a group is filled with paradoxes of its own and that the internal paradoxes are enacted in ways that are linked to the intergroup paradoxes, and vice versa. We have presented the view that the internal conflict that emanates from the inherently paradoxical tensions of group life is often displaced onto a group's external relations. The result is that the relations among groups are forever being experienced in conflict terms. These external conflicts then have to be coped with by the groups existing in this context. What often happens is that the groups take from their environment frames for understanding their own inner experiences, thereby bringing into their midst much of the cognitive and emotional material that they pushed out into their context in the first place. As a result, they treat as "other" that which is in large part "self." When groups use other groups as a system for understanding themselves, a self-referential loop has been created, setting up the possibility of intergroup paradox.

The effect of these dynamics is that the relations among groups are often a parallel playing out of the conflicts that exist within groups, and, in turn, much of what transpires within each group is a parallel enactment of these external conflicts. Groups transform their internal tensions into conflicts with others in the environment and create a parallel internal enactment of these conflicts. Perhaps more important, groups adopt the framework for understanding and managing their internal conflicts from the external environment and then use that same framework again in their intergroup relations. In the previous chapter, we discussed how this importation and exportation process occurred via the members of the group. In this chapter, we have attempted to describe how it can also occur directly at a group-as-a-whole level.

Part Three

Applying Paradox

In the last part of this book we are concerned with the implications of a paradoxical perspective on group life, for both the thinking and actions of leaders, consultants, managers, and group members. We have clustered the implications into two areas: (1) what new insights can be developed about how groups move from one condition to another when a paradoxical perspective is adopted; and (2) what actions become possible for an interventionist skilled in the art of paradoxical thinking, when working in an organization with groups that repeatedly paralyze themselves internally or that gravitate toward interactions with other interdependent groups in ways that are self-defeating both for themselves and for others.

Chapter Ten focuses on group movement, with an exploration of the proposition that attempts to *overcome* the conflicts that regularly paralyze groups only make those conflicts more entrenched and further immobilize the group. Here we articulate theory that moves our thinking away from the dynamics of conflict resolution and encourages instead an examination of how groups can be *released* from their paralysis. The key is not to learn how to avoid *becoming* stuck, but rather to learn how to progress and how to avoid remaining stuck. Often the efforts to avoid becoming paralyzed create the very paralysis that is being so energetically avoided.

In the final chapter, we explore a case in depth. The case is reported through the voice of the consultant who recounts both his understanding of the organizational groups and his thinking in paradoxical frames. Our purpose is to illustrate paradoxical thinking as it occurs in the reflections of an individual attempting to take meaningful actions in a particular organizational setting. This is not intended as a prescription for the translation of paradox into specific action. In this example we are eager to make a paradoxical frame accessible to those involved in taking actions in real settings, without oversimplifying the issues or implying that all one needs to consult adequately is a keen sense of the paradoxical.

10

The Cycles of Group Movement and "Stuckness"

Most theories of group development are strong in their descriptions of stages, phases, or cycles and weak in their analysis of the processes by which groups move from one condition to another. Movement is usually explained in terms of a "working-through" process. Rarely, however, is there any elaboration of what is meant by "working through." A paradoxical conception of group life contains within it a model of group movement. In this chapter, we will depart from the conflict-resolution approaches that have characterized group dynamic theories for several decades. In its place, we will elaborate the dynamics of release. To do this, we will explore the processes of both movement and stuckness. When referring to stuckness, we are concerned not with the temporary paralysis that may result from conflict over scarce resources or the existence of conflicting needs or goals. Rather, we are referring to the repetitive, often unconscious tensions that prevent a group from even doing the work of *problem solving* on scarce resources or *compromising* about conflicting needs. As will be evident in this discussion, the relationship between stuckness and movement, like the relationship between other opposites, has its own paradoxical qualities.

A paradoxical perspective suggests that the origins of both stuckness and movement are rooted in the ways individuals

207

and groups respond to the presence of coexisting opposites. The contradictory reactions evoked in members by the existence of a group create a variety of paradoxical tensions within individuals, within the group as a whole, and in relations among groups. The central dilemma for both individual group members and the group as a whole is how to survive and flourish in a social world defined in large part by the paradoxical contradictions it evokes. It is important to keep in mind that survival and growth in a world of contradictions involve not only the experience of paradox but the various ways of thinking about paradox that enable us to tolerate or manage contradiction and conflict. Precisely at the moment that we embark on a description of a *theory* of stuckness and movement, we need to be especially mindful of the power of the way we conceptualize experience as well as the power of the experience itself.

There are many ways to live in a paradoxical world, and this, we argue, is the world that faces those of us living and working with groups. Some of the choices we make in our efforts to cope with paradox are likely to produce stagnation and stuckness. Other choices facilitate movement. In this chapter, we explore the meaning of stuckness, movement, and progress in the context of a paradoxical conceptualization of group dynamics. We introduce this discussion with a metaphor, a description of a hypothetical living system that survives and flourishes in a world of coexisting extremes. The metaphor allows us to illustrate some of the characteristics of stuckness and movement in the paradoxical world of group relations.

A Hypothetical Jovian Organism

Imagine a hypothetical living organism on the planet Jupiter (Feinberg and Shapiro, 1980). The atmosphere on Jupiter is composed of layers of different gases, each with a different temperature. Our hypothetical Jovian organism lives in this atmosphere and has adjusted to a world of temperature extremes. It resembles a hot-air balloon. The living organism is the skin of the balloon, which is filled with an inert gas. As we first approach it, the organism is living in a hot, lower region of Jupiter's atmosphere. As the gas heats up, the balloon rises through this region and passes into a cooler one. At this point, the inert gas filling the living skin cools down, and the organism descends through the cool region into the hot layer, and the process repeats itself. The cycle continues as long as the organism can "feed" upon the energy in the hot region and deposit "waste" in the cold region. Whatever growth and development occur in the living skin of the balloon are predicated on this perpetual sojourn between the hot and cold regions of its world.

Our hypothetical Jovian organism lives in a world of coexisting opposites, and its growth depends on its ability to ascend or descend fully into the two different regions, because this immersion provides sustenance (as well as opportunities to get rid of waste) *and* because immersion is the condition that allows the organism to move through one region to another. Since both regions are a part of the organism's world and since the organism's survival depends on its ability to "get into" both regions, the process of full immersion in each region is critically important. Only through descending into the hot region can the organism rise into the cold, and only through fully ascending into the cold region can the inert gas cool down sufficiently to allow the organism to fall back into the hot region. Any attempt to arrest its ascension or descension would cause the organism to become "stuck" and die.

The metaphor is a useful one in a number of ways. Like the hypothetical Jovian organism, groups too are embedded in a world of coexisting opposites. Instead of hot and cold regions, group life is filled with coexisting and opposite reactions and emotions (dependence and counterdependence, inclusion and isolation, observation and involvement, creation and destruction). For groups, this world is partly of their own making, as the members struggle with the contradictory and conflicting reactions to collective life, and partly a legacy of the history and dynamics of the intergroup relations that surround any group. Like the atmosphere of Jupiter, group life is not *either* hot or cold, but rather a world in which both exist. It is a paradoxical world of coexisting opposites created out of the members' need to express the ambivalence associated with membership in a group.

The metaphor tells us something about movement in

groups as well. The Jovian organism oscillates between the hot and cold regions of Jupiter's atmosphere. From the outside, we can see the link between the two extremes, the framework that makes sense of the organism's path in and between the two regions. We can see that the oscillation is a necessary process to sustain the organism's life. But for the organism itself, the movement is always toward an extreme, toward a domain of discomfort. The Jovian balloon discovers the framework only by moving into each of the extreme and potentially risky places, and we can only speculate as to whether understanding the framework in which it lives and grows provides any comfort for the stress of living in such a contradiction- and conflict-filled world.

In groups, too, we are often unable to understand the paradoxical tensions, the polarities with which we struggle, until we immerse ourselves in the extremes that make it up and then learn, through this immersion, how to get outside the polarities to see the pattern created by the extremes. This immersion is risky and often filled with fear (of being consumed and of being isolated), but, as with the Jovian organism, the oscillation between the extremes may be a necessary aspect of the group's survival and growth. In order to discover the framework that links the opposing and contradictory elements in a group, the group must immerse itself in these same elements, but the fact that the framework is not clear at the outset makes the immersion even more risky and fearful. As a result, groups may choose not to immerse themselves in the extremes, thus not only reinforcing their stuckness but keeping themselves from ever discovering or creating a larger framework for understanding how their actions prevent productive movement.

Stuckness

The paradoxical condition in groups is a special case of coexisting opposites. As we have discussed, the oppositional forces in groups are often self-referential and apparently contradictory, creating the vicious circularity that can make paradox both intellectually and emotionally disturbing. The experience of stuckness in groups is a consequence of the various ways that groups and their members cope with paradox and specifically with their attempts to change the paradoxical circumstances. Faced with what appear to be mutually exclusive subgroups, beliefs, wishes, fears, or emotions, group members often try to undo or redesign this world of opposites. Attempting to undo the paradoxical circumstances often has the effect of further entrenching the oppositional forces and paralyzing the group.

Since groups evoke contradictory reactions, their expression is an important part of the emotional life of a group. But the expression of opposing reactions and feelings can also threaten the group, because members may, understandably, fear that conflicting and apparently mutually exclusive reactions will tear the group apart, at worst, and stymie any forward progress, at best. As the group struggles to "solve this problem" by reconciling the opposing forces or eliminating the contradictions, pressure is created in the opposite direction in order to ensure that the full range of contradictory reactions can be expressed. The more the group tries to eliminate contradictions, the greater the pressure to reassert them. A powerful, albeit unconscious, threat to the group is that only one side of group members' reactions to being in the group will be allowed expression. The other side will be held unexpressed, creating a potentially dangerous explosion if the forces containing these emotions prove to be insufficiently powerful. And the more powerful the forces of containment, the more explosive the feelings being contained. The fear of expressing only one side (and *suppressing* the other) provides a counterpressure against efforts to eliminate or weaken one side or the other of the group's emotional life.

The group's attempts to eliminate these contradictions are very understandable responses. The contradictions cause distress, conflict, pain, depression, frustration, and a feeling of helplessness, especially when they contain the paradoxical element, which adds both repetition and circularity to the experience of contradiction. The group's collective response to this is a group-level form of resistance, an unwillingness to fully explore the painful and distressing aspects of the group's psycho-

[handwritten margin note: Amy's dominance vs. My silent resentful submission]

logical world for fear of the consequences of what might be discovered. As with individual resistance, the fear is powerful precisely because the group *knows* both that the paradoxical contradictions are sources of pain and frustration in the group *and*
that they are an inevitable and fundamentally important aspect
of the group's existence.

There are a number of ways that groups attempt to eliminate paradoxical contradictions:

1. Group members may *try to compromise the emotions*
associated with the contradictions by finding a middle ground
that makes the contradictions disappear. In analogous terms,
this would be like the Jovian organism attempting to create a
"lukewarm" region in Jupiter's atmosphere. A compromise such
as this would be an attempt to reduce the intensity of the oppositional forces, but at the price of simultaneously forcing out
much of the group's vitality. The "hot" and the "cold" are
eliminated, and the lukewarm remains. Attempts to compromise these extreme forces create stuckness, because the group
ends up having to devote its energy to keeping itself in a narrow
region of "averages." The group is hemmed in by the intensity
of the possibilities. All of us have had the experience of being in
a group that could not move because its members believed that
they knew what they could not explore and were trapped by
this "knowledge."

2. Groups also *attempt to eliminate the contradictions*
by pitting the oppositional reactions against each other to see
which is "stronger" or more powerful in the group. In its simplest form, a concrete issue that seems invested with the power
of a particularly salient paradoxical issue may be brought to a
vote. Or the group may choose to hold an event at a time when
some of the members cannot attend, preferring to go ahead
with a "quorum" rather than take on the problem of "conflicting" time demands. As it attempts to subjugate one side of the
contradiction to the other, the group's process sets in motion
forces that reassert the conquered set of emotions or concerns,
for no one wants the group to become a place of emotional or
psychological domination, since each individual has ambivalent
reactions to the experiences of collectives. When one subgroup

seems to be on the edge of dominating the other (on issues of intimacy, commitment, involvement, and so on), the balance is restored. The process of competition merely strengthens the losing side, and the group experiences stuckness at the very times it appears ready to move on.

A striking example of this phenomenon occurred in a self-analytical group conducted as part of a course on group dynamics. The students knew nothing of "paradoxical theory" but did know that the course had a reputation of focusing on unconscious processes in groups. The "ideology" of the course was a matter of divided opinion even among the self-selected cohort that had chosen to take the course. Early in the life of the group, it was clear to everyone who were the "believers" and who the "skeptics." It appeared to the group members that a major ongoing battle in the group would be the one between these two subgroups. About halfway through the course, one of the "leaders" of the skeptic group announced that this "stuff" was starting to make sense to him and that he was beginning to "buy into" the ideology of the course. One could feel the balance begin to shift toward the "believers," but no sooner had the words been spoken than a member of the "believers" subgroup said, "When I hear you say that, it makes me want to buy out." By these two countervailing actions the balance was restored, bringing with it the feeling of stuckness that momentarily had the possibility of being released. What continued to elude the group was an understanding of the role of "belief" in the functioning of the group—that is, the framework in which the two opposing reactions were embedded.

3. Groups may also *use time to separate the contradictory elements*. A group with a very difficult struggle around authorizing and being authorized may find that two subgroups exist each of which is unwilling to authorize the other, so that neither can be authorized. Faced with making a specific decision, a group may elect to ignore or avoid the larger issue that divides them in their discussion of the merits of this particular situation. Subgroups appear to "put aside their differences" in the service of cooperation. However, one needs only to watch two consecutive meetings to see the ways in which a series of

decisions embodies the polarization that currently defines the group but that the group is attempting to overlook. Each "side" describes first one decision and then the next as a "victory" or "defeat" for one subgroup or the other. At the emotional level, the group feels stuck, and the concrete decisions merely perpetuate rather than dissipate the oppositional forces.

In each of these examples, stuckness is the result of the group's efforts to eliminate the paradox. In its attempts to "average" the contradictions, the group acts as if the elements of the paradox can be transformed, broken down into parts and recombined in a way in which only parts of each are retained. Take only 300 degrees from the 1,000 degrees in the hot region and combine them with −250 degrees from the cold region to produce a 50-degree temperature. In its attempts to have one side or the other dominate, the group acts as if it is possible to destroy or remove one element of the paradoxical tension. "Let's decide which environment is better, the hot region or the cold region, and we'll live in that one." In its efforts to separate the paradoxical elements, the group uses time to "split" the paradox, to separate the elements so that the contradiction and frustration can be avoided.

Such efforts produce stuckness because they seek to change the inherent character of collective life, a character that reasserts itself because the group's survival depends on its ability to serve as a forum for the expression of the *opposing* reactions evoked by group membership. Ambivalence can be more or less strong but is always the consequence of simultaneously holding opposite feelings about the same object or person. Similarly, paradoxical tensions in groups can be more or less strong, but they are always the consequence of coexisting opposite reactions in the group. If groups experience their realities as paradoxical and groups evoke contradictory reactions expressed through individuals and subgroups, then attempts to eliminate the paradox, to separate or split the elements and to divorce the two opposing forces from their common source, will create a reaction to assert the link and to pull the paradox back into the group so that both sides can be expressed. For groups trying to separate the elements of the paradoxical tension or eliminate them altogether, stuckness is an indication of the survival instincts of the group.

Groups both raise and provide expression for opposing, conflicting, ambivalent reactions. Taking away the opportunity for expressing and exploring these reactions creates a group that generates these emotions but has no way of "living" with them. These are the groups that struggle to deny or remove the paradox in the service of comfort and reduced anxiety. But these efforts, if successful, reduce the opportunities to express the opposing ambivalent feelings, and this heightens the forces in the group to reassert these opportunities. The stuckness cycle continues.

Movement

We have argued that stuckness is often a consequence of attempts to undo or eliminate the paradoxical tensions in groups. Now we argue that movement results from living within the paradox. This statement itself may seem paradoxical, since living within paradox would seem to entail endless circularity and frustration. However, by staying within the paradox, by immersing oneself in the opposing forces, it becomes possible to discover the link between them, the framework that gives meaning to the apparent contradictions in the experience. The discovery, emotional and intellectual, of the link provides the release essential for group movement.

What do we mean by movement? Movement is the exploration of new ground. In the case of the person or group that runs in place or walks in circles, there is motion but no movement. For individuals, motion without movement can be found in the repetitive patterns (often unsatisfying or counterproductive) that involve different settings, circumstances, or people but feel the same because the pattern of responding to these situations is the same. An example of this in psychoanalytical theory is the concept of transference reactions, where an individual's intrapsychic activities transform interpersonal events into relationships that evoke a repeated pattern of emotional responses brought to the present from the past. It is because there has been no movement in these emotional responses that the analysis of transference is a potentially useful therapeutic approach. Similarly, groups also develop patterns such that different situations produce a similar emotional response. A group confronted with an emotionally hot topic (for example, sex roles in the group, how to confront a popular but ineffective leader) may find that two of its most vocal members invariably become embroiled in an argument that feels familiar, long-standing, and all consuming. Or, in its relationship with other groups, a group may find itself inevitably disparaging the integrity of the other groups' members although it has little or no knowledge of them.

Movement refers to leaving old patterns, at least for a time, and exploring new psychological or emotional ground in the life of the group. It is not a condition defined as much by *what* is being discussed, confronted, engaged, or addressed as by *the patterns* used by groups and their members to discuss, confront, engage, or address. From a paradoxical perspective, movement in groups is the result of two major psychological processes occurring within individuals and within the group as a whole. The first of these is *the reclaiming of emotions and reactions that have been split off* and projected onto other individuals, subgroups, or groups. The second involves *immersion in and exploration of the polarities* that are part of the group experience.

Reclaiming split-off emotions and reactions is a very difficult undertaking. As we have discussed earlier, the process of splitting, while an attempt to "solve" contradictory or ambivalent feelings, actually contributes to the creation of opposing forces in groups. Through the mechanism of splitting and projection, members of a group simplify their ambivalent reactions to collective life by placing one "side" of the ambivalence in another person, subgroup, or group and retaining only the emotions on the other "side." The opposing forces that were once inside the individual are now inside the group, or those that were once inside the group are now inside an individual group member or in the relationship between groups. But the emotional simplification occurs only if the person or group can "lose sight of" the common source of these opposing reactions

—that is, the person or the group. Reclaiming split-off emotions refers to the reintegration of the opposing or contradictory reactions. In terms of our discussion of stuckness, this means struggling to acknowledge, when appropriate, the contradictory nature of our individual or collective reactions instead of trying (through splitting and projection, for example) to eliminate this contradiction.

It is important to note that reintegrating the split-off reactions does not translate into resisting the splitting and projective processes as they occur. Often it is impossible to know that these processes are occurring until after the consequences have been experienced. The question is not whether the splitting can be avoided but rather whether the recognition that splitting has occurred and is occurring can lead to efforts at reclaiming what has been split off. In addition, if taken to an extreme, efforts to prevent splitting may become a way of avoiding the paradoxical tensions at one level by focusing on the contradictions at another. If, for example, group members are so concerned about splitting and projection that they are unable to create roles in the group (Gibbard, Hartman, and Mann, 1974), they may see only individual ambivalence and never strong and opposing reactions at the group level.

To return to the hypothetical Jovian organism, reclaiming the split-off emotions is analogous to accepting the presence of opposing extremes in one's world. This acknowledgment is a necessary but not a sufficient step for movement, since the realization that individual and group life is, in our terms, paradoxical (composed of coexisting opposites) returns us to the question of how one lives in such a world without moving in circles or not moving at all. Here again the Jovian metaphor is useful. It points to the role of immersion in the movement process. In order to survive and to grow, the Jovian organism must immerse itself in one of the temperature extremes in its world. This immersion literally propels the organism into the other extreme, and the ability of the organism to immerse itself fully in both enables it both to exist and to grow.

In the case of groups, the extremes themselves may change in character over the life of the group as it struggles with dif-

ferent paradoxical tensions, but the need for the group to immerse itself in the extremes that comprise any given paradox remains. This immersion provides the experience necessary to
discover the connection or link between the extremes, if one
exists. When the group is struggling with a paradoxical tension,
the discovery of the link between two apparently contradictory
opposites provides a "reframing" of the relationship between
the two. This reframing brings with it new ways of "looking"
at the conflicts that have formed in the relationship between
the two extremes (individuals, subgroups, groups). In the following examples of interpersonal, group, and intergroup situations, the two processes necessary for movement are illustrated.
In each case, movement is the result of first holding the paradox
by reclaiming those conflicting feelings or reactions that have
been split off and projected out and then immersing the group
in the paradoxical elements and thereby experiencing a reframing of them.

    1. Relationships with parents are filled with paradoxical
tensions. From our earliest encounters with them, our parents
are simultaneously a source of satisfaction *and* frustration, of
love and hate. Our early ambivalent reactions give way in the
face of the anxiety aroused by our dependency on our parents,
and we begin to split these ambivalent reactions and to separate
the difficult and anxiety-filled emotions. Sometimes the split
leaves us loving ourselves and hating our parents, or vice versa.
Sometimes the split leaves us loving one parent and hating the
other, and at other times we end up hating our own family but
loving everyone else's. These splits remove the painful and scary
ambivalence but leave behind one feeling where once there were
two. The essentially paradoxical relationship with our parents
has been "undone," and in its place is a simpler but often stag-
nant one. As we grow older, we complain about the ruts into
which we fall when we are at home, and, unknown to us, our
parents lament the loss of openness and sharing that they hope
for but cannot seem to bring about.

    At some point in our lives, if we are lucky and attentive,
we may begin to reclaim what has been split off earlier in our
lives in the relationships with our parents. We begin to "see"

that our parents can be both frustrating and satisfying at times, lovable and not, divinelike and human. Our relationships with our parents contain both elements simultaneously, and while this seems impossible (how can one both love and hate one's parents?), there is some essential meaning of parent-child relationship that is captured in this coexistence of opposite emotions. If we allow ourselves to live in both sets of emotions when they arise, we often find that the relationship moves out of the patterns begun in childhood and into new emotional and psychological ground. It is not that we or our parents have grown smarter, but that we have reclaimed the paradoxical nature of the relationship and learned to live inside the paradox. The patterns kept in place by the efforts to change the paradoxical aspects of the relationship are more easily changed as the paradox is acknowledged, accepted, and explored.

parent + child relationship

2. A classroom group provides another example of how movement can be understood when using a paradoxical frame. Soon after the beginning of the semester in a twenty-person course on organizational diagnosis, students began arriving late for class or missing class entirely. Although it was not always the same students who came late, nearly half the class was always on time, so that class members began to be aware of a division: those who had been late and those who had not. Two weeks into the course, Daniel, the instructor, expressed his dismay at the tardiness and the absences, and a number of the "culprits" explained that it was job-hunting season and they had little or no control over interviews, call-backs, and visits to prospective employers. First the instructor and then class members who had not been late to class challenged these explanations and "encouraged" the latecomers to treat course time as sacred and to inform both the career office and prospective employers of this fact. The late-comers resisted this notion, convinced that it would succeed only in jeopardizing their job search.

The lateness and absences continued in spite of a similar follow-up conversation. The feelings on both sides remained the same except that, additionally, the whole class wanted the "problem" to go away, because it took class time to discuss it.

In spite of the disruption that this pattern presented, the futility of discussing it made the class avoid confronting it. Finally, the instructor expressed his anger and frustration and announced that the lack of commitment symbolized by the lateness made him wary about embarking on the field projects that were a large part of the course. It appeared to everyone that the class would "go around" on the issue one more time. A student from the "not-late" group said that concerns about committing oneself to the course might not be limited to the people who were coming late. She admitted to having mixed feelings about commitment as well and suggested that it would be less productive to continue the battle between the "committed" and the "uncommitted" than to examine what it was about the course that raised feelings in the area of commitment. In this regard, the appearance of an "uncommitted" subgroup, presented in the form of a number of class members who were having difficulty containing and managing their many commitments (work, study, classes, job searches, social life), became a collective method for the group as a whole to first avoid and then confront the difficulties involved in containing the many emotions stirred by the tasks of working with the people in the field projects.

The ensuing discussion focused on class members' anxieties about their competency to conduct the field project and their fears about the team-formation process yet to come. This helped release class members from the subgroup tensions that had developed in the class and triggered an exploration of the conflicting and often contradictory reactions evoked by their experiences and expectations of the course. This discussion in turn helped prepare them for the formation of teams and for the work of helping diagnose other peoples' experience in organizations. The apparent "regression" at one level facilitated the progress of the group.

3. Intergroup examples abound with similar paradoxical tensions. When a group is having difficulty managing its internal tensions, as in the case of the classroom example just discussed, it may become embroiled in struggles with authority figures. Daniel had memories of just such a situation the last time he taught this class. Confronted with a similar "tardiness" prob-

lem, the class had proposed a "solution." They suggested that Daniel go to the career office to negotiate a special arrangement whereby students in his class, because of their special circumstances, would get preferential treatment in the scheduling of job interviews.

Daniel felt trapped. If he attempted to negotiate with the career office and was unsuccessful, he would be seen by the students as someone unable to solve their administrative problems or as someone not powerful enough to influence the career office. If he were successful, he would be placed in an awkward position with respect to his faculty colleagues, who might resent the implicit statement that Daniel was making about the relative unimportance of attendance at other courses.

Daniel decided to describe his dilemma to the class and to return the issue to them with the interpretation that the class was in effect asking him to rescue them from their own internal group dynamics. As the students left the class, one of them suggested that a good teacher would never have allowed these emotions to surface and interfere with the course objectives. Joined by two other students, he decided to take his complaint to the dean. The dean listened patiently and then encouraged the students to "sit on their complaints" and get the most out of the semester. He did not tell the students to go to Daniel directly, nor did he tell Daniel about the conversation.

Three weeks later, some of the other students in the class who knew about this event and who considered themselves Daniel's supporters went to the dean to report how wonderful a teacher Daniel was. When the dean heard this, he became very confused, for now he had totally contradictory images of Daniel's work in the class, and he was eager to know which image was right. He was unable to see that each view was neither right nor wrong but that both were attempts by the group to "solve" their own internal dynamics by pulling in members of other groups with more power to "resolve" the situation. The paradoxical aspects of both the internal group and intergroup dynamics were, in hindsight, apparent.

In each of these three examples, the words belie the difficulty of the process. In some cases, the work of reclaiming split-off emotions can take hours, whereas in other cases it can take years. Sometimes we can, through a conscious act, choose to immerse ourselves in both sides of the conflicting reactions evoked by a relationship or a group, but at other times we are thrust into one extreme and must drag ourselves kicking and screaming to an exploration of the other. It is ironic that in order for split-off emotions to be reintegrated, the splitting process had to occur—and that to immerse ourselves in the contradictions, we must first know them and know our fears about exploring them. There is no movement without stuckness. There is no possibility of movement without the temptation of remaining where you are.

These examples also suggest three basic principles as a basis for movement in groups when understood in a paradoxical frame:

1. Go toward, rather than away from, the anxiety or fear associated with an issue or event (Alderfer and Brown, 1975). These emotions are often indications that the issue or event at hand should be engaged rather than avoided. The more a group struggles to avoid such issues, the more likely it will get stuck and the harder it is to move through them.
2. The role of leader in a group is one that facilitates the exploration of the full range of paradoxical tensions that arise. To be effective, the leader must be willing to explore his or her own contradictory emotions. The leadership role must seek to understand the relationship or link between seemingly opposite positions and to use this understanding to suggest actions that examine the patterns of stuckness that groups develop.
3. Groups will facilitate their own movement and growth when individuals recognize the ways they use others to define themselves and when groups recognize the ways they use other groups to define themselves. By defining "others" as the opposite of "self," individuals and groups, through the mechanisms of splitting and projection, constrain their ability to move in the service of reducing anxiety.

Group Release

Many theories have used the term *working through key conflicts* as the major descriptor of the processes involved in moving from one state of group development to another. As mentioned previously, what is involved in the actual "working through" is left frustratingly vague. We use this as a starting point in our discussion here.

The concept of "working through" has a particular meaning in the psychoanalytical literature. It refers to the repetitive, progressive, and elaborate explorations of the resistances that prevent an insight from leading to change (Greenson, 1967, p. 42). Working through sets in motion a variety of processes in which insight, memory, and behavior change influence each other (Kris, 1956a, 1956b; Greenson, 1967). Three of these elements are especially appropriate for understanding movement in the paradoxical circumstances that we have described. These are resistance, exploration, and repetition.

In groups, the resistance, both individual and collective, involves the desire to avoid the anxieties evoked by the powerful contradictory emotions inherent in group life. Holding opposing reactions creates anxiety, in part because it means accepting a "side" of oneself, one's subgroup, or one's group that has been systematically projected and denied. There is also the anxiety generated by the paradoxical tension itself, the fears of being trapped in a vicious circularity from which there is no escape and no apparent resolution. While repetition itself may be seen as the root pathology that must be overcome (as in the experience of the neurotic), it may also be the path to learning that, paradoxically, can make the repetition itself no longer necessary. Resisting the repetition because of its real or imagined consequences further entrenches a repetitive cycle at the level of resistance.

The exploration of these resistances is what we have called immersion, the process of fully living within these two sources of anxiety. The exploration process includes an examination of opposing paradoxical emotions as well as an exploration of the link between them. As is evident, the exploration process itself is filled with resistance, since, as in psychoanalytical practice, the process of exploring the resistance can be as threatening as the sources of the resistance themselves. It is this willingness to explore that is at the heart of movement in groups. Much like the working alliance in psychoanalysis, the members of a group (sometimes in concert with a consultant) have to come to the point of being willing to explore in spite of the anxieties that the exploration evokes. The exploration of paradoxical tensions in groups is based on a paradox, since the necessary willingness to explore is founded on an exploration of the paradoxes of belonging, engaging, and speaking.

The repetition of the exploration process helps the group gain experience in living with contradiction, discovering the link between the opposing forces, and finding ways to function and grow in the midst of a paradoxical environment. Each successive iteration provides learning, for individuals and for the group as a whole, about not only the difficulty but also the potential value of exploring paradoxes in groups. With repetition may come a gradual diminution of the pressure to eradicate or eliminate the paradoxical conditions that the group is seeking to understand and to explore. As this pressure diminishes, the group "gets better" at the exploration process and is more likely to benefit from it. Progress does *not* mean that a group will never experience the pain and disorientation of paradoxical tensions or even of a specific paradox; rather, progress can best be described as a process of learning to live through cycles of contradiction and paradox. Repetition aids this learning by providing opportunities for incremental experimentation in the process of exploration.

The concept of group release is based on the observation that energy in groups is catalyzed when that portion of an idea, emotion, or action that has been split off from itself in the service of managing the existence of contradiction is reclaimed or brought back. The energy devoted to maintaining the split is then freed up. Holding the contradiction uses this energy to explore and to reframe the paradoxical elements of the contradiction. The release provides the group with the impetus necessary to move out of a static and paralyzing experience of conflict. An analogy to nuclear fusion can be made. If enough energy can be marshaled to hold opposing forces together, in spite of the forces acting to drive them apart, a tremendous amount of energy can be released and a new "element" created.

Cycles

Movement in a paradoxical world is cyclical. The group is continually engaged in an oscillation between two poles of a paradox, and the movement, like the movement of the Jovian organism, is an ebb and flow first into, then out of, the paradoxical extremes. The repetition of the exploration process also contributes to the cyclical nature of this movement as new ground is covered in increasingly familiar ways. Ultimately, movement is heralded by the recognition that a cyclical process is inevitably part of each new seemingly contradictory situation.

There are numerous cycles in this paradoxical conception of group dynamics. In addition to the cyclical quality of the exploration process within any paradox, there are the cycles among paradoxes as well as the cycles among the paradoxical clusters. Just as the contradictory elements within a paradox are linked to each other, the paradoxes within each cluster are also linked, as are the clusters to each other. Although the links become more tenuous as we continue the process of aggregation, these connections give a cyclical quality to a group's movement among different paradoxes.

For example, the paradoxes of engaging are all concerned with the issue of participation in groups. There is a progression to the paradoxes of engaging: disclosure, trust, intimacy, and regression. Yet an exploration of the paradox of regression can be understood as working with an "earlier" paradox, such as intimacy or disclosure. As the group struggles to allow itself to regress, members talk about their reactions to events in a way that increases the level of self-disclosure. This in turn catalyzes the fears associated with disclosure in groups, and the group finds itself once again confronted with the paradox of disclosure. This "second encounter" with disclosure, however, will not be identical to the first, since the repetition of the process of exploration will have "moved" the group. Yet this encounter, too, will have a familiarity born of the sense of revisiting, cycling through once again, a recognizable though not fully known place. Within each of the clusters this cyclical progression is possible.

Across clusters, a similar pattern emerges. Our experience and the literature on group dynamics suggest that, as new groups are started, the likelihood is that they will encounter the paradoxes of belonging *before* the paradoxes of engaging, and that both of these will precede the paradoxes of speaking. This progression makes intuitive as well as empirical sense, since questions of membership often precede questions of participation, which most often precede the issues of influence and authority. Numerous authors have discussed the theoretical explanations for this progression (see, for example, Bennis and Shepard, 1956). This progression rarely proceeds without "interruption" and rarely concludes with a state of emotional equilibrium. Instead, the consequences of exploration within each of these clusters may evoke the contradictions of paradoxes in another cluster, and the group may find itself moving back and forth between clusters in still another type of circle.

Consider, for example, a group that has been struggling with the paradoxes of speaking and is now engaged in conflicts that have their roots in the paradox of creativity. As the group experiences the conflict between its creative forces and its destructive ones and searches, however haltingly, to explore the paradoxical relationship between these two extremes, members begin to feel uneasy about the level of disclosure being elicited by the discussion. To fully explore the current conflict (the paradox of creativity), each member comes to consider, once again, the conflicting feelings surrounding disclosure, trust, intimacy, and regression. For some, the uneasiness is brought on by the desire to uncover a creative side. For others, it comes from their participation in the destructive side of the group, an expression of their own destructive side. As the paradox of creativity is explored, the paradoxes of participation are evoked, and the cycle continues as the group learns more about itself and its members.

External events also trigger groups to shift to a previously encountered paradox. The addition of a new member, for example, may evoke one or more of the paradoxes of belonging as group members are left once again having to explore the implications of the addition of a new individual identity for the identity of the group. Changes in the status of individuals or subgroups within the group, as in the case of promotions or changes in marital status, may evoke a "return" to the paradoxes of speaking as the group struggles with the authority gained and lost by these changes.

The special complexity of a group's passage through its paradoxical existence becomes particularly visible when its relations with external groups change because of external forces or the reactions of external groups to how the group is living with, denying, containing, or deflecting from its paradoxical life. For example, a change in the status of the external groups to which members belong may shift the focus of the group from one set of paradoxes to another. Consider the situation where there are changes in the status of women in the organization in which the group is embedded. It may be that group members have to revisit issues of belonging, engaging, and speaking, so that it can continue living within this new context. These external changes may have specific effects on all group members, as in a major alteration of organizational policies, or they may have a specific influence on subgroups, as in the case of the change in status of minorities due to the formulation of organizational policies attacking discriminatory practices. The effect on the minority subgroup in particular will, in turn, draw the relations among all interdependent subgroups into a re-exploration of the previous patterns developed by the group as a whole to manage the paradoxes upon which its group identity was founded.

It may also be necessary for a group to revisit a previous paradox or cluster of paradoxes as a result of changes in the whole group's relationship to another group or to its environment. For example, on hitting a slump, an organizational group

long established as a profit center in an organization, and therefore highly valued, may find itself in a new relationship with the
senior management, who are eager to determine whether this is
a temporary setback or a permanent slide. Accustomed to a supportive environment, the group may have to deal with feelings
of threat and vulnerability that it has never had to confront before. This is likely to evoke fresh concerns about *belonging,* as
some members consider the possibility of losing their jobs;
about collective *engagement,* as the group struggles over whether to exert more effort to bolster performance, whether to remain loyal to the group, or whether to become resigned to a
fate seemingly beyond their control; and about *speaking,* as
internal authority patterns are shaken by the questioning of
external authorities.

   Finally, external relations may also contribute to the reasons behind the emergence of a particular group in a larger social system. Some groups are formed out of the need to band
together to deal with environmental forces that seem hostile to
individuals but more manageable when dealt with as a member
of a group. Other groups are formed as a result of members
being attracted to the opportunity to participate in activities
that are appealing. Such a group can be called an attraction
group. The developmental passages into and through the various
paradoxes may differ markedly for these two types of group.
For example, the major concern of a tenants' association in
forming itself is the task of confronting the landlords, a task
that may need to be adversarial. As a result, the group may
move quickly past belonging issues (mechanistically disposing
of them by simply delineating membership in terms of whoever
resides in a particular setting) and move on to how the group is
to develop a sufficiently forceful voice to be able to speak to
adversaries with authority. The process of developing a leadership ready to confront external relationship issues may take
precedence over concerns about how to nurture and regulate
internal needs. This will mean that many individuals will fold
into the paradoxes of speaking what is related to belonging and
engaging. In addition, the development of what membership
means, as opposed to the delineation of who belongs, may well

be linked to the level of engagement that individuals "promise" as the group considers how to do battle with adversaries. In this regard, belonging may well be defined in terms of members' stamina through the skirmishes destined to define the essence of this particular group.

In contrast, a group formed because of mutual interest in performing certain activities together, such as playing tennis in a recreational club, will place more importance on the process of joining and the matching of interests and resources than on the forming of leadership patterns for managing external relations (as in our tenants' association example). In fact, external issues may be sufficiently unimportant as to require no attention until the group as a whole has worked out how it is going to function internally. In this type of group, the paradoxes of engagement are likely to work out in the context of the belonging paradoxes, whereas, in the tenants' example, engagement became embroiled in the primacy of the speaking paradoxes.

The special point of these illustrations about the intergroup impact on internal group paradoxes is that we almost always are dealing with *paradoxes within paradoxes,* and that exchanges between groups have their own paradoxical and self-referential quality that is connected to, entangled with, or folded into the within-group paradoxes of the groups involved. These "between-group" paradoxes are themselves shaped by the images of group relations carried around in members' heads as a consequence of intergroup history and memory.

Conclusion

The cycles within and among the paradoxes create the ebb-and-flow process that occurs at many levels: within the individual, within the group, within a specific paradox or cluster, and across paradoxes and clusters. Progress or development can be measured in terms of the group's ability to (1) define and understand the opposing forces active in the group and (2) find the links between them, the framework in which *both* are embedded. The cycles provide repeated opportunities for the group to gain experience with the process of defining and understanding the role of oppositional, contradictory forces in groups. The experience makes it more likely that the group will be successful in its work with the paradoxical tensions it encounters, but the experience cannot substitute for this work, nor, by definition, can it substitute for the difficult and conflictual emotions that are part of the work itself. Rather than exempting the group from exploring certain issues or paradoxical tensions, experience with paradox often equips the group to engage them.

11

Using Paradoxical Thinking
in Organizational Analysis:
A Case Study

As a conclusion to this book, we explore how to use paradoxical thinking as a basis for reflecting on action with groups
in organizational settings. Although some readers may wish for
detailed prescriptions on how to increase group effectiveness,
we feel that this would run counter to the spirit of this book
and overwhelm it with the number of contingencies that would
have to be specified. We have chosen to illustrate how a paradoxical theory of group relations can shape one's thinking and
action in organizational groups by presenting a composite case
that represents an amalgam of dynamics drawn together from
several projects we have worked on, either separately or in collaboration. All names are pseudonyms, and certain elements
have been fictionalized to create the connective tissue necessary
to present this material as an integrated case. For simplicity,
our thoughts and actions are described from a single, third-
person perspective—that of Jansen, a consultant hired by the
organization AMPA. We summarize his observations and record
how paradoxical thinking shaped his understanding of the group
relations operating in this organization and informed his decisions about the actions that he took.

This case presents an application of thinking about action,

231

rather than a prescription for action. We are primarily concerned with illustrating the way in which a paradoxical perspective can enrich a consultant's thought about the interventions he or she makes in an organizational setting. It is not our purpose in this chapter to explicate a set of guidelines for action that flow from a paradoxical conception of group dynamics.

It is important to underscore that this case is intended to illustrate the role of a paradoxical perspective in a consultation project, but a paradoxical perspective is not the *only* conceptual framework present in the consultant's work. It is not possible, in our view, to work effectively with groups in organizations without a variety of other conceptual and practical skills, including but not restricted to those in the areas of interpersonal processes, intergroup theory, organizational diagnosis, power and hierarchy in organizations, and personality theory. What we have chosen to do in this case presentation is highlight the contribution of paradoxical thinking. This is not meant to suggest that an understanding of paradox is *sufficient* for work with groups in organizations or that the consultant in this case entered his work with only the paradoxical perspective described in this book.

Background

AMPA was in the midst of numerous organizational transitions. Laurent Pries, the chief executive officer, had sought consultant Jansen's help. "I don't quite know what we need, but I feel that our senior management group has gone through so much lately that we could benefit from stepping back and gaining perspective. We are all too close to do this for ourselves. We need the assistance of an outsider's eyes." As Jansen began his consultation, the senior management group, consisting of the chief executive officer and six senior vice-presidents, had assembled to review the agenda for the next board meeting. This was a ritual that took place every three months. The senior management group nervously anticipated the ways their lives "could be made miserable" by a board that, in their view, had "lost its way." "The board constantly sends us signals that are contradictory," was the perennial complaint. It had become increasingly difficult for them to accept the authority of a board whose views they experienced as confusing.

The senior vice-presidents respected Laurent Pries for his role in bringing AMPA to its current pre-eminent position in the industry. But they had grown weary of his nondirective leadership style. Pries was a member of the board and hence had the closest knowledge of the board's thinking. Yet he seemed unable or unwilling to translate the board's wishes into practical guidelines for the operation of the company. Whenever concern was expressed about where the company was going, Pries gave a detailed historical account of how far it had come in the previous ten years. The younger vice-presidents, more interested in the shape of the future than in history lessons, found this very frustrating. The older vice-presidents reacted with longing for "the good old days" when the company was small and everyone knew each other well.

One problem facing this group was that it had become divided, and its members did not know how to manage the internal cleavage: those responsible for the financial and administrative affairs, strongly committed to a good dividend for investors, were pitted against those involved in research, production, and marketing, who relentlessly emphasized maintenance and the advancement of quality. Recurring debates raged about whether to reinvest profits or pay greater dividends to stockholders. One side argued that easing up on quality would be AMPA's downfall. The other side countered that the constant insistence on growth of the work force, presented as a move to preserve quality, was sapping the company's resources. Each side acted as though its position were right and the other wrong. There was no one in the group who talked about profits *and* quality.

The internal split within the senior management group had deepened to the point where a great deal of energy had to be exerted simply to keep the two sides connected. Laurent Pries was of little help in these struggles. He tried to calm the troubled waters by walking a middle path, a strategy that left no one happy. When he left the factions to sort out their own problems, he was accused of being wishy-washy; when he took a firm position, he was labelled misguided by those on the other extreme. At the same time, skirmishes had been mostly contained to ritualized budgetary struggles and to rhetorical posturing prior to each board meeting.

Two paradoxical dynamics struck Jansen. (1) The internal split in the senior management group seemed to be masking the capacity of the group as a whole to hear messages in any way other than contradictory, because contradiction is what this group had become invested in preserving internally. If members actually heard external clarity, this group would be forced to acknowledge its own internal divisiveness. Theoretically, this seemed likely to set the stage for the paradox of authority. Such a group, Jansen thought, would be prone to reject its legitimate authorities in order to avoid having to acknowledge the ways it deauthorized itself. (2) It also seemed that this group, having difficulty creating interdependence among its own parts, would find being interdependent with another group (in this case, the board) hard to manage.

In the "good old days," when AMPA's earnings were minimal and when everyone was eager to establish a reputation, there was no split between profit and quality. Profits were small and the link between profitability and quality so self-evident that no one even thought to debate it. But with success, growth, and increasing specialization, profit concerns and quality concerns were carried by different people, with each subgroup becoming invested in aggressively representing its position. Each couched its actions in terms of simply doing what was best for AMPA as a whole and the external stakeholders that had to be satisfied, the investors or the consumers. This enabled the internal subgroups to avoid being accused of pushing self-interests.

"Don't Be Selfish"

Across time, another dynamic emerged: each subgroup profited more in the internal distribution of resources and rewards when the external stakeholders they "represented" were considered the most important. But the connection between self-interest and subgroup "success" was never acknowledged by anyone. Self-interest was not a legitimate reason for taking any position; hence, members of senior management were forever seeking ways to package their interests in terms of those external to AMPA.

The internal taboo that said "one must not be selfish" was very striking to Jansen as an observer. It was as though doing something for self—or, in this case, for the group that one was responsible for—would be automatically viewed as not being for the company as a whole. And "anyone not for the company was disloyal and therefore not deserving of the position that he or she occupied." It was as though everyone was obliged to adopt a personally sacrificial position to be seen as acting in the service of AMPA. Hence, when a vice-president wanted to push his or her own agenda, for whatever reason, the only legitimate way was to look around for some external stakeholder who would benefit from this and present the issue as the champion of that stakeholder's concern. Whether the particular stakeholder felt this way or not was apparently irrelevant. So long as the other AMPA vice-presidents could be so convinced, then the issue was accepted as legitimate.

To Jansen, this practice seemed insidious, and he felt that the senior management group needed to break out of this pattern and to start interacting with each other in a more grounded way. It seemed that this group was having its internal fights by setting up somewhat fictitious figures on the outside, presenting their interests as contradictory, and then fighting on their behalf, independent of whether or not those outsiders' feelings were accurately characterized. Jansen hypothesized that the taboo on "talking about being selfish" was stopping this senior management group from being straight with each other and was setting up an artificial split between what is "good for the parts" versus what is "good for the whole," and he decided to intervene by suggesting that they discuss how one might go about "being selfish" in this organization if they were so inclined.

"A selfish person wouldn't last long at AMPA," someone replied.

"Would they get fired?" Jansen asked.

"No. But they would be made so uncomfortable that they would simply leave."

"That seems a rather vicious way to get rid of someone!" Jansen ventured. "What's so wrong with firing someone outright simply on the grounds that he or she doesn't fit in?"

"Because it is hard to fire someone; it's so much easier for everyone if the misfit simply leaves!"

Jansen offered, "That seems understandable enough, but it also sounds incredibly selfish!"

Stunned silence.

Then someone asked, "What does that comment mean?"

"It seems that getting rid of someone can be experienced as being rather destructive—it's like wounding someone! To do that and not have to face the fact that the person in question has been hurt by AMPA is a rather selfish way of doing business! It sure seems to lack courage! This sounds like a way for people to protect themselves from looking at the destructive sides of their actions. That sounds selfish—very understandable but, nevertheless, selfish. The less selfish thing would seem to be to fire the person outright and face the pain of being confronted by his or her anger and the possible implications there were for AMPA!"

In this last intervention, Jansen was trying to tip the selfishness theme on its head by proposing that maybe "avoiding being selfish" was being mistaken for "being kind" and that they were actually acting out of selfishness but with a veneer of denial. Jansen did not know for sure what responses would be triggered, but he was convinced that they would reveal much about what was transpiring at the hidden level.

The exchange stirred a lengthy conversation about how most things at AMPA were done in a roundabout way. Jansen again asked how they might act if they were to be selfish. The response was, "Fight for your own interests without taking into account that others might be hurt by your gains!" This broke the "conspiracy of silence." In no time, both subgroups started accusing each other of doing just that. When the heightened volume in the room made it obvious that this was not going to be quickly driven underground again, Jansen asked each subgroup

to go off by itself for a while and to identify how it acted selfishly with justification and how it acted selfishly without justification. After completing this task, each subgroup was to list
how it saw the other subgroup behaving, using the same categories. After considerable time in the subgroups, everyone reassembled to share what was on their respective lists. This
proved to be a rather playful time. Each party felt freed up to
state directly what it thought of the other. It also became transparent that, while it was easy to see "unjustified selfishness" in
the other subgroup's behavior, it was hard to acknowledge its
presence in one's own subgroup.

Jansen suggested that their investment in always constru-
ing their actions to be for the "good of the AMPA as a whole"
might be serving no one's interest, that there was no reason why
a group's self-interest could not, on occasion, overlap with the
collective interests, and that refusing to allow this possibility
was robbing them of the opportunity to collectively learn about
the relationship between the interests of the whole and the interests of the part. The meeting ended, and all agreed to re-
assemble next week at their regularly scheduled time.

The Computer Fiasco

The next meeting of the senior management group was
hard to get started. It was as though there was resistance to getting back to where the group had been the previous week. The
board meeting that had stirred the anxious discussion the previous week had taken place, and there was lighthearted chatter
about the ramifications of two of its decisions. The implications to Jansen as an outsider seemed large, but no one was
speaking about them with any passion. It was as though all affect had been drained from the group. Jansen suspected that
behind this cool and nonchalant facade were deep emotions
that were being kept in check. The chief executive officer opened
the meeting with the proposal that they set an agenda of the
things that needed to be discussed following the last meeting
and the gathering of the board. This was a standard format following board meetings.

From the outset, it had been agreed that the normal work of this senior management group would continue while Jansen was involved with them. From time to time, Jansen would pause to reflect with them on what he saw happening when he thought this might be useful. At other times, he would simply sit as a silent observer. Jansen felt that it was important for them as a group to determine when to take time out to reflect on their actions. He had surmised that this group, like most having difficulty with authority, would find it hard to say "no" when they meant "no" and to mean "yes" when they said "yes." It would hurt no one if they practiced this art on him and the relationship he was about to develop with them. By this time, he had framed the work as an attempt to increase the collective capacity of AMPA as a whole to learn from its experience, to self-correct midstream if necessary, and to bolster the organization's capacity to store, remember, and retrieve its experiences in a meaningful way so that it could act out of a better understanding of both its internal and its external environments.

The meeting stumbled to a start. Laurent Pries was finding it difficult to get anyone to pick up on his initiatives. The vice-presidents, to a person, seemed as though they would prefer to be somewhere else. Jansen sat silently musing over whether something had recently occurred, maybe even at the board meeting, that had stirred the vice-presidents' anger toward Pries, since what was now in evidence seemed to be an outbreak of passive-aggressiveness, a sign of repressed anger. He backed away from this thought, because it just seemed a little too simplistic, even if there were some truth in it. Eventually someone said that they needed to discuss the ongoing problems of the new computer that had been installed. There were audible groans and eyeball rolling. Pries was quick to jump in. Developing a shared agenda for this meeting suddenly faded in importance for him. "You mean we haven't got that machine working right yet!" The next ten minutes were a barrage of complaints directed obliquely at the vice-president for administration, whose area was responsible, among other things, for AMPA's computing services. The content of these complaints was not particularly relevant. Their tone was worth attending to, though, because the comments seemed outrageously vindictive. No one appeared interested in improving their collective understanding of what was going wrong, what might be done to make things better, how various departments could help to alleviate an obviously horrible situation. The focus was on complaining, as if calculated to belittle one of their group, the vice-president for administration. Jansen began to wonder about the scapegoating energy in the room. The vice-president for administration was asked to explain what was happening, but, as he spoke, it was obvious that no one intended to listen to him.

Jansen subsequently learned that the installation of the new computer system, designed to store all information, personnel records, quality measures, inventory, production schedules, budgets, financial indicators, and so on, had contained a trap from the beginning. When this was eventually talked about, everyone claimed that no one was consciously attempting to sabotage the system, but the metaphoric fingerprints of several of the vice-presidents could be found all over the failure of the new computing system. It seemed that, from the outset, someone had decided that the new computer should be introduced in two phases. No problem. The vice-president for finance had volunteered to have his department incorporated second, because, as he claimed, "we already have a great system operating on our own computer. The financial procedures are straightforward and can be easily grafted on, once the more difficult software systems are up and running." Still no problem. A computer software consulting group was hired and briefed but was not told of the plan to include financial records. So the consulting group proceeded to design the architecture of the program with no awareness that it would be expected to eventually "house AMPA's financial world" as well. When this "oversight" was discovered, the reworking of the programming structure was set back many weeks. The error was so troublesome that someone needed to be held accountable for it, and *all* the finger pointing went toward the vice-president for administration.

After three meetings, Jansen noticed a curious pattern: when senior management was upset about something unidentifiable, the computer would be mentioned, detonating a mini-explosion that landed at the doorstep of the vice-president for administration. Jansen wondered what this group would do if the computer worked. He suspected that they would be lost, because the repository for these confused and murky emotions would have been taken away; could it be that another fiasco would be created to fill the role occupied by the computer? With that thought came the recognition that the computer problem might have been "created," albeit without their conscious awareness, to fulfill this function. He asked himself what emotion he himself would feel if he were one of them during a "dump on the computer and the vice-president for administration" routine. His reaction was that he would have been angry at Laurent Pries, leading him to hypothesize that the computer might be a smokescreen to camouflage their feelings (Jansen suspected angry ones) toward Pries. The vice-president for administration was being scapegoated, not viciously, but scapegoated nonetheless, and it would only be a matter of time before he would start to show signs of burnout.

The remainder of this meeting and the next two meetings dealt with "everyday administrative housekeeping," punctuated by an occasional outburst about the computer system. Jansen made no comments in these meetings but was busy formulating hypotheses about the role of the computer as a smokescreen and its links to repressed anger and scapegoating.

"It's Lonely Up Here!"

Jansen decided to stay within a paradoxical frame. Rather than address anything about what he suspected was the outgrowth of the vice-presidents' anger at Pries, he assumed that Pries's relationship with them was contributing to their keeping their anger at him unexpressed. So Jansen's next initiative was to try to explore with Pries, in private conversations, Pries's "apparent reticence" about his subordinates' expressing their anger. Raising this promised to be complex, but a nonthreatening way was to explore senior management's system of evaluation. Jansen thought that if Pries was afraid of the vice-presidents' anger—actually not their anger per se, but rather the consequences for everyone and AMPA as a whole if that anger were expressed—it might come through in how he dealt with giving his senior staff feedback during evaluation and salary review.

So Pries and Jansen began to talk about Pries's views of each of his subordinates: what he saw to be their respective strengths and weaknesses, what he imagined were their views of *his* strengths and weaknesses, how these were communicated, and so forth. Interestingly, three things emerged: (1) Pries was very unsure of what three of his vice-presidents thought of him; (2) he was eager to be seen as a "nurturing and supportive" boss, as in the "good old days"; and (3) he tried to avoid saying things at review times that could be construed as negative—"always accentuate the positive, and let the negative be self-evident in contrast" was his slogan. Jansen could see the chief executive officer's reluctance to have the complex emotions between him and his vice-presidents expressed. This, he suspected, would make it difficult for subordinates to be angry with Pries directly. The conversation prompted Pries to be curious about whether his view of the relationships he had described was accurate.

Jansen asked Pries, "How might you find out?"

"I have no idea!"

"Have you thought about discussing it with each vice-president directly?"

"No!"

"It must feel very lonely being so unable to talk about these issues."

This touched a chord. Pries went into a long account of how this was an inevitable part of AMPA's growth and that, while he had liked the earlier days when everyone knew well where each of them stood on all issues, that era was past. Jansen repeated his comment about loneliness. After a brief choking in Pries's voice, he told Jansen about the loneliness of his boyhood and how much he had missed his mother when she died in his late teens. The conversations that spun out of this exchange were continued across two further meetings. During this time, Jansen was thinking about how to help Pries feel his personal strength so that if the vice-presidents did acknowledge their anger at him directly, he would be able to absorb it and deal with it in a way that communicated that having such feelings was legitimate, a precursor to a sense of being authorized. In a paradoxical frame, Jansen was seeing their refusal to express anger directly and their covert resistance of Pries to be undermining their collective capacity to understand what was behind their resistance, which in turn was holding them back from the necessary launching into uncharted waters.

Jansen thought that it was possible that the vice-presidents were feeling dependent on Pries and were angry at him for those feelings but could not work out a way to free themselves from this bind. He thought that if the chief executive officer were strong enough to accept and absorb their anger, irrespective of the justifiability of their directing it at him, then the vice-presidents might come to understand something about their dependencies on him, a precursor to affirming their respective interdependencies with each other. This, Jansen reasoned, would give them at least a chance to break out of the cycle of undermining each other in which they had become so invested.

After Pries and Jansen had met three times, Pries asked for guidance about how to proceed. He was feeling impatient for some movement. Jansen suggested that there might be value in interviewing the vice-presidents to ask them the same questions about how they saw their own respective strengths and weaknesses and how they imagined that Pries saw them. Jansen told him that he thought so much energy was being poured into keeping feelings hidden that what was being kept out of sight might be significantly less dangerous than the explosive forces incubating in the effort to keep them hidden. Jansen could not know this for sure, though, and proposed that he himself talk with the vice-presidents as a precursor for further action. Pries agreed but said that he was afraid not everyone would be honest with Jansen and that, if they were, there might be some hurt feelings. Jansen responded by asking whether Pries felt that he himself had been honest in their conversations and, if not, why and, if so, why he imagined others might not talk as frankly. Actually, Jansen was delighted that Pries was so clear and direct in expressing his fears. Pries replied that he had felt he had been honest but that it had been hard "to be even that honest with myself, let alone you." Jansen said he thought that each person would have to struggle with the honesty question and that being confronted with this issue would benefit everyone. Pries was excited by this thought and suggested that Jansen proceed.

The Vice-Presidents' Views

When the vice-presidents were interviewed, two overwhelming issues surfaced. First, they felt that over the past three or four years Laurent Pries had become increasingly inaccessible to them. They understood why, but they felt that the organization had not been changed to distribute the authority and associated responsibilities to compensate for his unavailability. This, in their view, represented Pries's reluctance to accept others' authority, and it created intolerable bottlenecks at his office door. They experienced themselves as less and less able to work out what he wanted from them, yet they felt increasingly pressured to take more initiatives but with no ideas on how to combine their initiatives to avoid working at cross purposes.

Secondly, they felt the lack of feedback about their respective areas' contribution (or lack thereof) to AMPA's profitability. Their view was that the struggle between profit and quality was real but that there were no data to support either side of the argument. "We don't even have profit centers around here; if we did, then we would know who is right in this battle of profit versus quality! It's almost as though everyone is invested in keeping the answer to that question clouded over. What would we do with ourselves, the parts of us that seem to have to fight with each other, if we could actually produce an appropriate mix of profit and quality!" Jansen was reminded at this point of the descriptions provided in the therapy literature of families in "schizophrenic transaction," as Selvini Palazzoli, Boscolo, Cecchin, and Prata (1978) call it. Members of a family in schizophrenic transaction all work to keep the situation ill defined so that no solutions or resolutions can ever be created.

Heavy taboos are created that make the underlying dynamics undiscussible.

Interestingly, some of the vice-presidents were against the idea of profit centers, presumably because their departments would come out looking worse than the others if such data existed. When Jansen delved a little deeper into this, however, it seemed rather clear that those *in favor* of profit centers were in fact the ones most vulnerable to the data that would surface, whereas those who had reservations were the ones sure to come out looking good. This seemed very curious until it occurred to Jansen that maybe the battle between the profit and quality "camps" was some type of compensation system. Perhaps those "for" quality were the ones feeling most guilty about the level of profits that AMPA was making and were a little afraid that in reality they were "ripping off" the customer by producing a product that looked better than it really was. Their constant pushing of the quality issue was easy to do, because there was another faction looking after, as it were, the profit side. As a result, those speaking for quality but who deep down were actually as concerned about the profits as anyone else could be assured that the profit levels would be maintained, so they were free to garner the good feelings associated with being champions of quality. Thus, this subgroup was really invested in keeping the profit subgroup's position strong while acting as though they were trying to undermine it. Meanwhile, those outwardly identified with profit were very involved in undermining the position of the quality subgroup, because they felt contemptuous of the quality subgroup's "self-righteousness." The feeling was "they want all the benefits of our profitability but don't want to look like or feel as greedy as they act. I tell you, if we ever had to cut back around here, they would be the last to volunteer to make real cuts." So the "profit" subgroup resisted vigorously the "quality" subgroup because they did not like their self-righteousness; hence the investment in keeping everything ill defined.

The particular power of these thoughts for Jansen was that they opened up a new way of understanding why and how AMPA's senior management were so endlessly stuck in circles going nowhere, despite all the energy poured into making prog-

ress. Jansen was struck also by the unimportance of the original
questions he had started these interviews with—the relative
strengths and weaknesses they saw each other as having—though
it was clear that everyone's lack of knowledge about their relative standing with each other and their respective value to
AMPA as a whole remained absolutely central. Jansen decided
that the most useful thing he could do next was to help them
unfold the many layers that had them invested in keeping their
various positions on the profit issue clouded. He believed that
this would be a way to release some of the paradoxical binds
they had encased themselves in with their internal splits over
profit versus quality. It was unclear what such a release would
produce, but it was certain to throw them out of the grooves
that they were in.

The Task Force

At the next senior management meeting, Jansen suggested the value of exploring the various profit and cost profiles
for different parts of the organization. This emerged from his
reasoning that, while it was important to continue exploring the
relationships among internal parts of the organization, for the
time being it would be best to keep away from the subgroup issues that had been surfacing, the fights that had gone down
over the computer, the various hostilities felt toward Laurent
Pries, the reluctance to distribute responsibilities differently as
a result of changing authority patterns, and so forth. Jansen
thought that those issues would come out soon enough but that
for the moment it was more appropriate to get a larger organizational frame in place so that the struggles among the parts could
have some clearer context, which the vice-presidents could use
for drawing the essential linkages among their activities. Jansen
knew that they would have to actually work on issues central to
their relationships with each other while attending to the
themes relevant to AMPA as a whole, and this provided a way
for Jansen to keep out of struggles he could feel himself getting
drawn into.

Jansen proposed that this assignment be thought of not

in terms of who might end up with more or fewer resources or what would become the next growth center within AMPA but as a means of understanding how the organization's collective blind spots tended to grow. He reasoned with the group that their investment in keeping where profits were coming from and where resources were going unclear was having the undesirable consequence that *all* decisions were being made on the basis of internal politics, which led to the seeking of behind-the-scenes deals with the chief executive officer, which kept the waters of their relations with each other excessively muddied and reinforced the very patterns of authority distribution that they were complaining about.

Jansen knew that it would be hard to do this work, because the computer system was not functioning in the way planned, which of course was originally meant to produce the very data needed to explore this issue. He thought that it was possible that senior management might be unconsciously sabotaging the attempts being made via the new computer system to develop the information that would eventually throw them out of the cycle that was proving to be so problematic. It was obvious that many struggles would have to be engaged simply to decide what proportions of collective costs to allocate to which work division and so on. This intervention was designed to break the pattern of spoiling for fights that no one would ever have and to trigger their approaching the shared resistances located in the computer system—to creep, as it were, behind those resistances by coming at the issue another way. Jansen suspected that if the task force could uncover the critical data, the value in undermining the computer system would be taken away and problems that were simply technical in nature would be readily fixed. This proved to be the case. Over the next few weeks, there were very few conversations about the computer; there were no public ritualized gyrations about the computer and "floggings" of the vice-president for administration; to everyone's surprise, the elusive technical solutions suddenly appeared.

The next few weeks around AMPA were difficult. However, there was a sense that critical work was occurring. The "reorganization task force" was like a new elite in that its potential influence was seen as enormous, which was true only at a perceptual level and then only because of the way everyone had colluded in keeping the situation ambiguously defined. One surprise that surfaced was that the divisions that had been most vocal about quality were the ones actually bringing in the largest profits. Hence, the position of profit *or* quality began to lose its power as a symbol, and an old pattern of thinking was destroyed. Subtle but significant shifts in alliances were triggered by this revelation, making several vice-presidents nervous about how their units would be seen in the future and how resources would be allocated as a result. This immediately gave a groundedness and authenticity to feelings of anxiety, as opposed to the various imaginary anxieties that had existed in their relations with each other for so long.

As the task force finished its work, there was a lot of interest in the possibility of some organizational restructuring. This posed a different kind of threat, because it was impossible to know in advance whose departments would benefit and whose would suffer in any reorganization. Jansen was also nervous about this, because he sensed that each vice-president was assuming that a new structure would remove the problems they had been having with each other. That is, it seemed probable that they would seek a structural solution as a substitute for the necessary hard work of wading through the difficult processes that would enable them to grow as a collectivity. While Jansen was sure that his caution about this was well founded, another reality was equally convincing. They were invested in not falling back into the same old patterns with each other. Some new type of energy was being released, and they wanted to capitalize on it.

Several new organizational structures were proposed, four of which were to be explored seriously. Two could be effected internally by the chief executive officer in concert with the senior management group; but two had implications that the board would have to deal with, so that the ultimate decision would have to be theirs. There was some reticence to kick the issue up to the board level because of doubts about the board's

awareness of the key issues and the possibility of their making a
decision that would not be management's preferred option. In
Jansen's thinking, this was an important event, because it was
forcing senior management to confront their reservations about
the quality of direction they were getting from the board. He
felt sure that many issues around authorizing would be stirred
and that the group would get a chance to see how senior management helped to authorize the board to make high-quality decisions and how it deauthorized the board and therefore itself.
The issue, Jansen felt sure, would be whether the board would
be given maximum information in readily digestible form so
that it could delve into the issues and make the decisions appropriate to its authority position, or whether management would
try to make the decision itself and politically set it up so that its
desires would be the only option the board was able to take
seriously.

These possibilities surfaced in the minds of the senior
management group as they started the debate, and Jansen cau-
tioned them to be careful not to deauthorize themselves by deauthorizing the board. It was a little hard for them to grasp
what he was driving at, but ultimately they caught onto the idea
that there was certain work that they had to do and certain
work that the board had to do, that the line between these was
rather fine, but that everyone would be impoverished if their
parts were not done fully. This was a somewhat new thought to
many of the vice-presidents, who had found it so difficult across
the years to see the board in anything other than adversarial
terms.

"I'm For the Group!"

As senior management commenced its work on restructuring proposals, informal word was sent to the board to expect, at its next meeting, an agenda item involving the possible
restructuring of AMPA. The board's response was interesting.
No one attempted to speak with Laurent Pries. Rather, they
sought out one of the younger vice-presidents, Vince Broadbent. He had a high profile and was occasionally mentioned as

a future chief executive officer when Pries retired, an event that was still years away. The board's informal contacting of Broadbent felt strange to him, and he experienced it as potentially very undermining of both Laurent Pries and the senior management as a whole. Broadbent immediately called a special meeting of the senior management group to tell them that this had occurred and that he had resolved to have no contact with the board other than via Laurent Pries, senior management's spokesperson.

The group was surprised by this action. It had been common for the board to use both formal and informal channels, and the vice-presidents were prone to do this themselves in their relationships with subordinates. In general, they were very reluctant to ever look at the consequences of this, how their immediate subordinates might feel undermined, how they regularly sent messages down through the system that said "use the formal channels or use backdoor methods as you see fit." They had picked up on modern rhetoric about "managing by walking around," responding, of course, to years of frustration caused by formal channels that did not work. Everyone was so convinced that the formal system would not work that they immediately took actions to circumvent that system, thereby weakening it so that it was never even given a chance to work, and then, naturally enough, using the resulting failure as justification for the circumvention.

Broadbent's action created a lively debate within the senior management group. Someone ventured the interpretation that Pries might not have been contacted because he was seen as a very powerful figure and thus potentially an adversary for the board in these restructuring deliberations. This statement was laughed at, almost as if to imply the opposite, though no one said anything to this effect. Someone then suggested that perhaps the board was trying a "divide-and-conquer" strategy— "after all, what a stroke of genius if they could get half of us feeling loyal to Laurent Pries and the other half loyal to Vince Broadbent!" To Jansen, the interesting thing was that the senior managers were looking only at the side of this that implied combat with the board. "It's almost as though you as a group want to have a fight, but it is unclear what the battle would be about. Is there something particular you want to have out with the board, and, if so, what is it?" But the thing Jansen was really wondering about was "how it felt to have one of your group say so boldly that he was placing the interests of the group as a whole ahead of any of the personal kudos he could derive by building stronger personal and informal links to the board. And, in particular, what does it feel like to have this level of visible support for Pries expressed in a time of such considerable uncertainty?"

Jansen's strategy at this moment was to confront the group behaviorally with the paradoxical interpretation that their investment in an external fight might be a flight from the terrifying internal group feelings that were arising from the intimacy that came when an influential individual supported rather than undermined Pries and affirmed the group's importance at a time when he was being singled out as individually important. Jansen felt that if they could see how their fear of group unity and intimacy was stimulating their undermining of authority and their search for an external group fight, new patterns of thought and action might be possible.

This set the metaphoric "cat among the pigeons." For the next hour, this group had a conversation about things never before discussed openly, including people's feelings about not knowing when Pries was representing his own view on issues or when he was acting as the agent of the board and implementing their wishes; the reluctance of anyone to point out when someone was doing a poor job; the feeling that the company was driven more by history and precedent than by reasoned positions; the fear that the only way to get ahead was to be an "insider" in an informal club whose membership was always ambiguous; the sense that supporting Pries would be viewed as being a "yes person," while opposing him would be viewed as being a "rebel looking for a cause"; a sense that the more energy they put into AMPA, the more frustrated they got with its "immovability"; the feeling that the board was too old to learn about the contemporary issues facing AMPA; Pries's sense that the vice-presidents sought his advice but were reluctant to follow it when it went counter to their wishes; the overwhelming frustration of having too much work and not enough time to do it; and their anger about their inability or refusal to set priorities.

At the end of the meeting, there was an amazing sense of relief, as though pent-up emotions of the years had been expressed. The conversation had commenced with a very acrimonious tone, but, by the end, members of the group were no longer complaining but rather were simply talking with each other about their experiences in the group and AMPA. Pries, who had started the meeting feeling defensive, commented at the end that he felt refreshed by the openness of the discussion. Most importantly, the group made the decision to work on the restructuring proposals together and to create a subcommittee of three, including Pries and Broadbent, to manage the relations with the board around these proposals and to keep the senior management group informed.

From a paradoxical point of view, the action of Broadbent to interpret his being approached by the board not solely as an individual event but as one with enormous group and intergroup implications led to numerous outcomes that were beneficial to everyone. It brought increased support for Pries in particular and the role of the chief executive officer in general rather than diminishing both the individual and the position. It helped the senior management group as a whole to affirm its groupness, and it opened up exploration of topics that this group desperately needed to discuss. It augmented Broadbent's position in the group while heightening the importance of others at the same time. It highlighted the need to build a different kind of link between the board and senior management to facilitate their relationship during this period, and it prevented the group from mindlessly fighting with the board and helped it to examine the tensions in its own group.

"We've Got a Preference"

The next few weeks were spent studying the implications of the various restructuring options. Senior management was gravitating toward a particular option for reasons that were not completely clear, but the flavor of the conversation indicated that members of the group believed that this would give AMPA management greater freedom and autonomy from the wishes of the board. For some reason, this group was feeling that such an outcome was desirable. Jansen ventured the interpretation that "going for" more independence from the board might get them less independence in the long run. He reasoned that their motive of less connectedness with the board would be so transparent that, irrespective of the merits of that particular structuring option, the board would reject it in a kneejerk manner and force an option that was more restrictive to management's autonomy. Jansen suggested that if senior management went the other way and looked at how being dependent on the board would be beneficial for all concerned, rather than how it would be detrimental, other reasoning would probably result, and the relationship with the board could be enriched simultaneously. Senior management accepted Jansen's comment and worked for a while on the option that would build on their dependency rather than deny it.

Interestingly, they again came up with the same option. Jansen commented that it was ironic that the option they had seen as giving them "less autonomy" was also the one that seemed to offer more possibilities for constructive interdependence with the board. He wondered aloud what this might be telling them. After a while, the group began to talk about the restructuring possibilities in terms of how the various organs and levels of AMPA would benefit under each of the restructuring plans. This led to the creation of a very full grid identifying the various consequences, positive and negative, for all groups in AMPA, the board included. When this was completed, senior management found that they had a clear preference.

The question was what to do with the information on the grid and the senior management's preference. Initially, the decision was simply to give the board one recommendation with the reasons supporting it and a catalogue of the shortcomings of all the other potential options. The right decision, they felt, was so evident that it would be wasting the board's time to ask them to review all the relevant materials. After deciding this, someone asked what they were being so defensive about. Was this an attempt to avoid having the board decide? If this were remotely a motive, the senior management group acknowledged, it would constitute a refusal to accept their own followership role, which would ultimately deauthorize both the board and themselves. They eventually decided to give the board a complete summary of all the pros and cons of each option and to accept whatever the board decided.

This was a very interesting moment in their evolution as a group. But Jansen was a little less sure that they would accept the outcome if the board came up with a decision that differed from their own choice. Still, he thought that the learning that would result for everyone if this happened would benefit AMPA as a whole. So he said nothing.

The Board's Reluctance

The board was given the relevant information, and every one awaited its response. From senior management's viewpoint, this board meeting went poorly. Board members argued about many trivial issues, refused to engage the decision-making task at hand, indicated a preference for an option that management did not like, concocted another option, and instructed Pries to provide the relevant information to enable this new option to be evaluated.

When senior management reassembled, they were in a strange mood. Some of them were furious at the board and were very acrimonious about having believed that the board would be competent to decide. Others were less hostile, suggesting that maybe the board was just having a bad day. Pries was philosophical. "For years I've watched that board. They never grab a good idea straight out. They invariably take two steps backward before they take three steps forward. This is all so new to them, and they need time to try on the various options. Though I must admit I think next time we should go to them with our preference clearly stated." After some struggle, senior management fell in behind the position that Pries was presenting, although there were a few moments when it looked like they would erupt into a fight.

Jansen found this to be interesting, for it often happens that when a group enters a serious exchange with another group and comes away without getting what it wants, it splits internally and starts to fight with itself. To overcome the internal split, the group adopts a combative stance with the group that it feels beaten by, making, of course, the external battle a displacement for the internal one. He was impressed on this occasion that senior management did not fall for this trap. It was also striking that they listened so intently to Pries, accepting that his long experience with the board gave him a wisdom worth respecting. And Broadbent, whose influence in the group was growing almost daily, was not pulled into a polarized position vis-à-vis Pries. He willingly took a back seat, and the group let him do this.

Jansen had never met the board, had very little information about its members, and knew virtually nothing about its history. But theory suggested that it probably had its own difficulties struggling with the paradoxes that we have been discussing in this book and that the board members might well have to manage splits in their own group before they could come to any decision about the restructuring proposal. Jansen resolved to find out more. However, circumstances were such that he could not visit AMPA again until just two days before the next board meeting, when presumably the restructuring would be discussed again and possibly decided upon.

Two days before the next board meeting, Jansen met with the three-person management subcommittee handling board-management relations, the one that included Pries and Broadbent. Pries seemed amazingly anxious. Despite his earlier philosophical position, he now wanted to take a hard line. His position was "let's go in there and tell them what we want, present the arguments, and try to force a decision!" Jansen was somewhat amazed and felt that it was time for a strong intervention. He asked Pries what he was so afraid of and why he was being so combative. After much probing, the following facts emerged. The discussion turned into a very emotional event for everyone.

"Keepers of the Faith"

Pries had been brought to AMPA by Barry Argos, a very charismatic man who had been a towering figure in this industry. Argos had been a significant mentor to Pries and had provided him numerous opportunities to obtain the experience that prepared him for the role of chief executive officer, an appointment that Argos had orchestrated while he was chairperson of AMPA's board. A triangle made up of Pries, Argos, and another mentee, Chris Rolland, who also served on the board, had totally transformed AMPA from a fledgling company into a giant. Argos was a visionary who managed to capture the imagination of many people, and this triangle was very much like a father and two adopted sons. When Argos had died of a sudden heart attack five years earlier, everyone had been eager to continue playing out the dream that he had begun. Rolland was the logical person to take over as chairperson and, together with Pries, had "kept Argos alive" by continuing to build AMPA into a memorial to him. Neither Pries nor Rolland was a visionary like Argos, and in most ways they were more than willing to simply play the role of custodians of the organization that they had inherited. They were dedicated to "keep the faith" as good "sons of Argos."

This had caused no problem, because "AMPA had been built on rock, its architect knew how to create wonderfully gracious moments out of angles and lines, and the construction overseer had made sure every brick was laid by a craftsman," as the eulogist had said of Argos at his funeral. But that was five years ago, and time was marching on. While Pries and Rolland were happy to continue as the enacters of the Argos dream, they both had ideas of their own, ambitions that needed to be fulfilled. The relevance of this was perhaps a little more acute for Pries, since Rolland spent only a small portion of his life on AMPA affairs, having a whole career of his own as director of the Argos Center for the Performing Arts, named after the benefactor whose death had brought such an infusion of money that a small community theater company was in the process of being transformed into a major performing and educational facility. So for Rolland, the issue of producing some structural change in AMPA meant something different from what it meant for Pries. Pries had not quite brought this into consciousness, but change for him meant the possibility of deviating from the course set by Argos. The question was whether changes could be seen as building a fuller embodiment of the Argos vision or whether they would mean taking the organization along a different path. If the latter, how would he deal with the part of him invested in "keeping the faith of the father"?

Many questions came to Jansen's mind as he heard this story, but his greatest concern was that somehow Pries would take on the role of advocating change and innovation and that Rolland would be pulled into preserving what Argos would have wanted. If this happened, Jansen predicted, the board and senior management would simply become pitted against each other in a power struggle that would be an acting out of tensions that had been created in the Pries-Rolland relationship as they continued to do homage to their dead mentor. Jansen did not think that Pries was ready to look at or understand this possibility, but he wanted to try to avert a fight at the board meeting that would set in concrete a pattern that might take an eternity to recover from.

Jansen suggested to Pries that the board needed time to reflect and that to push a decision too quickly would be folly, despite senior management's impatience about "getting on with the future." He said that he felt sure that as the board struggled with reorganization issues it would be tempting for Pries and Rolland to begin to fight. If Pries found his own fighting instincts welling up within him, Jansen suggested he get suspicious and back off from the fight, even if it meant that the board might decide on an option that Pries would find hard to accept or live with. Jansen felt hopeful that if Pries and Rolland could hold off from fighting at this time, it would be possible to get into the deeper issues in a way that would be helpful to AMPA in the long term. Accordingly, he suggested that Pries's own role be merely one of attempting to orchestrate as full an exploration as possible of all options, and Pries agreed.

The board meeting turned out to be hard for Pries, because the board was very feisty, and, sure enough, Rolland was eager to tear holes in the thinking that senior management had presented as to why restructuring was necessary. Pries had done a good job holding back and not taking the bait, although afterwards he was very angry at Broadbent, who he felt had not spoken up nearly as strongly as he might in presenting senior management's views. However, the board finished the meeting recognizing the need to study the issues further. The reports of this meeting confirmed for Jansen that the board had many internal dynamics that they had to work through before they would be in a condition to make a decision.

An Intervention

Jansen decided that it was time to take an initiative. He suggested that he have a meeting with Pries and Rolland, to get a firsthand experience of the tensions in their relationship and to explore a way that they could integrate the respective roles that they carried from the Argos legacy, rather than mutually tearing at the fabric of this organization they loved. Pries agreed to such a meeting; when Jansen called Rolland to introduce himself and the proposal, he got a favorable response to the idea.

The meeting turned into a special event. The two men talked about the history of AMPA and the dilemmas that they now faced. Jansen thought that it was possible that the two of them could get caught in the paradox of creativity: that one would espouse the need to move on while the other would get locked into the position of trying to preserve the past as a way of continuing to honor their dead mentor. He also feared that their failure to understand this dynamic could lead to the board's adopting, on Rolland's behalf, the "preserve the status quo" position while senior management would push the "it's time to change" perspective on Pries's behalf. Jansen said this to them directly. It rang a bell. It was true that Rolland felt more than Pries the burden to keep AMPA in the form Argos had left it in. They were, however, quickly able to agree that Argos would have wanted the company to continue to grow and that he had entrusted them to mold the organization as they saw fit as well as to carry on the traditions he had left them with.

The fascinating issue that emerged in this conversation was that the board had a split within it as potent as the one in the senior management group. Rolland indicated that there were three members of the board who had been appointed since Argos's death and who had no investment in the intense emotional legacy that Pries and Rolland were carrying. These three board members were all for change, but they felt that Pries was not going far enough in his proposals for reorganizing. They felt that he was too conservative and accordingly resisted his proposals because they were insufficiently radical. The other board members had rejected their extreme views, so that the board became stuck and felt angry at senior management for putting them in this position. None of this had come through to Pries. All he had seen was the resistance of the board, the "radical trio" included, and he had coded everyone's response in the same category of "reluctance to support change." Rolland pointed out that these three board members in fact saw both Rolland and Pries to be the problem. The core difference between Pries and Rolland ("advocate of change" and "preserver of the status quo," respectively) was very small in the eyes of others, who saw instead their alikeness—namely, "fixation on serving their dead mentor."

At this point, Jansen began to recognize the special irony associated with those wanting change. Sometimes people's hopes for change are so intense that they will reject the small opportunities being offered because they do not match the levels of change desired. They fear that to accept a small change will be to "sell out" on their hopes for larger transformations; hence the resistance to change by those most outspoken about the need for it. Of course, such a posture unwittingly makes conservatives out of those presenting themselves as radicals, because there always seem to be fundamental inadequacies in what is being proposed, leading to the imperative to reject the initiatives of those in authority, or to reject the authority, in the hope that something more significant might be forthcoming.

However, the authorities, sensing only the resistances, see these individuals as not supportive of change and therefore as one more obstacle to overcome when anything new is to be considered. Both parties invested in change fall into a conundrum of their collective making without any recognition of their mutual roles in creating the very thing that they are attempting to alter.

After significant conversation, Pries and Rolland recognized the need (1) to collaboratively authorize their relationship to move from being merely the preservers of an earlier dream to shapers of a future that might deviate from that dream and (2) to work *with* rather than *against* the splits in both the board and the senior management group. They agreed that the restructuring had to be done together and that it should not be viewed as the burden of the senior management *or* the board. They proposed the creation of a joint board–senior management committee, to be chaired by Broadbent, to bring the decision to the next stage. This happened without fanfare, and three months later a restructuring that had not been in the mind of senior management or the board when this event began was implemented, with the explicit support of everyone.

Implications for Action

The case just presented is not exclusively about the application of paradoxical theory to an organizational dilemma, but aspects of the case and the consultant's behavior illustrate a number of issues that arise as one applies a paradoxical perspective to common problems in groups. In this final section, we discuss some of these issues to begin an articulation of a theory of action based on a paradoxical conception of group life.

Attending to the "Fault" Lines. The key to the discovery of the important paradoxical issues in this case was attention to the "splits" that existed inside the senior management group, inside the board, and between the management group and the board. We can think of these splits as occurring along fault lines, or issues that separate two sides from each other. The double meaning of the term *fault* also applies, because the splits that divide a group are often accompanied by a great deal of blame. By attending to the issues that are surrounded with strong and reciprocal blame, one is likely to discover the processes of splitting and projection, which point to the self-referential contradiction of paradox.

In this case, there were many such splits: between the profit subgroup and the quality subgroup, between the board and the management group, between selfishness and selflessness, between Pries and Rolland, between the factions on the board, and even between the "good old days" and the present. Through the consultant's eyes, many of these splits turned out to have their roots in common paradoxical tensions, and it was through the cumulative attention to and exploration of each of these fault lines that the connections and meaning became clearer.

The splits deserve attention also because their presence suggests that both sides, and therefore the group or system as a whole, are likely to experience events and perceive information in terms of the issues dividing them. This ethnocentrism means that the subgroups will have difficulty seeing their similarities and equal difficulty seeing their internal differences. The blame that surrounds these splits makes it even more unlikely that a subgroup will acknowledge its connections to another subgroup.

In the AMPA case, the causes of these splits could be traced to a variety of sources, including the company's rapid growth, the senior management's displacement of its internal tensions, the conflict over how much change the organization should undertake, and the historical division of the founder's investments into two roles. These are common dilemmas facing organizations and groups. The fault lines represent the ways the collective has split the contradictory elements of the dilemma in an attempt to manage the uncertainty and tension. They provided the consultant with a starting point from which to explore *backward* to the paradoxical issues that spawned them.

Searching for the Link. Much of the consultant's work in the AMPA case was a search for the link between a series of conflicting and apparently contradictory positions and opinions. These links are often hard to see, overwhelmed by the apparent absence of common ground. Like the groups and subgroups involved in the case, the consultant too is often hard pressed to perceive or understand the connections. Instead, he or she is quickly able to perceive the differences and the lines of "fault."

The consultant must be able to begin with the "problem" at hand but be willing to develop a relationship with the group that allows *both* the consultant and the group to explore the issues fully, to immerse themselves in them in a search for the patterns that *might* connect. Since the "solutions" to the "problems" are often driven by unconscious forces in the group, the links between competing and contradictory solutions, the "sides" along the fault lines, can be drawn only if the group can begin to learn how their actions and reactions are expressions of unconscious as well as conscious wishes and fears. It is the domain "beneath" the problem that includes the potential for discovering the paradoxical link between the problematic but persistent opposing forces in the group.

This search, in the domain beneath the problem, for the link between opposites was most striking in the examination of the battle between the "quality" and the "profit" subgroups in the senior management. The search for the link took the consultant and the group on a long odyssey that was hardly apparent to either the consultant or the group when the project began. The debate was obviously significant for the group as measured by its intractability, but the reason for its importance seemed to elude everyone. In a major way, it was the consultant's *reluctance* to hang on to his initial interpretation and his decision to continue to explore additional but seemingly unrelated events and emotions that led to hypotheses about the links between the two issues and the two subgroups. The uncovering of the link between Pries and Rolland had a similar flavor.

The Consultant's Temptation. The consultant in this case often faced the temptation to adopt the framework used by the organization to understand the "problem" and to "solve" it. When one is confronted with deep and emotional splits within

groups and between them, it is tempting to use familiar approaches to conflict resolution (for example, compromise). In
our terms, there is a great temptation to "import" a nonparadoxical framework and its attendant solutions to the problem
of coexisting opposites. In this case, the inability of the system
to "solve" certain recurring "problems" (for example, conflict
within the management group, conflict between the management and the board, frustration with Pries's leadership style,
conflict over the computer fiasco) led to the request for consultation in the first place. At a number of points along the way,
the choice to resolve one conflict or another would have obscured the paradoxical issues driving the conflict. The consultant's efforts to resolve the conflict would have taken him away
from the work of exploring the conflicts and of searching for
the unconscious links between the opposing sides.

The temptation to enter into a nonparadoxical framework is intensified by pressure from within the consultant as
well as from members of the organization. The consultant may
find it hard to choose inaction over action even when his or her
judgment suggests that there is important "in-formation" yet to
be formed. Since consulting effectiveness is often defined by
the *actions* taken (Pries, in this case, tells the consultant that he
is "anxious" for the consultation to provide some results) and
the paradoxical aspects of group life are often obscured by
either/or frames of reference, there is significant pressure, particularly in the early stages of work with groups, to produce results within the existing framework rather than to explore the
effects of the framework itself. To the extent that the consultant gets pulled into the existing framework, he or she further
entrenches it.

Facilitating Movement. Throughout the case described
above, the consultant worked to facilitate the expression and
exploration of the strongly held but conflicting thoughts and
feelings in the management group. When this was possible (for
example, the "selfishness" discussion, the discussion of whether
to give *all* the restructuring information to the board, the face-
to-face meeting between Pries and Rolland), the group experi-

enced some release from the repetitive, unproductive cycles that had become paralyzing. In each instance, the consultant searched for a way to help the group affirm and legitimate what was being negated and considered illegitimate. When *both* kinds of reactions or opinions could be expressed and tolerated, when opposing forces could coexist (selfishness *and* selflessness; desires to preserve the status quo *and* desires for change; a need to protect a personal legacy *and* a need to enhance it; the primacy of quality *and* the primacy of profit), the group was able to move. Prior to this release, the group's description of its struggles suggested lots of motion and very little movement.

The Consultant's Skills. It would require more space than we have here to address the skill and training required for the kind of work described in this case. But one general observation can be made as we explore the implications of a paradoxical perspective. The case points out that paradox exists at many levels of human experience and across these levels as well. Individuals in the case struggled with their own internal contradictions, as did subgroups within groups and groups in their relationship with each other. In addition, each of the levels was connected to the others such that the ways individuals managed their internal struggles with paradox influenced what happened in the group and intergroup relations. The reverse influence was also evident.

Much of the consultant's work involved the search for these cross-level manifestations of the paradoxical tensions that we have described in this book. It is clear that the consultant must be willing and able to recognize and work with the influence of paradoxical tensions at each level, both in the client system and in his or her own work with the client. Since the consultant too is simultaneously an individual, a member of a variety of groups, and an intergroup representative, he or she must develop the capacity to apply a paradoxical framework to both self and other. If the consultant is unable and/or unwilling to do this, his or her work with the client is likely to be constrained by his or her own unconscious fears or inadequacies. It is not that the consultant needs to be free of paradoxical tensions, but rather that these tensions, at multiple levels, must be open to the same degree of scrutiny and exploration as those residing in the client system.

Role of Authority and Power. There are contradictory messages in the AMPA case about the role of formal authority in "authorizing" the expression of strong emotions. The consultant worked with Pries to help him understand the ways in which his behavior might be inhibiting the exploration of precisely the reactions and feelings that he, Pries, was interested in. In preparing Pries for a meeting in which these feelings, some of them negative and critical, would be expressed, the consultant clearly believed that how Pries behaved would have a significant influence on the behavior of his subordinates. On the other hand, the consultant's work with the senior management group included efforts to influence their behavior vis-à-vis the board, and it is clear that here the consultant believed that it was possible to send influence up the organization as well.

Again, we are tempted to ask, "Which way is best, top-down or bottom-up?" But the message of the case is that levels of analysis and levels of hierarchy are connected. Both top-down and bottom-up approaches implicitly adopt a framework that assumes that each level can explore *its* paradoxical tensions in isolation from the others. The case argues strongly that this is not possible. The splits within each group (senior management and board) are placed into the relationship between them. The relationship is then used by each group as a frame for "understanding," denying, or displacing its own internal dynamic, creating in the process the self-referential, circular, and repetitive patterns that we have been discussing. To the extent that we try to split the interdependent groups or subgroups in an organization, especially along the dimension of power and authority, we run the risk of trying to separate the elements of the paradox (for example, the paradoxes of authority and dependency). If we then address our efforts to either the top or the bottom, we have joined one of the opposing "sides" of the paradoxical tension and have become part of the framework that paralyzes the system.

"But you have to start somewhere," cries a voice struggling with the implication of this observation. True. But it may be less important where you start than how you proceed once you have begun. If the consultant can be authorized and authorize the group at the same time to explore the opposing forces and the meaning that their coexistence conveys, the path will inevitably lead both up and down.

References

Adler, A. *The Individual Psychology of Alfred Adler.* (H. L. Ansbacher and R. R. Ansbacher, trans.) New York: Harper & Row, 1956.

Alderfer, C. P. "Group and Intergroup Relations." In J. R. Hackman and J. L. Suttle (eds.), *Improving Life at Work.* Santa Monica, Calif.: Goodyear, 1977.

Alderfer, C. P. "An Intergroup Perspective on Group Dynamics." In J. Lorsch (ed.), *Handbook oj Organizational Behavior.* Englewood Cliffs, N.J.: Prentice-Hall, 1986.

Alderfer, C. P., and Brown, L. D. *Learning from Changing.* Beverly Hills, Calif.: Sage, 1975.

Andolfi, M. "Paradox in Psychotherapy." *American Journal of Psychoanalysis,* 1974, *34,* 221-228.

Bales, R. F. *Personality and Interpersonal Behavior.* New York: Holt, Rinehart & Winston, 1970.

Bales, R. F., and Cohen, S. P. *Symlog.* New York: Free Press, 1979.

Bateson, G. *Naven.* Cambridge, England: Cambridge University Press, 1936.

Bateson, G. "A Theory of Play and Fantasy." *APA Psychiatric Research Reports,* 1955, *11,* 39-51.

Bateson, G. *Steps to an Ecology of Mind.* New York: Ballantine, 1972.

Bateson, G., Jackson, D. D., Haley, J., and Weakland, J. H. "Towards a Theory of Schizophrenia." *Behavioral Science,* 1956, *1,* 251-264.

Becker, E. *The Denial of Death.* New York: Free Press, 1973.

Becker, E. *Escape from Evil.* New York: Free Press, 1975.

Beisser, A. "The Paradoxical Theory of Change." In J. Fagan and I. Shepherd (eds.), *Gestalt Therapy Now.* New York: Harper & Row, 1970.

Benne, K. D. "From Polarization to Paradox." In L. P. Bradford, J. R. Gibb, and K. D. Benne (eds.), *T-Group Theory and Laboratory Method.* New York: Wiley, 1964.

Bennis, W. G., and Shepard, H. A. "A Theory of Group Development." *Human Relations,* 1956, *9,* 415-437.

Berg, D. N. *Intergroup Relations in an Outpatient Psychiatric Facility.* Ann Arbor, Mich.: University Microfilms, 1978.

Bion, W. R. *Experiences in Groups.* London: Tavistock, 1961.

Bowen, M. *Family Therapy in Clinical Practice.* New York: Jason Aronson, 1978.

Bradford, L. P., Gibb, J. R., and Benne, K. D. *T-Group Theory and Laboratory Method.* New York: Wiley, 1964.

Brown, J. R. *I Only Want What's Best for You.* New York: St. Martin's Press, 1986.

Brown, N. O. *Life Against Death: The Psychoanalytic Meaning of History.* New York: Viking Books, 1959.

Campbell, D. T. "Common Fate, Similarity and Other Indices of the Status of Aggregates of Persons as Social Entities." *Behavioral Science,* 1958, *3,* 14-25.

Cartwright, D., and Zander, A. (eds.). *Group Dynamics: Research and Theory.* (3rd ed.) New York: Harper & Row, 1968.

Coleman, A. D., and Bexton, H. B. (eds.). *Group Relations Reader.* Washington, D.C.: A. K. Rice Institute, 1975.

Coleman, A. D., and Geller, M. H. (eds.). *Group Relations Reader 2.* Washington, D.C.: A. K. Rice Institute, 1985.

Cooley, H. C. *Human Nature and the Social Order.* New York: Scribner's, 1922.

Coser, L. *The Functions of Social Conflict.* New York: Free Press, 1956.

Delbecq, S. L., Van de Ven, A. H., and Gustafson, D. H. *Group Techniques for Program Planning.* Glenview, Ill.: Scott, Foresman, 1975.

Deutsch, M. *The Resolution of Conflict.* New Haven, Conn.: Yale University Press, 1973.

Feinberg, G., and Shapiro, R. *Life Beyond Earth.* New York: Morrow, 1980.

Foerster, H. von. "On Seeing: The Problems of the Double Blind." First annual Gregory Bateson Lecture, Philadelphia, Oct. 1, 1985.

Frankl, V. *The Doctor and the Soul: From Psychotherapy to Logo Therapy.* New York: Knopf, 1965.

Frankl, V. "Paradoxical Intention and Dereflection." *Psychotherapy: Theory, Research, Practice,* 1975, *12,* 226-237.

Freud, S. *Group Psychology.* Standard Edition, vol. 18. London: Hogarth Press, 1922.

Freud, S. *Group Psychology and the Analysis of the Ego.* London: Hogarth Press, 1949.

Gibbard, G. S., Hartman, J. J., and Mann, R. D. (eds.). *Analysis of Groups: Contributions to Theory, Research, and Practice.* San Francisco: Jossey-Bass, 1974.

Glidewell, J. C. *Choice Points.* Cambridge, Mass.: MIT Press, 1970.

Gödel, K. *On Formally Undecidable Propositions.* New York: Basic Books, 1962.

Goodman, P. S. "Social Comparison Processes in Organizations." In B. M. Staw and G. R. Salancik (eds.), *New Directions in Organizational Behavior.* Chicago: St. Clair Press, 1977.

Greenson, R. R. *The Technique and Practice of Psychoanalysis.* New York: International Universities Press, 1967.

Gustafson, J. P., and others. "Cooperative and Clashing Interests in Small Groups. Part I. Theory." *Human Relations,* 1981, *34* (4), 315-339.

Hackman, J. R., and Morris, C. G. "Group Tasks, Group Interaction Process and Group Performance: A Review and Proposed Integration." *Advances in Experimental Social Psychology,* 1975, *8,* 45-99.

Haley, J. *Uncommon Therapy: The Psychiatric Techniques of Milton H. Erickson.* New York: Ballantine, 1973.

Haley, J. *Problem-Solving Therapy: New Strategies for Effective Family Therapy.* San Francisco: Jossey-Bass, 1976.

Hare, P. A. *Handbook of Small Group Research.* (2nd ed.) New York: Free Press, 1976.

Hofstadter, D. R. *Gödel, Escher, Bach: An Eternal Golden Braid.* New York: Vintage Books, 1979.

Homans, G. C. *The Human Group.* New York: Harcourt Brace Jovanovich, 1950.

Horwitz, K. "Projective Identification in Dyads and Groups." *International Journal of Group Psychotherapy,* 1983, *3,* 259–279.

Hughes, P., and Brecht, G. *Vicious Circles and Infinity.* New York: Penguin Books, 1975.

Jackson, D. D. (ed.). *Therapy, Communication and Change.* Vols. 1, 2. Palo Alto, Calif.: Science and Behavior Books, 1968.

Jaques, E. "Social Systems as a Defense Against Persecutory and Depressive Anxiety." In M. Klein, P. Heimann, and R. E. Money-Kyrle (eds.), *New Directions in Psychoanalysis.* London: Tavistock, 1955.

Jaynes, J. *The Origin of Consciousness in the Breakdown of the Bicameral Mind.* Boston: Houghton Mifflin, 1976.

Jourdain, P.E.B. "Tales with Philosophical Morals." *Open Court,* 1913, *27,* 310–315.

Jung, C. G. *Answer to Job.* Princeton, N.J.: Princeton University Press, 1958.

Jung, C. G. *Memories, Dreams, Reflections.* New York: Vintage Books, 1965.

Karpman, S. "Script Drama Analysis." *Transactional Analysis Bulletin,* 1968, *26,* 39–43.

Kernberg, O. *Internal World and External Reality.* New York: Jason Aronson, 1980.

Kierkegaard, S. *The Concept of Dread.* (W. Lowrie, trans.) Princeton, N.J.: Princeton University Press, 1957. (Originally published 1844.)

Klein, M. "Our Adult World and Its Roots in Infancy." *Human Relations,* 1959, *12,* 291–303.

Klein, M. "Notes on Some Schizoid Mechanisms." In *Envy and Gratitude and Other Works, 1946–1963.* New York: Delacorte Press/Seymour Laurence, 1975.

Kris, E. "On Some Viscissitudes of Insight in Psycho-Analysis." *International Journal of Psycho-Analysis,* 1956a, *37,* 445–455.

Kris, E. "The Recovery of Childhood Memories in Psychoanalysis." *Psychoanalytic Study of the Child,* 1956b, *11,* 54-58.

Laing, R. D. *The Politics of the Family.* New York: Vintage Books, 1969.

Landsberger, H. A. "The Horizontal Dimension of Bureaucracy." *Administrative Science Quarterly,* 1961, *6,* 298-332.

Lawrence, P. R., and Lorsch, J. W. *Organization and Environment.* Boston: Graduate School of Business Administration, Harvard University, 1967.

Le Bon, G. *The Crowd.* New York: Macmillan, 1895.

Levine, R. A., and Campbell, D. T. *Ethnocentrism.* New York: Wiley, 1972.

Lipset, D. *Gregory Bateson: The Legacy of a Scientist.* Boston: Beacon Press, 1980.

Luft, J. *Group Processes.* (2nd ed.) Palo Alto, Calif.: Mayfield, 1970.

McGrath, J. E., and Altman, I. *Small Group Research.* New York: Holt, Rinehart & Winston, 1966.

Maslow, A. "The Need to Know and the Fear of Knowing." *Journal of General Psychology,* 1963, *68,* 111-125.

May, R. *The Courage to Create.* New York: Bantam Books, 1975.

Mills, T. M. *Group Transformations.* Englewood Cliffs, N.J.: Prentice-Hall, 1964.

Minuchin, S. *Families and Family Therapy.* Cambridge, Mass.: Harvard University Press, 1974.

Montaigne, M. De. *The Complete Essays of Montaigne.* (D. Frane, trans.) Stanford, Calif.: Stanford University Press, 1958. (Originally published 1595.)

Mozdzierz, G., Macchitelli, F., and Lisiecki, J. "The Paradox in Psychotherapy: An Adlerian Perspective." *Journal of Individual Psychology,* 1976, *32,* 169-184.

Newman, R. G. *Groups in Schools.* New York: Simon & Schuster, 1974.

Nietzsche, F. W. *Thus Spake Zarathustra: A Book for Everyone and No One.* Baltimore, Md.: Penguin, 1961. (Originally published 1911.)

Ogden, T. H. "On Projective Identification." *International Journal of Psycho-Analysis,* 1979, *60,* 357-373.

Ogden, T. H. *Projective Identification and Psychotherapeutic Technique.* New York: Jason Aronson, 1982.

Perls, F. *Gestalt Therapy Verbatim.* New York: Bantam Books, 1976.

Polster, E., and Polster, M. *Gestalt Therapy Integrated.* New York: Vintage Books, 1973.

Rank, O. *Will Therapy and Truth and Reality.* New York: Knopf, 1936.

Redl, F. "Group Emotion and Leadership." *Psychiatry,* 1942, *5,* 573-596.

Rice, A. K. *Learning for Leadership.* London: Tavistock, 1965.

Rice, A. K. "Individual, Group and Intergroup Processes." *Human Relations,* 1969, *22,* 565-584.

Sarason, S. B. *The Creation of Settings and the Future Societies.* San Francisco: Jossey-Bass, 1972.

Sartre, J. P. *Critique of Dialectical Reason, a Theory of Practical Ensembles.* Atlantic Highlands, N.J.: Humanities Press, 1976.

Satir, V. *Conjoint Family Therapy.* Palo Alto, Calif.: Science and Behavior Books, 1967.

Schermer, V. L. "Beyond Bion: The Basic Assumption States Revisited." In M. Pines (ed.), *Bion and Group Psychotherapy.* Boston: Routledge & Kegan Paul, 1985.

Schutz, W. C. *FIRO: A Three-Dimensional Theory of Interpersonal Behavior.* New York: Holt, Rinehart & Winston, 1958.

Schwartzman, H. B. "Research on Work Group Effectiveness: An Anthropological Critique." In P. S. Goodman (ed.), *Designing Effective Work Groups.* San Francisco: Jossey-Bass, 1986.

Seltzer, L. F. "The Role of Paradox in Gestalt Theory and Technique." *Gestalt Journal,* 1984, *3* (2), 20-30.

Selvini Palazzoli, M., Boscolo, L., Cecchin, G., and Prata, G. *Paradox and Counterparadox.* New York: Jason Aronson, 1978.

Sherif, M., and others. *Intergroup Conflict and Cooperation: The Robbers Cave Experiment.* Norman, Okla.: University Book Exchange, 1961.

Simmel, G. *Conflict.* (K. H. Wolff, trans.) New York: Free Press, 1955.

Slater, P. E. *Microcosm.* New York: Wiley, 1966.

Smith, K. K. *Groups in Conflict: Prisons in Disguise.* Dubuque, Iowa: Kendall/Hunt, 1982a.

Smith, K. K. "Philosophical Problems in Thinking About Organizational Change." In P. S. Goodman and Associates, *Change in Organizations: New Perspectives on Theory, Research, and Practice.* San Francisco: Jossey-Bass, 1982b.

Smith, K. K. "Social Comparison Processes and Dynamic Conservatism in Intergroup Relations." In L. L. Cummings and B. M. Staw (eds.), *Research in Organizational Behavior.* Vol. 5. Greenwich, Conn.: JAI Press, 1983.

Smith, K. K. "Epistemological Problems in Researching Human Relationships." In D. N. Berg and K. K. Smith (eds.), *Exploring Clinical Methods for Social Research.* Beverly Hills, Calif.: Sage, 1985.

Stierlin, D. *Separating Parents and Adolescents: A Perspective on Running Away, Schizophrenia, and Waywardness.* New York: Quadrangle, 1974.

Sutherland, J. D. "Bion Revisited: Group Dynamics and Group Psychotherapy." In M. Pines (ed.), *Bion and Group Psychotherapy.* Boston: Routledge & Kegan Paul, 1985.

Tillich, P. *The Courage to Be.* New Haven, Conn.: Yale University Press, 1952.

Tuckman, B. W. "Developmental Sequence in Small Groups." *Psychological Bulletin,* 1965, *54,* 229–249.

Walton, R. E., and Dutton, J. M. "The Management of Inter-Departmental Conflict: A Model and Review." *Administrative Science Quarterly,* 1969, *14,* 73–84.

Watzlawick, P., Weakland, J., and Fisch, R. *Change: Principles of Problem Formation and Problem Resolution.* New York: Norton, 1974.

Weeks, G. R., and L'Abate, L. *Paradoxical Psychotherapy: Theory and Practice with Individuals, Couples and Families.* New York: Brunner/Mazel, 1982.

Wells, L. "The Group-as-a-Whole: A Systematic Socioanalytic Perspective on Interpersonal and Group Relations." In C. .P. Alderfer and C. L. Cooper (eds.), *Advances in Experiential Social Processes.* Vol. 2. New York: Wiley, 1980.

Whitaker, D. S., and Lieberman, M. A. *Psychotherapy Through the Group Process.* Chicago: Aldine Press, 1964.

Whitehead, A. N., and Russell, B. *Principia Mathematica.* 3 vols. (2nd ed.) Cambridge, England: Cambridge University Press, 1910–1913.

Wilden, A. *Systems and Structure: Essays in Communication and Exchange.* (2nd ed.) London: Tavistock, 1980.

Yalom, I. *The Theory and Practice of Group Psychotherapy.* (3rd ed.) New York: Basic Books, 1985.

Zander, A. *Groups at Work: Unresolved Issues in the Study of Organizations.* San Francisco: Jossey-Bass, 1977.

Zander, A. *Making Groups Effective.* San Francisco: Jossey-Bass, 1982.

Index